How Do You

MW00398651

Recipient of Outstanding Non-fiction Award,
2012 Southern California Writers' Conference

"A compelling, well-written memoir. The opening chapter will grab
you and the small flashbacks and memories that follow will take
you deeper into the story and bring it alive."
—Judy Reeves, author of *A Writer's Book of Days*

"As an author with a mother who was also a 'nut case,' I relished
Sharon Hicks' book, *How Do You Grab a Naked Lady?* She presents
her mother vividly, but with an underlying compassion—surely the
best way to depict a relative who is both loony and someone you
love. Readers will relate to Sharon's well-written story."
—Maralys Wills, author of *Higher than Eagles*

"A marvelous book. Sharon Hicks, whose mischievous sense of
humor keeps bubbling out, has written a touching memoir. It is a
compelling case study of what it is like to live with an impossible
parent."
—Dr. Elaine Hatfield, Department of Psychology,
University of Hawaii, author

"Once I started reading this book, I did not want to put it down.
Something unexpected unfolded in every chapter, and I could not
wait to turn the next page. A great read underlying the survival
spirit within all of us."
—Dr. Doris Ching, community leader, educator, and author

"For any of us who have struggled, silent and alone, with a mentally
ill family member, this book is like a window thrown open to air out a
musty room. It made me laugh, it made me cry, but more than anything,
it reminded me that I am actually *not* alone. Help and understanding
are only a few doors down."
—Linda Hamilton Krieger, JD law professor,
University of Hawaii, civil rights advocate, author

David, age 7, and me, age 3

To my brother, David,
for endless enthusiasm and loving encouragement

Acknowledgments

A special thank-you to my dear friends who read my drafts, offered suggestions and assurances, including Puchi Romig, Lani Lofgren, Dr. Doris Ching, Wendy Lagareta, Annette Dung, Malcolm Koga, Carol Kleinman, Alice Ann Parker, Robert McEwan, Dr. Alan Howard, Marilyn Whitehorse, Jeff and Ingrid Gryskiewicz, Laura Williams, Paddy Dunn, Susan White, and Carol Horne.

I want to thank Frank South for suggesting the title of my book when I told him the story about a department store guard yelling: "How do you grab a naked lady?" Frank said: "That's your title, Sharon." The title stuck and proved relevant throughout my memoir.

A special thank-you to Heidi Emerson Altree for reading the wordy second draft and for her brilliant suggestions needed for the polish.

✺

I am indebted to my family for their encouragement, patience, and stories—especially to my daughter Julie Cooper, my daily sounding board, reader, and advisor. To my daughter-in-law, Julie Larson-Hicks, for suggestions and OMG reactions. To my son, Guy Larson-Hicks, for not judging his own mother. To my grandchildren, Mahina Kahalewale, Makana Kahalewale, Adri Kinhult, Mykel Hicks, Mario Kaluhiokalani, Hunter Hicks, and Keaton Hicks for their devotion and excitement.

To my cousins, Julianne, Janie, and Jim Nowell, for their unwavering love and support.

To my niece, Kathy Hicks Cannon, for her undying encouragement. And to my nephews, David L. Hicks, Tom K. Hicks, and Michael P. Hicks, for contributing stories and reminding me of the rippling effect Mother's craziness has on all of us.

To my sister-in-law, Jeanie Hicks, for her understanding. Welcome to the family!

✺

And, finally, thank you to my friends at Abbott Press.

Mother, age 30

If you can't get rid of the skeleton in your closet, you'd best teach it to dance.

—George Bernard Shaw

Part One

1940–1960
Hawaii/California/Hawaii

"SHARON, I AM WRITING A BOOK! The title is *Fuck!*"

Fuck was Mother's favorite word.

"*F* is *for*, *U* is *you*"—she points at me—"*C* is *see*"—she points to her eyes—"and *K* is *clearly*." She spoke deliberately. An. Emphasis. On. Every. Word. "Come on, Sharon! Don't you get it? For. You. See. Clearly. Everything is so fucking clear to me!"

She plopped down next to me at the kitchen table while I was eating an afternoon snack of milk and cookies. Her green eyes were wild and frenetic; sharp as cut glass, they darted about as though they were looking for a place to land. I was terrified of her eyes, and instantly my stomach clenched.

This was how it started—enunciating every word in slow motion, and then the restlessness and the itching. Her bright-red polished nails tap-tap-tapped on the tabletop. She was a watch wound too tightly; it was only a matter of time until the spring popped. Mother laughed at her own cleverness, then leaped from the kitchen chair and began pacing.

I had to admit it: it was clever—the way her mind worked and the way she saw things differently from most people. Still, at sixteen, I was more interested in the fact that I was homecoming queen for Roosevelt High School and that the football game on Saturday was against our biggest rival, Punahou School. I was more interested in imagining my dress. How it would be strapless and pink, with loads of crinoline and dyed shoes to match. How I would be smiling and waving, and the entire city of Honolulu would be cheering for me as I rode around Honolulu Stadium in a horse-drawn carriage.

"Sharon, are you listening to me? I had a twenty-four-karat gold necklace made for me with the letters *FUCK* to dangle across my chest. It costs fifteen thousand dollars. Let's go pick it up."

I shoved another cookie into my mouth and became intensely interested in the scratches on the table. The good news: we were still sitting at the table, which meant this wasn't actually a problem—yet. Still, my stomach knotted.

I didn't want to go with her. I never knew how to handle her when she started careening out of control. There was no telling what she'd do, and it was her unpredictability that left me unbalanced. *Will she hurt me? Will she hurt someone else? Will she hurt herself?* Still, there was that split second when I thought that maybe this time she would hold it together, as though she had a choice, as though she controlled her brain rather than the other way around.

"Come on! What are you waiting for?" Mother slapped the table.

The room began to pitch and roll. I gripped the sides of the table, trying to keep my balance. Mother filled the room; she pressed herself into every corner. It suddenly felt claustrophobic in our wide-open kitchen, even though it was surrounded by windows and sliding-glass doors. I twisted my head and looked through our kitchen sliding-glass door, out past our backyard and its pristine green lawn, out past the palm trees swaying in the breeze to the blue of Maunalua Bay. Out there, all was calm and serene. Peaceful.

"Let's go, Sharon!" Mother's voice slung shot me back into the kitchen.

Suddenly, I was in our convertible hurtling at breakneck speed down the middle lane of Kalanianaole Highway, broken yellow lines on either side. Mother winked at me. "This is my special lane." Horns honked loudly and insistently at us for being in the wrong lane, the lane used for passing vehicles only. Mother shook her fist like a dictator. "Don't they know who I am? Some people can be so stupid!" I crouched in the seat and gripped the door handle with both hands.

Mercifully, ten minutes later, we pulled into the parking lot. Mother had barely turned off the engine when she leaped from the car and shot, like a bullet, through the front doors of the upscale department store straight for the fine jewelry department. Then, for reasons unknown, I followed her.

The cool of the air-conditioning hit me in the face as I stepped through the doors. It took a moment for my eyes to adjust to the lighting. I saw Mother standing at the jewelry counter talking to a tiny Japanese saleslady. I'd be willing to bet the word *fuck* had never once crossed her lips. I positioned myself behind a rack of women's Hawaiian dresses. My eyes peeked out just above the metal bar of the clothes rack.

"I'm sorry, Mrs. Hicks," the saleslady said in her breathy, friendly voice, "but management would not allow us to make the necklace."

Mother stiffened. I pressed myself deeper into the clothes rack, camouflaging myself in silk prints of red hibiscus and golden pineapple. My heart pulsed in my throat. Other shoppers milled about—perfectly manicured housewives. They were innocents. I felt a bit jealous. The air around Mother warped and then expanded, like a balloon being stretched beyond its capacity. She was bristling.

"Oh, yeah? Well ... fuck you!"

The balloon burst.

"Fuck you! Fuck you! Fuck you!"

The words rained down on me like gunfire. It happened that fast. One minute I was sitting at the kitchen table enjoying a tidy little snack of milk and cookies, and the next I was hiding inside a rack of women's clothes while my mother sprayed startled customers and salespeople with "Fuck you!" like Howitzer gunfire.

Without warning, my mother spun around and headed for the escalator to the second floor. When she reached the top, she positioned herself behind the Plexiglas barrier directly above the fine jewelry department. A smile inched its way across her face. I wanted to close my eyes. Some things children should never witness. But it was like a train wreck: you know you shouldn't stare, but you're compelled to, just in case someone asks you about it later and you should have all the facts straight.

Yes, Officer. Yes, she did pull her muumuu over her head. No, no she wasn't wearing any underwear. Yes, sir. Completely naked. No, she never did this before. Yes, sir. This was the first time she stripped naked in public. May I go home now, please?

It happened in one swift, fluid motion. Mother pulled her muumuu over her head and then let it flutter over the railing, where it settled gracefully on the fine jewelry counter below. There she stood, my mother, on the second floor, behind the see-through Plexiglas barrier, naked.

My heart crashed to the floor. I took a deep breath and clenched both fists to my chest, where my heart once dwelled. My world stopped abruptly and then fast-forwarded when I heard Mother scream, "Fuck all of you!"

She threw her head back, then started to descend to the first floor on the escalator. All eyes were fixed on her, just the way she liked it. As she paraded down the escalator, she yelled, "You're all a bunch of shitheads! All of you! Shitheads!"

Shithead was Mother's second-favorite word.

When she was almost to the bottom of the escalator, I started to leave my hiding place to get her muumuu that was resting on the fine jewelry counter. But I hesitated. If I moved, then people would know she was my mother.

Still, I recognized that at thirty-nine, my mother was seductive and curvaceous. She was round in all the right places, and this was a sticky point for me because I looked an awful lot like her. All right, I liked being attractive. I would need that to land me a husband in a few years. I just didn't want anyone thinking that the resemblance between my mother and me was anything more than cosmetic.

I stood hidden in the clothes rack. She was reaching fever pitch now, her arms flailing as though that would add more force to her words, more momentum. Two blue-uniformed security guards arrived, one at the top and one at the bottom of the escalator. When Mother saw them, she smirked. In the midst of my mortification, I realized that to her this was just a game, an afternoon of fun. She pedaled backward on the escalator and then pranced down a few steps. Up a few, down a few. She kept up this awkward little dance for hours, or so it seemed. Down. Up. Down. Up.

"Come on, you fuckers. Come and get me."

The guards hesitated. The one closest to her, the one at the bottom of the escalator, yelled, "Hey! How do you grab a naked lady?"

A third guard arrived with a blanket. He threw it around Mother and grabbed her. She twisted and threw off the blanket. The guard threw the blanket on her again and held her firmly.

I hurried to rescue Mother's muumuu from the top of the jewelry counter and followed her and the security guards. While the guards took Mother inside the manager's office, I stood inside the doorframe, her muumuu over my arm. Mother threw the blanket off and sat in a chair, legs crossed. She narrowed her eyes at the security guard, a dare. The security guard wrapped her with a blanket again. This time, Mother smiled and tittered, sounding like a little girl.

"Are you her daughter?" the store manager asked me.

"Yes, I am." My voice was calm and even.

Out of the corner of my eye, I saw my mother waggling her foot, willing me to look at her, to talk to her. I fixed my gaze on the manager.

"Is there someone you can call?" he asked.

"Yes, thank you. I'll call my father. He knows what to do."

The manager clicked his pen nervously, as though he wanted me to say or do something else.

"I'll need her purse and her jewelry," I said with an air of authority and resignation.

Mother knew the drill. She giggled and batted her eyelashes at the store manager and security guards while she slipped the rings from her fingers. I stuffed her jewelry inside her purse and then turned to walk out of the office, my feet feeling like concrete blocks. I ambled down the hallway, anxious to put some distance between Mother and me.

Her voice chased after me. "Sharon! Sharon! They pissed me off! Dammit! I was counting on that FUCK necklace. It's the title of my new book! Shitheads!"

~∞~

Later that evening, Dad told me that Mother was not arrested but committed to Kaneohe State Mental Hospital, locked in a secure ward. These incidents with Mother were taking a toll on him; he looked haggard and worn. It pained me to see him this way. He deserved better. *I will never be anything like my mother! I will never disappoint my dad, like she does.*

MY DAD LIKED TO TELL me it was love at first sight. He was visiting his best friend, Louie, when he saw Mother sleeping on the living room couch. That couch was the only piece of furniture in their rented apartment. Grandmother Nowell moved constantly, trying to find the cheapest apartment for her and her three youngest children of twelve: Louie, Mother, and Ernie.

It was 1933, and times were tough. The only work available for a single mother in Los Angeles was as a maid. Grandmother Nowell scoured the morning papers for a cheaper apartment; then, when she found one, she piled the kids in the car and relocated. They moved fifteen times in three years, hence the dearth of furniture; it was easier to pick up and leave if all they owned were the clothes on their backs.

"I'm going to marry your sister," Dad said that afternoon in Louie's apartment.

Just like that.

It was one of the things I admired most about my dad—the way he knew what he wanted, the way he wasn't afraid to snatch it up and make it his own. Whenever he told me this story, I thought of Sleeping Beauty. Only instead of chaste little pecks on the cheeks or lips, Mother and Dad necked like crazy in the back of Louie's car, much to the consternation of Louie's girlfriend (and future wife), Mackie, a die-hard Catholic. Mother never was what you would call a proper girl.

Anyway, I thought Dad the perfect Prince Charming with the way he rescued Mother from her life of poverty. She was fifteen, and Dad was seventeen. They married the next year. But I sometimes wondered if she regretted getting married so young. Maybe if she had waited a few years—waited until she was a little older, waited a little longer to have kids, to have me. Maybe everything would have been okay.

8

IT WASN'T THAT I BLAMED myself for her illness. But according to Dad, it all started when I was born in December of 1940 on Friday the thirteenth. Not entirely an auspicious beginning.

I liked to imagine that before I was born, Mother, Dad, and my brother, David, were this perfect little American family, similar to the one showcased in *Father Knows Best.* I pictured Mother and Dad smiling sweetly at one another as they clinked their glasses together at dinner to celebrate their good fortunes. I saw David with his hair slicked back with pomade and his feet dangling from the chair that was too big for him as he reached forward to join the toast with his glass of milk. Everyone was happy. Content.

And then I showed up and Mother didn't leave her bed for an entire year. She had the baby blues—times ten. She didn't have baby blues with David's birth four years earlier. Not that I compared us. Not that I think this had anything to do with why she seemed to love him more than me.

In 1940, Dad worked for May Company as a buyer of women's clothes. He had been working for May Company for nine years, ever since he graduated from high school at age fifteen. It was a step up from his days of hustling newspapers and getting paid to tell johns where to get the girls on the streets of Los Angeles. (Sometimes it was hard for me to imagine my dad as a ten-year-old pimp.) As a buyer, Dad took the train to New York City for weeks at a time. On those train trips and in New York City, Dad was exposed to men with drive and ambition. He became enamored of these go-getters, longed to emulate them. Already an avid atheist, drive and ambition became his gods.

Because of her depression, I imagined the separation was especially hard on Mother. But a man with ambition was what she wanted. She wanted to connect to it, to make love to it, to marry it. In the 1940s, women were expected to stay at home, raise their children, keep their mouths shut, and defer to the whims of their husbands. That was definitely not my mother. She could mix it up with the best of them. She loved the rapid-fire logic of a man's mind; she loved to think and reason and debate. I thought it was the thing Dad loved best about her. It made her unusual. Special. A partner rather than a subordinate.

Grandma Hicks, Dad's mom, told me that during my first year, while Mother was sidelined by her depression and Dad was busy building the American dream, I was left alone in my crib most of the time. Grandma said when I "messed my pants," I twirled my "mess" in my hair and smeared it all over my crib and anyplace I could reach behind my crib. First thing Grandma did was raise the blinds and bring the sunshine into my room. Then she bathed and dressed me, prepared my bottles, fed me, and scrubbed my room while Mother stayed in bed. Grandma brought me love.

It was Dad who explained that after a year of Mother being depressed, he took her to a psychiatrist. Dad described the doctor as a big, redheaded Irishman who took one look at Mother and threw her on the couch. Wham! She had her first electric shock treatment. On the drive home, Mother couldn't stop talking. She couldn't wait to fix dinner for all of us. Shock treatments were a medical wonder. Dad was a believer.

Our family life wasn't always bad. There were lots of good times when I was young. I guess that was why it was so hard, because I knew that normal was possible.

Like the times when David would organize a puppet show for all the neighborhood kids. Dad built the stage, and Mother sewed the curtains. David named his puppets Stepin Fetchit and Bozo the Clown. At four years old, it was my job to sell the tickets to the neighborhood kids and to pull the curtains at just the right time—a real family affair.

And at dinner, the four of us gathered around the table in our mismatched dining room chairs. (Mother insisted we each pick our own chair at the furniture store. I picked a lightwood one that had indentations on the ends of the arms where my thumbs fit. Plus, it felt good on my bottom.) Mother, Dad, and David talked and laughed about the puppet show and batted ideas around for the next one. Dad asked David about his various adventures in the neighborhood and reprimanded him for trampling Mr. Pingston's lawn. I sat there swinging my legs in my special chair, marveling at the way the three of them packed a room.

Sundays were my absolute favorite. We woke up very early and piled into the car. David settled himself over the hump on the floor next to the backseats and breathed in the gas fumes on the way to Griffith Park. When we arrived, David jumped from the car (presumably for some fresh air) and headed straight for the stream to catch crawdads. I chased after him, desperate to be included in everything he did. We explored trails and paths, ran up and down hills, and played catch. At home, David was always ditching me, treating me like a real nuisance. But on Sundays, I had my big brother's attention.

Our favorite picnic spot was next to a sparsely wooded area. The table and benches were rugged and weathered, but I loved them because somehow, when we sat around that table together eating our breakfast, we were equal. No one was more special than another. Everyone mattered the same.

Over an open fire, Mother cooked breakfast: eggs, bacon, and pancakes. Dad watched, smoking his pipe. I loved to listen to the gurgle and hiss of the coffee as it percolated over the fire. I was too young to drink it, but the aroma warmed my insides. The food tasted better in the open. Maybe it was the freedom of the outdoors, the way the blue sky ran forever. No limits. No boundaries, a great big openness. Like you would never run out of air to breathe.

It was so dark. I hated being in the closet. *What did I do?* I always tried really, really hard to be a good girl. I ate all my breakfast, and I played quietly by myself so I wouldn't make Mother mad. That was one of the rules: never upset Mother. I wasn't like David. He'd always get into trouble, like when he pulled my hair. Or like that time he shot the arrow through the neighbor's window and it landed in that man's bowl while he was eating his cereal. Mother whipped David with a wooden coat hanger. And then, when it broke, she got madder and hit him with another hanger.

But I was a good girl. I knew how to be silent and invisible. I knew how to not matter. But, I ended up in the closet.

When I curled up real tight in the dark closet and held my breath, I could hear my own heartbeat. It sounded like a drum. Ba-bum. Ba-bum. Ba-bum. If I laid down flat and squished my cheek against the floor, the light peeked under the door, and it made me feel better. Sometimes I could only see darkness, and I was so scared. I wondered when she was going to let me out or if she remembered where I was. I knew how to be still—still enough not to disturb the spiders because they were creepy, crawly, scary, and ugly, with big bellies and hairy legs. If you squashed one, their guts got all over, or sometimes little baby spiders ran from their belly in all directions. I was afraid to move, even a little bit. I waited an eternity for my rescue and rolled into a ball listening to my heartbeat: ba-bum, ba-bum, ba-bum.

And then there were the times Dad took us fishing on the Santa Monica Pier. We left before sunrise, and the neighborhood was quiet. I remember the chill in the air—the way my skin tightened with goose bumps. Dad packed the fishing gear in the back of the car, and Mother gave us a thermos full of hot chocolate. She never went with us. I'm not sure why, although I remember the way the edges of Dad's face softened as we pulled out of the driveway and away from the house. And the little knot that always sat in my stomach like a sack of stones went away for a little while.

The best part of the day was sitting on the pier with Dad watching the daybreak. I thought the sun slept in the desert on the other side of the mountains, and I stretched my arms way over my head to help it wake up. The salted air mixed with the hot chocolate running down my throat. The waves beneath the pier slapped and sucked the water. I felt the warmth of Dad's hand wrapped around mine as we walked across the weathered planks among the fishermen, complimenting them on their catches. Dad had such an easy way about him. Even though I was very young, maybe five or six, I could see how people warmed to him, how they relaxed around him, and how my heart felt so full I thought it would burst.

As I looked into the buckets of caught fish that lined the pier, I saw the fish thrash and gasp, fighting for their lives. I felt sorry for them. Once I asked Dad to throw them back, to save them. But he said they were supposed to be in the bucket, that it was their fate. I reached into the bucket and ran my fingers along their sides, and a few scales stuck to my fingertips and glistened in the rising sun. They looked like diamonds.

"Time to go outside, Sharon."

Mother pushed me through the back door. Her hands were mean. The door shut and made that clicking sound that meant I couldn't get back inside the house. I didn't know why she put me outside today. She never told me. She just said, "Time to go outside, Sharon," and then she shoved me outside. She always locked the door.

I sat on cold stone steps by the back door with my fists bunched under my chin. And I waited. I was good at waiting. Then I lay down on the lawn, where it felt warmer. I loved the smell of the grass and the way it tickled the edge of my nose. I liked to watch the bugs. I wondered what I looked like to them. I wondered what they ate. I wondered what their parents did and if they went to school. I made up stories about the bugs. But I never shared the stories with Mother and Dad because they were never as good as David's stories.

I sat up and looked around the yard for my puppy, Timothy, an Irish setter with a bright, shiny red coat. He was my best friend. He liked to jump all over me and lick my face, and it tickled. Timothy made me laugh. I loved him, and I knew he loved me.

I wandered around the yard. "Timothy, Timothy. Where are you?"

Where was he? I knew he wasn't inside because Mother said animals were never allowed inside because they were dirty. "Timothy?" I tiptoed across the lawn, whispering Timothy's name. I didn't want to disturb Mother by yelling. I looked in his doghouse. I only saw the alarm clock Dad had put there.

⋘◦◦⋙

"You don't need to worry about Timothy, Sharon," Dad said as he wound the alarm clock.

I didn't believe him. I thought I needed to worry about Timothy sleeping outside in the dark alone. He should be sleeping inside with me.

"The ticking of the clock will make him feel safe," Dad said. "Here. Listen. Tick-tock. Tick-tock. Doesn't that sound nice? Just like a heartbeat."

I wanted to tell Dad that it wasn't a heartbeat—that a heartbeat was warm and goes ba-bum, ba-bum and that a clock was cold and goes tick-tock, tick-tock. They were definitely not the same. And I wanted to tell him I didn't think Timothy was that stupid, that he knew the difference between a real heartbeat and a clock. But I didn't say anything because I didn't want to hurt Dad's feelings. I saw the way his eyes saddened when Mother talked back to him, and I didn't want to make him sad like she did. That was another rule: don't talk back.

Dad wrapped the clock in a blanket and put it in the corner of Timothy's doghouse. I didn't feel any better, but I hugged Dad's leg and said thank you because that was the right thing to do.

∽o∼

I couldn't find Timothy anywhere. *What if he gets out? What if he runs away?* A funny little fluttering in my chest and my hands made me sweat. I kept thinking about the story in the newspaper that Mother and Dad had told me about last night—the one about the grandpa who sawed his granddaughter's friend into little pieces and then stuffed her in a suitcase.

What if he finds me all by myself in the backyard? And what if he cuts me up too? I rubbed my eye with my fist. I wished Timothy were there. He would protect me. I wanted to knock on the door and ask Mother to please let me in, but I didn't because she'd get mad and then she might put me in the closet again. Or she might make me do things I didn't want to.

Like the times she made me suck her.

She made me climb into her lap, and she put her breast in my mouth and held me tight against her clammy skin. She pinched me hard and told me to suck. And then she made these weird noises and I thought I was hurting her, so I stopped sucking, and then she pinched me again. Even when I started crying, she made me suck more, and she kept making weird sounds. Her body shook and her voice changed pitch, and I panicked. I wished Dad and David were there, because she never made me do this when they were home.

∽o∼

Bang! Bang! Bang! David was home! I heard him knocking on the front door. When Mother didn't answer, David came tearing through the back gate and started banging on the back door. Bang! Bang! Bang! Mother opened the door; her forehead was beaded with sweat. She leaned forward and gave David a hug.

"Hey, there," she said breathlessly. "How's my little man?"

Timothy bolted from the house with his tail between his legs, whining. He ran into his doghouse. Mother wrapped her arm around David's shoulders and ushered him inside the house. I followed them, wondering: *What did Mother do to Timothy?*

WE LIVED ON MARBURN AVENUE on one of the largest lots in a new development called Windsor Hills, in Los Angeles. Mother and Dad were the youngest married couple on the block. Everybody loved them, said they were "darling." They especially loved Mother because she was so beautiful.

Mother was also an excellent cook. She made bread and cookies from scratch with fresh ingredients. Milk, butter, and eggs were delivered to our back porch. The butter came in big white blocks. Together, Mother and I mixed in the yellow food coloring, dribbling it in until it swirled like ribbons of sunshine. Mother called the eggs "chicken abortions."

We made ice cream in our ice cream maker. We filled the big silver bucket with eggs, cream, and milk, and then we flavored it with fresh fruit, hunks of chocolate, or vanilla. Dad poured big chunks of rock salt over the ice that sat around the steel bucket. And then we cranked the lever. Around and around and around. Sometimes my arm was tired (and sometimes I pretended it was tired) and Dad helped me turn it. His big hand covered mine and folded over with little squeezes. Even at six years old, I understood my dad was an attractive man. Women loved him much the same way men loved Mother.

Dad said, "Keep going, Susie!" (His pet name for me.) Together we spun the lever. I pressed myself into Dad's chest and smelled his sweat, which gave me this funny tingling in my stomach. I thought I might float right off the ground because I knew I would never love anyone more than I loved my dad.

∽∘∾

I knew it was time to sing when Mother motioned for me to sit with her at the piano. I waited for Mother to give me the cue. Then our voices harmonized loud and clear, twined together like shimmering strands of pearls singing, "M-O-T-H-E-R, a word that means the world to me" (Howard Johnson and Theodore Morse, 1915).

"Sharon, this is our special song. It tells me how much you love me—how much I mean to you."

Mother's cheeks shined and reddened; her voice was rich and full. We repeated the song many times so I wouldn't forget the lyrics. I sat very tall so I could sing at the top of my lungs because I wanted her to know that I loved her.

Suddenly, "Okay, that's enough." Her voice was not sweet anymore but as rough as sandpaper scraping me. "Time to go outside." She hustled me out the back door.

Click.

Just like that, we were done. I sat on the cold stone steps.

～∞～

Mother was positively tingling with excitement because her brothers were in town for a family party. Two of her brothers, Gordon and Ernie, with their wives and children had flown from Hawaii. Her twin brothers, Marvin and Melvin, and stepbrother, Abe, flew from Utah with their families. Louie and his family drove forty-five minutes from Sunland. She bustled with excitement when her six brothers came to our house. The Nowells were an exclusive club: smarter, prettier, richer, and more talented than anyone else. According to Mother, Uncle Ernie, and Mormon genealogy, the Nowells were descended from the kings of England. David belonged to the club. I did not.

"Too much like your dad," Mother said to me. "Too much like a Hicks; a step above white trash."

Mother said this about Dad and me because Grandpa Hicks and his second wife, Myrtle, had chickens in their kitchen and living room where they lived in Torrance, California. Chicken shit was everywhere. They were a real, live Ma and Pa Kettle. Mother didn't like messes. She liked everything to be neat and orderly, as in a museum.

Mother hummed as she unfolded and spread her lace tablecloth on the dining room table. She twisted linen napkins into gold napkin rings to match her gold knives, forks, and spoons. She placed ashtrays and goblets for water and wine at each place setting. Flowers sat in a vase at the center of the table with two skinny red candles lit on either side. Mother really knew how to make a table look inviting.

She wore her favorite white, low-cut peasant blouse, and she tucked it into a sleek pair of black shiny slacks. Gold buttons adorned her ears. Her dark, wavy hair brushed from her face highlighted soft-angled eyebrows and ruby-red lips. With an easy elegance, she served roast beef, mashed potatoes, green beans, and gravy. She made rolls and her famous chocolate cream pie. Mother reminded me of a top model on the cover of a fashion magazine. The way she held her head, tilted delicately to the right with her lips slightly parted as she listened to Uncle Gordon. The way a smile sneaked across her face and bloomed like a flower when Dad rubbed her shoulders. She seemed happy. Joy filled me like water spilling into a glass. There was food and laughter, and I wished it would always be like this.

After dinner, Mother sat down at the piano. The air crackled when Mother started to play the piano and sing. She threw her head back in delight when her brothers joined her on ukulele, guitar, banjo, harmonica, and gutbucket. All their voices harmonized:

There'll Be Some Changes Made.
—W. Benton Overstreet and Billy Higgins, 1921

Mother's strong alto voice filled our little house on Marburn Avenue, and I swelled with pride. I held my breath and sat on my hands to keep from wiggling too much. Even though she was different from other moms, even though she might not always be the mom I wanted or needed, she was mine.

I didn't know that hidden between the lyrics of her favorite song was a warning: things were going to change. Drastically.

On that autumn night in the hills of Los Angeles, surrounded by aunts and uncles and grandparents and cousins, I thought:

No one else has a mother as beautiful, creative, and talented as mine.

I must be the luckiest girl in the world.

DAVID AND I CREPT DOWN the steep stairs in front of our house. David wrapped his hand tightly around mine. I turned my head and looked back at our front door. David felt my hesitation and turned to me, his face a portrait of impatience.

"Come on," he said, tugging on my arm.

"I'm scared," I whispered.

"Stop being such a fraidy cat, Sharon. Stop shaking."

I tried to pull my hand from his. He gripped it tighter.

"Do you want to see them or not?"

I thought I did. I hesitated. Still, whatever was down there couldn't be worse than David teasing me. I squared my shoulders; time to be brave. David threw me a wicked grin. The fear in his eyes startled me. He didn't really want to do this either, but he was a boy and boys were strong and brave. Even if he was only ten.

With each step we took, the light of day retreated into darkness. Our destination: David's bedroom at the back of the garage where he had moved a month or so earlier. The room wasn't part of the house—more like an addition to the garage. The only way to get to it was through the garage. To get to the garage, we went outside, down the stairs leading from our front door to the street, and past the big bushes where the bogeyman lived. I never saw the bogeyman, but David assured me he existed and that if he saw us, we were goners because he liked to eat little kids.

We stepped off the last step and onto the pavement. David squeezed my hand.

"Ready?" he asked.

I barely heard him over the fear pulsing in my ears. I nodded.

"Ready ... set ..." He crouched down. I didn't know why he did that, but I did it too. He blew out a big breath of air. I did too. He yanked my arm. "Go!" We ran as fast as we could to the garage door. David pulled the garage door open. We rushed inside. David flicked on the light, slammed the door shut, and locked it behind us. We both leaned against the closed garage door, our knees shaking. We had made it halfway without being eaten.

19

"You stay here," he said as he put his arm protectively in front of me. As if he believed I was actually going to stand there by myself.

He bobbed up and down a couple of times. I did the same. Then he tore across the garage and kicked his bedroom door open. I was right on his heels. We flattened ourselves against the door and scanned the room for intruders. David checked under his bed, underneath the desk and chair, and in every corner. I stood flat against the door, my heart hammering in my chest.

He looked at me, his eyes as wide as saucers.

"Quick, Sharon. Up here!" He motioned to the top bunk of his bed. I scrambled up after him. He had his BB gun loaded and cocked. We lay flat and motionless on the mattress. And we waited.

"They don't come out during the day," David whispered. "I don't know where they are during the day, but I see them here every night."

I was too busy watching the shadows to say anything. I held my breath and waited for them to move. Then, I saw one. Two beady little eyes glinted in the fading light. It was the size of a small football. It scurried across the bedroom floor, dragging an impossibly long tail. I screamed at the pop of the BB gun, wrapped my arms around David in a death grip, and buried my face in his shirt. Apparently he wasn't lying about the rats.

~∽~

Three days earlier

"Sharon," David said, "don't ever tell Mother there are rats in my bedroom. I don't want her to know. Promise. It'll be our little secret."

Our little secret? I nodded my head solemnly, wondering how I was going to keep a secret as important as this one.

I ran to Mother.

"Mother! David has rats in his bedroom. He's scared. Can he please share my bedroom with me? Please?"

"I don't believe there are rats in his bedroom," Mother snapped. "He's just telling you that so he can sleep in the house again." Mother dismissed me with a wave of her hand. "He's staying in the garage, and I don't want to hear another word about it."

Disappointed, I ran to tell David the bad news.

"Sharon," Mother called after me. I turned to look at her. "Tell David that Timothy can sleep in his bedroom. I think that's a good idea." She winked at me. I clenched my hands into fists to keep from squealing with excitement. Best not to show too much emotion around Mother.

"Thank you, Mother." My voice was flat and toneless.

I ran to tell David the good news.

"Ha!" David said. "I knew it would work. I knew you would go tell her. Still wish I could come back in the house, but it'll be better out here with Timothy." He patted me on the head. "Good job, Sharon."

∾∘∾

I wasn't sure there were rats. I thought maybe he had invented the story, like Mother said, so I made David promise to show me the rats, to prove to me that he was telling the truth. Now, three days later, I watched a giant black rat scurry out of range of David's BB gun.

I was angry with Mother. She didn't even care if those rats hurt him or if the bogeyman ate him. I knew he was scared to walk down to the garage by himself, and I knew he was scared to sleep out there alone. When I told David I was mad at Mother, he just shrugged his shoulders. Then he popped off another round from his BB gun.

∾∘∾

Another time

David's room stunk.

"Phew, David!" I said, crinkling my nose. "It smells like pee in here!"

David laughed. "Yeah, I know. I don't have a bathroom, so I pee in these jars." He pointed to a row of jars filled with something that looked less like pee and more like a putrid witch's brew.

"That's gross!" I yelled. "Yuck! What's that dark ugly stuff on top?"

"I don't know. Think it fermented."

I waved my hand in front of my nose.

"What was I supposed to do, Sharon? I can't go upstairs in the dark because the bogeyman is waiting for me in the bushes. I was peeing through a hole in the wall, but that started to stink. So Mother told me to pee in the jars instead. She says at least that way I can get rid of it."

"How long do you keep them?"

"As long as I can stand it. I don't let Mother see them. She wants me to bury them in the hills. I don't want to touch them. Nasty!"

I rolled my eyes. "Why don't you just tell her you want to share a room with me? That way you can use the bathroom like the rest of us." I pinched my thumb and forefinger over my nose.

"I can't, Sharon. I don't want her to know that I'm scared. Besides, I think she does know, and I have to prove that I can do this."

I plopped on the floor and settled my chin in my hands.

David sat beside me and said, "Look, it's best I don't say too much. I don't want to get locked in the closet. I hate it when she locks me in there."

The closet. I nodded thoughtfully. I put my hand on his knee and rested my head on his shoulder to show him I knew. To show him I understood.

∽○∽

Later, David woke up and spied Timothy sleeping on the floor next to his bed, on his back, his paws straight up in the air. David touched Timothy's paw to wake him. Timothy's whole body rocked back and forth; he was stiff and dead.

Fat tears cascaded down my cheeks as Dad dug a hole in the backyard. I cried for Timothy, and I cried for David. My puppy was dead, and David would be alone in his garage bedroom. Alone with the rats and the bogeyman.

Mother sat on the porch, a glass of lemonade in her hand.

"Whew!" she yelled. "He stinks! Bury him deep, Harold! Bury him deep!"

I looked at David. He shrugged his shoulders.

∽○∽

After Timothy died, David brought stray dogs home. He desperately wanted another pet. Sometimes the dogs mysteriously died. More often Mother coaxed the dog into the car. David and I tumbled into the backseat. Mother drove us to the barren brown hills above our home.

"Open the door, and let the dog out!" Mother said after she pulled to the side of the road. After a moment of hesitation, David opened the back door, the dog bounded from the car, and Mother sped away. "The hills are the best place for animals," she said.

David and I scrambled to our knees and perched along the back window of the car. We stared at the dog chasing after us through clouds of dust. The dog became smaller and smaller, until it was the size of a pebble and then disappeared. Devastated, my heart ripped in two. I wondered whether our newfound pet would be safe from coyotes. I wondered who would feed him and take care of him when it was dark. I wondered why Mother was so mean.

IN 1949 IT SNOWED IN Los Angeles. That rarely happened. It wasn't a lot, not enough to make snowmen or snowballs, not enough to really stick to the ground, but that didn't matter; I was entranced. I pressed my nose against the chilled glass of the living room window and watched the tender white flakes dance and whirl about like miniature faeries against the gray afternoon sky. My breath left little frosted haloes on the glass.

I wrote to Mother and Dad because they weren't home to see the snow. They would never believe it! The previous week they had sailed on a big boat called the *Lurline* to Hawaii because Mother wasn't feeling well again. At least that was what Dad called it when she stayed in bed or when she sat in the chair in the living room and stared blankly. She looked lost. Dad told me if I ever got lost, I should stay put, sit real still, and wait for someone to come find me. Maybe that was what she was doing. Besides writing about the snow, I told them I hoped they didn't get seasick and that I missed them. I included five rows of Xs and Os just to make sure they wouldn't forget about me.

Grandmother Nowell had said she would stay with me but not David because he was too much trouble. David went to Utah to stay with Mother's twin brothers, Melvin and Marvin. I was content in our home alone with Grandmother Nowell. Although she was stern and proper and not as cozy as Grandma Hicks, I admired her independence and fearlessness—and I loved her stories. As a teenager in Utah, Grandmother was a maid for widower, Oliver Nowell, and his five sons. When she was nineteen, she married Oliver and bore six more boys and one daughter (Mother), an even dozen. Grandmother became a fabulous bread maker from necessity—to save her family from the Indians. Periodically the Indians circled their home, whooping and hollering. When she heard the ruckus, she ran outside to give them hot bread. Satisfied, the Indians rode away on their horses.

That afternoon Grandmother and I made scones. I pushed a chair next to the stove and watched Grandmother drop balls of dough into the hot grease. They tumbled and rolled in the yellow oil, and a few minutes later she scooped them up, tossed them in sugar, and served them with butter and jam.

"Go on, Sharon, have one."

I pinched one between my fingers. It burned. It slid from my fingers as I lifted it to my mouth, so I pinched it harder. And then my mouth exploded with hot, sugary, buttery goodness. It was what I imagined heaven tasted like. But I would never tell Grandmother Nowell that because she didn't believe in heaven.

"Don't believe in all that religious stuff, Sharon." Her voice was flat, not warm and cozy to match the chewy softness of the scones. "Church is all a show. Ever watch them on stage? It's all an act!" She shook her head. "Why, I saw a man the other day in Montrose who looked just like an ape. We're not far from the apes."

I didn't believe her. God created all of us. That was what Grandma Hicks said. Grandma Hicks believed, and I did too. I thought maybe Grandmother would get mad if I talked to her about God, so instead I licked the jam and butter from my fingers, grabbed another scone, and headed back to the window to watch the snow flutter to the ground like fallen angels.

∽∘∾

A week later, Mother and Dad returned from Hawaii. Mother pulsated with excitement. "The weather! The water! You've never seen anything so blue!" She jabbed her finger at me, and I recoiled. My stomach curled itself into a fist. I never meant for my stomach to get so tight. More than once Dad had carried me around the house because I couldn't walk, my stomach hurt so bad. "And it's so warm it's like taking a bath in the ocean! Imagine!" Her voice clicked like a typewriter, clackety-clackety-clackety-clack. "We must move there! Immediately! Life will be grand there! You'll see."

∽∘∾

The propellers were on fire. I knew we were going to die. I knew without a doubt that my short life of nine years was ending. The whole plane rattled, shook, and groaned. I seized the arms of my seat and waited for the window to pop and to be sucked into the vastness of the blue sky. I visualized myself spinning and falling toward the ocean, to my deep blue grave. I pulled my eyes from the window. Instantly the plane felt too tight. There was no place to run, no place to hide, no place to get free. I decided right then and there that if I survived, I would never fly back to California, never spend another ten hours in this death trap. I hoped I liked Hawaii because I would be stuck there forever.

David was excited. All he talked about were his stupid nylon swimming trunks. They were chartreuse and bright green and visible for miles. He wore them on the plane because as soon as we landed, he planned to jump into the ocean.

I must have fallen asleep because the next thing I knew, people were shouting: "There it is! There it is! We are here!" We came around Diamond Head crater and saw Waikiki with two big buildings on the white, sandy beach. One was pink, and someone called it the Royal Hawaiian Hotel. The other one was white and called the Moana Hotel. I wondered if we were staying in one of them. As we started our descent, I watched the crystal waters licking the white sand on the beach and imagined the warm waves dribbling over my toes. I relaxed. My stomach unclenched.

The first thing I noticed when I stepped off the plane was the gentle Hawaiian breeze caressing my face, pregnant with moisture. I craned my neck around the people standing in front of me, looking for Dad. (He had left California about a week earlier to begin building homes with Uncle Ernie.) I finally found him in the sea of people and waved madly. Mother, David, and I squeezed and squirmed our way through the crowd, and Dad swept me into a big hug.

"Missed you, Susie!" he said as he kissed me on the cheek.

"Missed you too, Dad!" I nuzzled my face into his neck.

Dad put me down and draped a flower necklace called a lei around my neck. "These flowers are plumerias, and they grow on trees all over the island. Susie, you can pick them off the ground by the armful."

I buried my nose in the yellow and white flowers and inhaled their spicy sweetness. And then it happened. It took me totally by surprise. Something exploded; little fingers of delight tickled my insides, and I knew there was new life here. I didn't know how I knew, but the times of being locked in closets, of being locked outside of the house, of feeling alone and dismissed, of David sleeping in the garage were over. I was certain of it. In Hawaii there were uncles and aunts and cousins and miles of beach, and the Pacific Ocean stretched to eternity. There was sunshine and openness, and everything was green and lush and full of promise. I breathed in the tropical trade winds of my new home. Hawaii would fix everything.

IT DIDN'T TAKE ME LONG to relax into the rhythm of Hawaii. There was something about the aina (the land)—the way she wrapped her arms around you and gathered you into her womb. For the first time in my life, I felt protected.

We lived in a one-bedroom apartment while Dad built us a home in the country. Our apartment was across the street from the Ala Wai Canal in Waikiki. David and I explored the canal in a little dinghy; the blades of our oars dipped, swept, and sent ripples across the water's surface. I wore my one-piece swimsuit, and David wore those chartreuse swimming trunks that glared like a beacon. We marveled at the huge Samoan crabs scuttling along the canal's concrete edges, the schools of mullet, and at the locals with their bamboo poles and wads of white bread for bait. There was a calm simplicity here in the islands—an easy flow that lulled me into believing that our life in California might not have existed. Mother seemed different, happier. Dad seemed happier. David didn't run and leave me behind. Sometimes while David rowed in circles, I tilted my head back and took a long, deep pull of the sweet Hawaiian air and then gave myself a little pinch just to make sure it was real.

In the evenings when the sky streaked of deep corals, oranges, and yellows, we strolled on Waikiki beach. We passed the tourists and the locals. I wasn't a tourist but I wasn't a *kama'aina* (local) either. The locals called the tourists and newcomers *malihini*. Some people said you became a *kama'aina* when you lived here for seven years. Others said when you ate *poi* and *laulau* for the first time. Still others said when you ditched the white socks and shoes for *slippas* or understood when a local said, "Eh, what school you grad?" or "Where you stay" or "You know, brah, *da kine*." Basically, you became *kama'aina* when Hawaii felt like home. If so, then I became *kama'aina* the moment I stepped off the plane.

Mother, Dad, David, and I often walked along the main drag in Waikiki. I tried to match Mother's graceful stride, and my bare feet slapped the pavement a few paces behind her. Mother "talked story" (chatted) with the locals and the tourists. She smiled, laughed, and giggled. She made perfect strangers think they were important to her. I smiled, giggled, and skipped after her, wishing she would fold my hand into hers so people would know I was her daughter.

Fridays were "kill a *ha'ole* day" at school. David and I were *ha'oles*, meaning "without breath." When the first foreigners arrived in Hawaii, they did not know or use the *honi*, a Polynesian greeting by touching nose to nose, inhaling, and sharing each other's breath. To share breath was to share life. Foreigners were aloof and ignorant of the local ways and were considered not to have any spirit or life within. They also stole the land from the Hawaiians, which did nothing to endear the white folks to the locals. Locals would say, "The missionaries came to do good, and they did very well." Consequently, the *ha'ole* way was held in contempt. We were seen as invaders, intruders—those who took without asking. We were seen as brash and cocky and without regard for anyone but ourselves.

It happened on the first day of ninth grade for David. The kid called David a cocky *ha'ole*. Thankfully, Jack—everyone called him Big Jack—liked David on that very first day. "You beef my friend, you beef me," Jack challenged the boy after school as a crowd gathered around, eager for bloodshed. But that was the end of the fight. No one messed with Big Jack.

No one wanted to beef with me in fifth grade. I wasn't cocky. I was quiet and shy—invisible. I melted into the background. I became scenery. It was how I survived. I learned that being invisible had advantages, primarily that when you were invisible, no one wanted to kick your ass.

On Sundays, my aunts, uncles, cousins, Mother, Dad, David, and I went to Aunt Pudie and Uncle Ernie's house on Diamond Head Circle. We barbecued, sang, played music, and swam in their pool. I splashed around in the pool with my twelve cousins and laughed until my face hurt. Cousin Julianne (who was one year younger) and I helped with our one-year-old twin cousins, Keiki and Lani. We felt so grown up as we straddled the babies on our hips and took them inside the house to change their diapers. Keiki was my favorite. I watched her like a hawk to make sure she didn't fall into the pool, hoisted her onto my lap, and brushed her hair. In the bathroom, I took her diaper off and spanked her until her *okole* (bottom) was bright red, until she sobbed and sucked in great, hiccupping breaths. The slap felt good against my hand. I felt powerful. I gathered her in my arms and pressed her tightly to my chest. I held her until she stopped crying and told her everything was going to be okay.

〜〇〜

In September 1951, we moved into our new home that Dad had built for us in the country on Maunalua Bay. At night I treasured the times when Dad and I lay on the lawn in our backyard. The air was warm and moist, cooled by ribbons of trade winds. I leaned against Dad's chest, my head rising and falling with the rhythm of his breathing. Dad folded his hands behind his head.

"Look, Susie, out there in space. All humans share the night sky. No matter where you are, in the mountains and lakes of Canada, on the plains of Africa, in the desert of Central Asia, or on a little island here in the middle of the Pacific Ocean, the night sky is seen and enjoyed."

I loved these stimulating conversations with my dad. They made me think I was part of something limitless and grand. They made me feel important. As his chest inflated with a deep breath, I thought about how lucky I was to have such a wonderful and handsome dad. My eyes tripped over the twinkling stars. I tried to take in the enormity of it all. I nestled deeper into his chest.

"There are just so many stars and stuff," I said.

"That's right, Susie. No beginning, no end, no middle. Here we are, you and me looking at the wonder of it all."

Dad's chest pillowed and deflated again. He smoothed back my hair with his hand. It was warm and comforting on my forehead. I was at peace, out here in the open, underneath the night sky. I closed my eyes and listened to Dad's heartbeat, to my heartbeat, a syncopated rhythm. When I opened my eyes, a star shot across the sky.

"Make a wish," Dad said.

I wished it could always be like this. Calm and predictable. Relaxed and free. I reached up and wrapped my fingers around the night sky. Then I pulled my hand back and clutched it to my chest, a fistful of hope.

〜〇〜

Puchi, Lani, and I were best friends. We formed a club. We were the older girls of the neighborhood, so forming a club made absolute sense. Puchi lived next door to me, and Lani lived next door to Puchi. Our club was special. Not everyone could join. In fact, we were the only members. We spent hours and hours trying to settle on a name: PSL or SLP or LPS or any combination of our three initials. I preferred having my initial in the middle. I felt safer that way for some reason. We played and laughed and splashed in the swimming hole in our bay. We stripped and exchanged bathing suits in the water because we believed the whole world revolved around us and *won't the neighbors be shocked when we return in different suits!* We scrambled up the beach, speckled with salt and sand, and ran across the three-lane county highway to play with the cows that lived in the pasture. The three of us lay flat in the middle of the field, shivering with delight, hands pressed over our mouths to stifle the giggling. Soon several curious cows would lope over to where we hid in the grass. We held each other's hands, snorted, and giggled. Then, suddenly, we leaped to scare the cows. The cows bolted, running for their lives, scared to death by three little girls who were doubled over, hysterical with laughter.

On some nights Dad, David, and I fished with torches in Maunalua Bay with our neighbors. Carefully, we waded through the still, shallow water, searching for dark shadows that streaked below the surface. I straddled a surfboard and held the lantern while Dad pushed me around, protecting me from whatever lurked in the water. I swirled my feet in the tepid water, bits of *limu* (seaweed) tickling my toes. David would take off alone. He didn't need protection because he was fourteen and almost a man.

The flames of the lanterns danced across the surface of the water, creating the illusion of natural light. The reef fish darted upward, propelled toward the light by instinct—an instinct to feed, to live. They were confused. Mesmerized. Tricked. Dad raised his spear. He watched and waited, motionless. I shivered with excitement. I don't know what it was about watching my dad frozen, spear hovering, poised for the kill. Maybe it was the primal energy of the hunt, the focus in Dad's eyes, the way his tanned muscles glistened in the lantern light, but at that moment, I knew everything was really okay. Dad sucked in his breath and hurled the spear at the surface of the water. He smiled as he pulled the spear from the water. Impaled on the end was a thrashing fish.

Life was good. Scratch that—life was great.

AND THEN IT WASN'T. There was no end in sight. There were too many of them. I scratched the tip of my nose with the back of my hand and then plunged my hand back into the basin of soapy water. Mother had told me to wash and dry every dish in the house and then to sweep the floors and clean the sliding glass doors, no streaks, no smudges. I pulled the last plate from the sink, rinsed it, and set it on the counter to dry. I had already cleaned three hutches full of dishes and knickknacks. I had just finished the dishes in the cupboards.

Mother had planned a surprise anniversary party for Dad that night to celebrate seventeen years of marriage. It was my job to clean the house. Mother's job was to sunbathe on the lanai.

"My pretty tan will make me ravishing tonight," she had said.

I climbed down from the stool, dried the last dish, and put it in the cupboard. I peeked through the sliding glass doors and saw Mother flip onto her stomach; the Hawaiian sun caressed her beautiful, shapely thirty-three-year-old body. I glanced down at my ten-year-old skinniness and wondered how I would look as a mature woman. I wondered if I would be an olive-skinned beauty with curves in all the right places like Mother. I wondered if men would stare at me the way they stared at her.

Mother shifted and threw her arm over her eyes to shield them from the sun. I looked at my fingertips, which were swollen and wrinkled, and dragged my hand across my forehead. Mother had been sunbathing all day. It was now 3:00. Other than three hutches and cupboards full of clean dishes, there wasn't a single shred of evidence that a party was planned for tonight. I opened the refrigerator door and clung to the possibility that food for the party was tucked and stacked neatly on the shelves, that somehow I had missed seeing it when I checked the refrigerator an hour earlier. No such luck. I knew I shouldn't do it, knew I should have just left it alone, but I worried, so I tucked a strand of hair behind my ear and went outside to the lanai.

"Mother, there's no food in the house. What will the guests eat?"

She turned over and stared at me through her black-and-white polka dot–rimmed sunglasses. Then she pulled them down to the tip of her nose and stared at me with a look of impatience and pity, as though she were assessing the level of my stupidity and wondering why I didn't already know the answer. She crooked her finger at me and beckoned me closer. Instinctively, I took a step back and tripped over my own heels. Mother's eyes flicked up and down, running the length of me. They darted, frantic, unsettled.

"God. Will. Provide," she said, her words crisp. "Don't you worry about a thing, Sharon. God will provide. He told me so himself."

"I bet Dad will be surprised," I answered, trying to find something to say. Mother bolted upright. Even as the words left my mouth, I realized I had made a horrible, irreparable mistake.

"Another thing: your dad is not your dad," she snapped. "I really don't know who your father is—certainly not that weakling of a man I married." Her words, sharp and razor-like, sliced me open.

Mother ran her fingers through her hair and adjusted her bikini top. "After this party, I'm getting a divorce. Can't stand your father. Can't stand to live with him anymore." She paused to allow the words to gain weight. Then she frowned. "But I don't know if I can live without him." She shrugged her shoulders and laughed. "Can't live with him, can't live without him. How 'bout that!"

She leaped from the lounge chair and trotted into the house, snapping her fingers and humming a little tune. She was a flurry of motion. I stood there, frozen.

≈≈≈

At around seven o'clock, the guests began to arrive: friends, neighbors, and relatives. When the doorbell rang, I flitted across the room, opened the door, and smiled at each guest. "Good evening, thank you for coming. So happy you could join us." I invited them into our home with a gentle, graceful wave of my hand. I was the perfect hostess. Mother and Dad were having drinks at a neighborhood restaurant with their friends Ed and Esther. They were due back any minute, and it was my job to orchestrate the "Surprise!" part of the surprise party.

In between tending to the growing number of guests who wondered where the food and drinks were and questions to which I had no ready answer ("God will provide" didn't seem like the right thing to say), I kept watch at the front window. At about half past seven, the headlights of our car swept across the driveway, and I sprang into action. I flipped off the lights and ushered everyone together in the living room, ready to surprise Dad. The doorknob clicked, and we all crouched a little lower. The door opened, and I threw on the lights. Everyone shouted: "Surprise! Happy anniversary! Seventeen years! Imagine! Congratulations!" Hugs. Kisses. Handshakes. Dad grinned, and Mother clapped her hands madly.

Mother smiled, her teeth gleaming white against her red lipstick. She fluttered from guest to guest and thanked them for coming; she kissed each on the cheek. The room was instantly more vibrant because she was in it. But terror started to grip me. I wasn't sure how, but I knew something was going to happen. The unpredictability of it all sucked me down like an undertow, leaving me kicking and screaming and gasping for air.

It didn't take long.

Suddenly Mother announced, "I'm hot. I'm going to take a shower," her words clipped and hard. It happened without warning, without reason, like someone had flipped a switch. It was that fast. I watched her prance off to the bedroom. And in the way animals hunker down when they know a storm is brewing, I squeezed myself into a corner in the living room and waited.

A few minutes later, Mother glided from the bedroom wearing a pink see-through negligee, her burgundy nipples straining through the fabric. A teddy bear was nestled in the crook of her arm. Anxiety, panic, and embarrassment clobbered me. I pressed myself further into the corner and held my breath.

Mother floated through the room to Dad and gave him a little peck on the cheek. Then she sashayed among the guests, nodded her head, and waved like a queen. The entire house fell quiet except for some random throat clearing and a few surprised giggles. People looked at their feet, at the ceiling, at each other, and at Dad for some sort of explanation. They stared at anything to avoid staring directly at Mother, who was stark naked beneath the negligee. She made one final sweep through the crowd and then danced back to the bedroom.

The guests milled around with tumblers of ice and amber liquid in their hands, and for a moment I rose from a fog of confusion to wonder who had brought the liquor. The doorbell chimed, and I blanched at the thought of anyone else being exposed to (and by) Mother. Dad opened the door, and in walked the most handsome man I had ever seen. He was a bit taller than Dad, and his liquid blue eyes stood out against his deep Hawaiian tan. Dad motioned for me to come, so I peeled myself out of the corner and on shaky legs, snaked my way through the crowd. Dad introduced the man as his friend from the Aina Haina Lions Club. As I shook the man's hand, I heard a strangled gasp behind me and turned to see Mother floating out of the bedroom again, this time in a see-through white negligee, a triangle of hair clearly visible through the sheer fabric, the teddy bear still cradled in her arm. She spied Dad and his friend and immediately glided over to us, her hands sliding seductively down her body. My stomach twisted and flipped, and I felt the color drain from my face by degrees.

Mother gave me a rough shove and extended her hand toward Dad's friend.

"So nice to meet you," she purred. "We're so glad you're here."

Mother slipped her arm through the man's elbow and pressed her hips and breasts into him. I glanced at Dad. His jaw was clenched, and his eyes were hard and tight even as he managed to smile. A soft hand slipped over my shoulder, and I turned to see Esther standing behind me. She winked at me then turned to Mother. "Time to eat, Carolyn."

Eat? Where did the food come from? I craned my neck around Mother and saw Aunt Pudie and our next-door neighbor, Beulah, carrying big trays of food into the kitchen.

Mother's face went dark.

"I don't want to eat now!" she hissed. "Take that food away!"

I cringed behind Dad's leg. Mother turned to Dad's friend and ran her finger along the collar of his shirt.

"Come on, Carolyn. Let's get some food," Dad urged. He took Mother by the elbow to pull her away from his friend.

"Get your hands off me! You shithead! Can't you see I'm busy?"

Dark, stinging tears swelled up behind my eyes. Mother was ruining the party. She was humiliating us all. I suddenly felt flattened, drained, and deflated.

From across the room, Uncle Ernie yelled, "Oh, leave her alone. She's fine. She's just having a little fun, feeling good."

Mother wrenched away from Dad and darted back to the bedroom.

I grabbed my gut to relieve the tightness. Maybe I hadn't cleaned the house and dishes to her satisfaction; maybe I shouldn't have talked with her that afternoon. Maybe I set her off. I folded my hand into Dad's and squeezed an apology.

The handsome stranger knelt down next to me and looked me straight in the eyes. He had the kindest eyes I had ever seen, and I was overcome by an urge to curl up in his lap. "Let's go next door," he said, and he took my hand from Dad's and led me from the house.

I didn't know where David was all evening, but suddenly he was there with me, sitting on the couch at our next-door neighbor's house. Dad sat on the loveseat, his head down, looking at the floor. He looked as though he'd been whipped. The handsome stranger sat down next to Dad and folded his hands in his lap.

"I'm not just your dad's friend," he said. "I am a doctor. My name is Dr. Paskowitz, and I came tonight to observe your mother."

Even though his voice was gentle and soothing, I could not relax. The events of the evening were still skittering in my head, and I only vaguely understood what he was saying. I was terrified of what Mother was probably doing at that very minute, in front of all those people.

"Your mother is sick," Dr. Paskowitz continued. "There are many diseases, and she has a disease of the mind. We need to treat her as if we are treating any other disease—like cancer or heart disease."

Sick? He said she is sick.

It took a moment for the words to register, for understanding to take hold. There was an answer. An explanation. It was not my fault. The house was clean enough. She had a disease. The words were like a salve. They were magic words. They were words of absolution. I heard David exhale beside me. *What was he thinking?* Like Uncle Ernie, he always believed Mother was having fun.

"Do you understand, child?" he asked me.

"If she's sick, that means she can get well, right? Like with a pill or an operation?"

"Yes, she can get well."

I was in love with Dr. Paskowitz. Relief opened like a paper fan. I allowed myself to imagine that maybe, once she was well, I could finally call her Mom. The very thought of it left me dizzy with delight. And even as I curled my tongue around the word to keep it safe, I could not imagine what it would be like. To be held and kissed and rocked to sleep. To have her brush my hair and ask about school and my friends. I gorged myself on the possibilities.

"I need you to listen very carefully." Dr. Paskowitz's voice pulled me from my daydream. "Some things are going to happen right now that might look very scary, but they will let us help your mom."

He said *mom* like it was already real.

"I have called an ambulance," he continued. "We are going to take her to the hospital. There will be men in white coats, and they will strap her down. She will probably scream and yell, but we have to strap her down. It's for her safety. She doesn't know she is sick."

This last statement threw me. *If she doesn't know she is sick, then how will she know when she is well?* The balloon of hope started to hiss and shrivel as this question tumbled around unanswered in my mind. It occurred to me, momentarily, that this all might be too good to be true.

And then suddenly we were home again. Mother had changed again, this time into a black see-through negligee, the teddy bear a permanent accessory. I waited nervously for the knock at the door, for the arrival of the men in white coats. My ears pulsed with anticipation.

Mother latched on to Dr. Paskowitz again and ran her forefinger down the length of his chin. "Where have you been, you naughty boy?"

Dr. Paskowitz smiled and took Mother's hand in his.

There was a knock at the door. I flinched and flicked my eyes between the front door and Mother.

My memory of what happened next played like an old, scratched film reel that ran too slowly—all warped and distorted, sounds and images out of alignment, tumbling over the other. A blur of white coats. Hands. So many big, strong hands that grabbed, gripped, restrained. Mother screamed: "Shitheads! This is my house! Help me! Don't just stand there. Somebody help me!"

The teddy bear fell from Mother's arms. I lunged forward to rescue it. It was all I could think to do. I was helpless. I wished she would stop screaming and jerking. I wished she would go quietly— not because I was afraid they were hurting her but because she was being strapped down against her will. Because we both were powerless to stop it. And I didn't want to watch.

"Carolyn," Dad called, his voice cracking. "Darling, it's for your own good. You need help. Please. You need help."

Mother twisted toward Dad. "Harold! You are the biggest shithead of them all! I'm just having some fun. Why do you want to spoil my fun? It's my party. I can do whatever I damn well please! Goddamn you! I want a divorce!"

Hands and white coats wrestled and strapped my mother onto the gurney. Her eyes were wild with fear as she struggled under the restraints all the way to the ambulance. The ambulance doors slammed shut and sped away.

And then there was silence.

THE HOUSE REMAINED quiet and somber—filled with Mother's absence. Once in a while, I thought it was all a dream, the disjointed way it all unfolded, the way it felt like I was underwater the whole time. But it wasn't a dream. It was real.

Dad and I piled into the car and drove to Kaneohe State Mental Hospital to see Mother. It had been three days since the anniversary party. We didn't talk about it much, but I knew Dad's heart was breaking. He was lost without her. On the other hand, I was hopeful and relieved that she was sick. I couldn't stop smiling and chattering incessantly. *What do you think she'll be like? Do you think she'll hug me? Ask how I'm doing? What will the doctors say? Will she be able to come home with us today? Everything will be okay now, won't it?* I held Dr. Paskowitz's promise in my hands with a death grip. He had said she would be cured, and I believed him. How could it be any different?

I didn't ask Dad those questions. I actually didn't say anything at all because Dad looked tense. I decided that I must be a comfort to him rather than a burden like Mother. As the questions tumbled around in my mind like gleeful puppies, I sat quietly and folded my hands in my lap. I glanced out the car window and was struck by the beauty of the day: the way the sun shone in the clear blue sky, the way the blue waves turned to white foam as they crashed along the beach along black lava. We drove by Hana'uma Bay and then through Makapu'u and Waimanalo. As we turned into the long drive that led to the hospital, toward the Ko'olau Mountains rising like green pillars behind the hospital and shrouded in gray mist, one more question joined the fray: *Will she love me now?*

I can't tell exactly when it happened. It probably wasn't any one particular moment but rather a slow meander toward the realization that my mother didn't really love me—not in the way other mothers loved their daughters. I knew this through very careful observation: there were no hugs, no kisses, no warm hands rubbing slow, lazy circles across my back when I was sick or in need of comfort. There was, quite frankly, no apparent concern for me at all. I was simply in the way. Now I understood she was sick, and maybe this sickness in her head also made her sick in her heart. It wasn't that she didn't want to love me; it was that she really didn't know how because she was sick. And Dr. Paskowitz had promised to fix that.

∞

My first thought when I saw her was: *There's been a horrible mistake. Something is terribly wrong. Someone messed up.* Her fingers were curled around the aluminum chain link fence that bordered a green grassy area of the hospital. Her hair was matted, her hospital gown tattered and stained. Eyes wild and sharpened. This was not the mother I had imagined. This was not what Dr. Paskowitz had promised.

Mother spotted us and rattled the fence. I swallowed my disappointment so hard my throat hurt. I pulled Dad's hand. I didn't want to go inside. There could be others like her in there. This was not what I came to see.

"Hey!" she yelled. "Shitheads!" Fear pulsed through me. Dad's face dropped. This was not what he came to see either.

Mother hiked up her tattered hospital gown. "Look at this! Someone fucking bit me!" She pointed to her upper thigh, which was black and blue and indented with a neat row of teeth marks.

We left her hanging on the fence and entered the hospital. Dad and I walked down hallways, through double doors, down more hallways, past other patients who were shuffling and mumbling and chattering and smacking the sides of their heads with their hands. My eyes fixed to the cold linoleum floor. I was afraid to look at these people. I wished I could tuck and fold myself until I was small enough to hide in Dad's pocket. I was suddenly in the grips of an irrational fear that I might someday end up in a place like this.

Dad and I finally reached the giant locked door with "Secure Ward" stenciled in big, black letters. Dad pushed the buzzer, a nurse opened the door, and we walked down a series of halls until we reached Mother's room. She waved us into her room with a grand sweep of her arm, loped around us in circles, and then hopped up on the bed.

"There was a ball! I am the queen!" She leaped from the bed and darted across the room to retrieve a paper crown. She smashed it over her dirty hair and then flopped back into the tangle of sheets on the bed. "You must bow to the queen!" She pointed to the floor.

I flattened myself against the cold brick wall. I breathed like a compressor: short, spasmodic bursts. This was not what I had expected. She was supposed to be better. Calmer. Better. Normal.

Suddenly Mother bolted upright and flung herself across the room again.

"I am an art-e-e-st! A fucking genius! We must sell these paintings, Harold. We'll make millions!"

She threw crumpled papers at Dad's chest. I caught a glimpse of her paintings: pages filled with swirls and swipes of chaos and confusion, like her brain had thrown up a Crayola box. Dad sat them down on a table, the only flat-topped piece of furniture in this tiny room. He ran his hand through his hair. Mother talked a blue streak—unintelligible, incomprehensible blabber. She never looked at me. She never talked to me. I was invisible. I slid down the wall and tucked my knees into my chest. Disappointment spilled from me by the bucketful and pooled around my shoes.

I didn't know much of what happened to Mother in the hospital, only that she stayed there for three months and that, according to the doctors, she could still get well. After I saw my mother raging and splitting in all directions, I wasn't sure I believed them. She wasn't sick. She was crazy. And I didn't think there was a cure for crazy.

∽⚬∾

I stood on my tiptoes, reaching and straining. I flipped the pants over the clothesline. Opened the clothespin. Attached the clothespin. Stepped off the stool. Moved it over a few inches. I loved hanging the clothes outside in the warm sun. I diligently counted each piece as I hung them on the clothesline. In the kitchen sink, I dipped the shirts in starch and hung them outside to dry. When they dried, I sprinkled them with water, rolled them in a towel, and put them in the refrigerator. Note to self: *don't forget to iron tomorrow*. Next, the beds: Mother and Dad's bed was huge. Dad had built it especially for them. It was low and firm, like a wrestler's mat. I flipped the custom made sheets, spread them out, and pulled them tight. I heard *her* voice: *a clean and orderly house is a clean and orderly life.* I washed another load of laundry in our wringer washer, rinsed them in one tub, and rinsed them again in another tub. I squeezed them through the ringer. *Careful, now! Don't snap the buttons! Don't twist the zippers!*

Dad came home. "Hi, Dad. How's your day? Sit down. Relax. Put your feet up. Don't you worry about a thing; I've got it covered."

I sliced the spam into a casserole dish and topped each slice with a pineapple ring, sprinkled each slice with brown sugar, and popped the dish into the oven. I knew Mother couldn't make this. I had learned this at school. After dinner, I cleared the dishes, cleaned the table, washed the dishes, scrubbed the sink, and swept the floor. Then I collapsed into bed, exhausted. When I woke up, I started again. This was good. This was working. Dad was happier. I guess it sort of happened by degrees, the way I disappeared. My focus narrowed and sharpened on pleasing Dad, on making things right, on filling the space that was once shaped like Mother. My needs were suddenly irrelevant. They were clutter, so I boxed and stored them in the carport next to the unpacked dishes.

⌇

A month or so into Mother's hospitalization, the doctors said she was an excellent candidate for a lobotomy. They assured Dad that many reputable psychiatrists all over the world performed thousands of lobotomies. The side effects were loss of emotions, loss of personality, and loss of self. In other words, she could become a vegetable. She might not come home. Dad declined because he didn't understand how an ice pick to her brain would bring back the woman he loved. He wanted his wife back. And I wanted a mom, as promised.

⌇

Three months later, Mother came home. They had given her a round of shock treatments. She was confused, disoriented, and groggy most of the time. She didn't know where she was, how to get to the grocery store, how to wash dishes or do laundry, or even on which side of the street to drive. (The fact that she was even allowed to drive during this time still baffled me.) She mostly limped along in a series of shuffled lurches and jerks, her face a permanent question mark. Dad told me it was my job to help her remember. I took her hand and reminded her again who she was, who we were, and how we chopped carrots.

MY PERIOD STARTED. I didn't want to talk to her about it. I felt afraid: afraid of the blood pouring from me, afraid of Mother's reaction. We didn't have that kind of relationship where I could talk to her about things that mattered to me, about things that scared me. I didn't want to make her mad. Still, I hoped this would connect us—would give us a loving mother-daughter moment.

At her bedroom door, I saw Mother stretched on her wrestler-mat bed. I couldn't help but admire her: her long and slender legs, her toes painted bright red, her wavy hair, and her smooth, olive complexion. I hoped that someday I would be as beautiful.

She patted the bed next to her. An invitation. I sat down on the edge of the mattress. My head started to tingle, and I couldn't tell if I was nervous or excited. Chances were she would ruin this moment, this opportunity for the two of us to connect.

I blurted it out: "I'm bleeding."

"Sharon, dear. My sweet Sharon. My little girl is changing into a woman. And do you know how wonderful that is? To be a woman?" She stroked my hair away from my face. She never stroked my hair.

"What do you mean, Mother?"

She cupped my face in her hands.

"When you are a woman, you attract men. This is what is happening to your body now, and this is what your body is for—to attract men, to satisfy men."

She smiled at me.

"My little girl. Do you understand?"

At the moment I thought I might get what I had always wanted, I immediately wished it would go away because the reality of it was so different from how it had played out in my head.

"Sharon," Mother continued, oblivious to the fact that I had stiffened to the point of rigor mortis. "When a man sticks his hard penis in you, it will drive you crazy! I can't describe the feeling … mmmmm … it's just pure ecstasy!"

44

The word *penis* bounced around inside my head like a rubber ball. I tried to hold the word still, but it wriggled and squirmed and then nested in the corner of my mind. It was an intruder that had snuck in through an open window I thought was closed.

"But Mother, why am I bleeding?"

"Why, dear, don't you know?"

I shook my head, terrified of the answer.

"You're preparing for a man's hardness."

Then there was no blood. By the next morning it was gone. Thank goodness. I didn't want to be a woman. I didn't want a man's penis inside me, driving me crazy. I was only in the sixth grade. I wanted to be a little girl.

Before first recess, I felt something wet and sticky on the seat beneath me. I shifted to the side a little and looked. I saw a pool of blood all over my seat and on my skirt, a crimson stain. I scrubbed my seat with my skirt and ran to the school nurse, praying no one found the mess I had created. I needed to hide.

But the kind and gentle nurse explained what was happening to my body. She told me how to clean myself, how to wear a pad, how often to change my pads, and how to track my periods on a calendar.

She never used the words penis, hardness, or ecstasy.

IT HAD BEEN THREE YEARS since Dr. Paskowitz had promised me a mom. She was in the "normal" stage—that stage after the numbing effects of the last shock treatment wore off. She was calm, subdued, hollowed out. Normal, in our house, teetered precariously on the edge of a very thin fence. Mania lived on one side and depression on the other, and no one ever really knew what was going to tip the balance. And believe it or not, these times were the worst because she looked like (mostly) and acted (very nearly) like a real mom. The resemblance was striking, convincing, and made you want to reach out and touch her to make sure she was real. Even though she wasn't. She was no more a real mom than I was a real girl.

∽∘∘∾

I sat on the edge of the bathtub, one leg laid out on the edge, the other inside the tub for stability. David straddled the edge. He looked me in the eye, and then brandished a razor from his back pocket. "It's time," he said.

He set the razor down and began lathering my stretched-out leg with soap.

I nibbled my nails.

"You need to act your age, Sharon. Start taking care of yourself."

He looked at me solemnly, blue eyes glinting. I nodded solemnly. This was a very solemn occasion.

"You're in eighth grade now. It's time for you to learn how to be a young lady."

David dragged the razor up the front of my shin to below my knee. I flinched because it tickled. David scowled and then cut another swath of bare skin up my leg.

"Just like this, okay? Always up, never down and never across. Remember that." He handed me the bar of soap and the razor.

I held the items delicately, as if they were breakable. Once I did this, there was no going back. I would be a young lady. I slathered

46

soap up and down my leg, all the way to my knee. I looked at David. He nodded. I drew in a ragged breath and placed the razor on my ankle. Just then, Mother shuffled by our bathroom in Dad's oversized, faded T-shirt. She paused at the bathroom door. Her empty, hollowed eyes swept across the white tile.

"We need a hat rack," she said to no one in particular.

David and I looked at each other, eyebrows raised.

"By the front door. So I can hang up my panties." She sniffled. "I have nowhere to hang up my panties. And visitors have nowhere to hang up their underpants. No one should wear underpants. Not in my house."

Mother shuffled back the way she had come. Her bedroom door clicked shut.

David and I shrugged.

I pulled the razor up the length of my leg.

"Good, Sharon," David said. "Very, very good."

A few days later, David called me into the bathroom again. His was blond hair slicked back, and his eyes shimmered pools of blue. At seventeen, he was quite handsome, a real catch. When his friends came to our house, I could hear them comparing and counting. *How far can you squirt? How many inches are you? How many girls have you had? How many times?*

When Mother felt well, David regaled her and Dad with stories of his girlfriends, proudly displaying the notches on his bedpost. He and his friends discussed their penis size and the pliability of Betty or Jane or Sandra's breasts. Mother and Dad listened, asked questions, and offered advice. Sex permeated the air. It always had. I had long been aware of my parents' sexual energy; they often disappeared into the bedroom for "long naps." Hours later they came out of their bedroom, spent and flushed. As early as I could remember, conversations around the dinner table had centered on the pleasure of sex, the ecstasy of orgasm. While I was told to keep my legs shut in order to avoid becoming "used goods," David was encouraged to have as many girls as he could. And he did. Mother and Dad couldn't have been prouder. David was becoming a fine young man. He knew what men wanted in a woman. I would learn from him.

David stood in front of the bathroom mirror, an assortment of Mother's lipsticks lined up on the counter like little soldiers.

"If you want boys to start paying attention to you, Sharon, then you need to make yourself more desirable."

He thrust a tube of lipstick at me. I raised my eyebrows, excited and uncertain. I twisted the tube. Bright red. Like candy canes. Or red jellybeans. I smeared the lipstick across my face, wielding the tube like a crayon. David supervised.

"Not too much. No, that's too red; boys will think you're easy. Lighter. Try again. That's better." David handed me a folded tissue. "Now blot. Like this. Gently. Good." He stepped back and smiled, satisfied.

I surveyed myself in the mirror. My bright red lips jutted from the rest of my face. I felt older and sophisticated. I smiled, frowned, and licked a bit of lipstick off my teeth. I pursed my lips together in a mock kiss.

David punched me in the shoulder.

We found Dad relaxing on the couch in the living room. I jumped up beside him.

"Look!" I practically shouted. "I'm wearing lipstick."

I made my mock kissing face at him. Dad frowned. I pulled back. By now the need to please my father had settled into my bones. Any hint of disappointment from him sent me spinning.

"Susie, you can always tell when a woman wears her makeup properly. It doesn't show. No woman should hide her beauty." He smudged the lipstick from my lips with his thumb. "Class in a woman isn't found in her makeup. It's found in her manner, how she dresses, how she walks and talks. Women who wear lots of makeup do it to show off for other women or to cover up their own insecurities."

Dad ran his thumb over my lips again and removed whatever color was left.

My lips felt naked.

Dad winked at me.

"You don't need to wear lipstick, Susie. You're already a beautiful girl."

Now I was the one who was disappointed. I wanted him to see me as a beautiful young lady. I was thirteen!

∽o∾

We settled into a routine, a rhythm that mostly involved walking around on eggshells and holding our breaths as we swung along the arc of Mother's moods. Dad worked long hours, building a hundred homes a month. His construction company, Hicks Construction, was thriving because Dad was the first to offer predesigned, affordable homes in Hawaii. David left for college. He hopped a plane, hopped out of our lives, hopped out of the chaos and landed at Fresno State College in California.

I went to high school and took piano and hula lessons. I dated Roy. I dated Hank. I dated Danny. Dad worried. Mother laughed: "Who is it this week, Sharon?"

HE WAS DARK, quiet, and serious. He was not like the other boys—the silly boys. At sixteen, I was tired of dating boys. I wanted to date a man. Tom was a senior: a jock, a star football player. He was strong and solid. Sturdy. There was a solemnity about him that made him seem mysterious, as though he understood how heavy the world was, as though he understood that frivolity was just an illusion.

He was dating Sandy, the cutest cheerleader in school. He flirted with me in the hallways, in class, in the cafeteria. I flirted back, smiled, and batted my eyes. I tilted my head and swayed my hips, hands clasped behind my back. I had watched Mother flirt for years. I knew how.

Tom asked me out. I said yes. He was now dating me, not Sandy.

He was uncomplicated—easy. I liked that about him. When I was with him, the specter of Mother's illness disappeared for a while. When I was with him, I was content to simply be me. Dad frowned a worried look but said nothing. Tom and I talked on the phone every night. Mother set a timer.

Tick. Tick. Tick. Ding.

"Get off the phone, Sharon! Now!"

I didn't care because I knew she would never ruin this. He wanted me. He needed me. He couldn't live without me. To him, I mattered. To him, I was everything. We would spend the rest of our lives together.

THE DAYS EBBED AND FLOWED like the tide in response to Mother's moods. I never knew when I came home from school how I would find her. One day I found her naked while she painted the living room, her slender body flecked with paint. Another day I found her staring at a picture of Harry Belafonte on his record album.

"Sharon, I am in love with this man. Going to fuck him."

More meds. New meds. Couldn't find the right combination. Then I found her curled up in the bed sheets again. Drowning in sadness, in nothingness.

Dad told me, "Susie, learn to go with the flow or you will drown. Remember when I taught you how to float in the water so if you were caught in an undertow or exhausted from swimming, you could lie on your back and float. Don't fight against the current. Float."

I trusted Dad. He read the *Encyclopedia Britannica* just like another person read a novel. He read every volume, from A to Z, then from Z to A. I wanted to be like him, a reader. I made a promise to myself to read the *Encyclopedia Britannica* too.

Dad also said: "Buddhists say to bend with the bamboo. The bamboo sways with even the slightest breeze. Their bodies are hard and firm, and their trunks stay rooted firmly in the ground. In time, even the strongest wind tires itself out, but the bamboo remains standing tall and still."

I got the go with the flow, but bending with the bamboo required strong roots. I felt more like the tumbleweed, uprooted and scattered over a desert floor. I kept these thoughts to myself, because I was only sixteen and sure I would find roots. The answer was in finding a husband who was normal and smart, like Dad.

≈

In September 1957, David was marrying Barbara, the sweetheart of Sigma Chi, which was his fraternity at Fresno State College. He was marrying her because she told him no—no to his charm, no to his advances, no to his hand sliding down her pants. Dad told me boys would always try to get into my pants. That was what boys did. Girls should protect their reputation; remain pure and chaste. Unsullied. That was what good girls did. Barbara had said no. That made her good wife material. She was nineteen and getting her MRS degree. I made a mental note to always say no so I could earn my MRS degree too—a husband like Dad.

～o～

Mother and Dad sent me to California in July to be fitted for my bridesmaid's gown that Barbara's mom, Daisy, was making for the wedding party. She laughed at my measurements: "You have a big bust, Sharon." She showed me the measuring tape. "Look how big you are!" Heat rushed to my cheeks. I had always been "blessed" in that area. I developed young, and I developed quickly. "None of the other girls in the wedding party have a bust like you!" she said. I managed a weak smile, filled with adolescent awkwardness.

Daisy's hands flew over my breasts, cupping and shoving, and all the while she kept crowing about my big breasts. And I liked it not because she thought I was stacked but because she fussed over me. No one ever fussed over me. She was a flurry of energy and laughter and smiles and kindness. I smoothed my hands down the side of my pencil skirt, pulled my shoulders back, and let her feel me up for a few minutes more.

～o～

Daisy took Barbara and me to San Francisco for a day in the city. The three of us twirled through the streets. After lunch, we went to a play starring Mary Martin as *Peter Pan.* Mary Martin flew through the air, gliding and dipping, sailing and floating. Graceful. I was enthralled, hypnotized. I could almost feel the wind brushing against my cheeks, whipping through my hair. I wondered what it felt like to be that free.

(Right about now in Hawaii, Mother would be taking her afternoon nap, oblivious to anyone but herself.)

When the play ended, the three of us skipped to the pastry shop. *Éclairs! Delicious!* As we drank our tea and dabbed éclair crème from the corners of our mouths with napkins, the constriction of my life in Hawaii began to uncurl. As my stomach untwisted, I gulped breaths of freedom. In an instant, I was Peter Pan, flying through the air, unhindered, unrestrained. Soaring.

Daisy and her mild-mannered-accountant husband, Virgil, lived in Northern California with their four children: Barbara (the oldest), Tom, Arlene, and Diane. Their home oozed love and laughter. That night we gathered around their dinner table. "Please pass the meat. Pass the potatoes and gravy. How was your day, Sharon? Did you enjoy the city? Did you enjoy the play?" They sat in rapt attention while I answered their questions.

I spent my days in the bubble of this normal family. And inside this bubble, I was real, with weight, substance, and dimensionality. Immediately, I was addicted to normal. It burrowed into my bones, and I became jittery with wanting.

—∞—

I dated a friend of the family even though, technically, Tom was my boyfriend. But I was two thousand miles away, on an adventure, having fun, being free, and tasting normal. I sat outside Barbara's house in a parked car with … well, I can't exactly remember his name, but I liked him. He was handsome and exuded masculinity. He was in college—smart and driven. He spoke in complete sentences, not like the boys in Hawaii speaking Pidgin English. His (really wish I could remember his name) English, by comparison, flowed like threads of spun satin.

This boy with his perfect English fascinated me. I practiced saying no inside my head. He didn't actually try anything yet, but I wanted to be prepared. I stared at him, marveling at the way his lips molded around the words as he talked. I smiled and batted my eyes. I crossed my legs and then uncrossed them. I folded my hands in my lap. I laced my fingers together, hoping I looked more sophisticated and knowledgeable than I felt. He talked. And then he talked some more. I was smitten. Wedding bells chimed inside my head. I tried not to think of Tom, how he was waiting for me, and how his Pidgin now made him seem foolish.

And then, just as I thought my reputation (sadly) was safe for the evening, Mr. Perfect English closed his eyes and leaned forward, head tilted, lips parted. My heart twisted and tumbled inside my chest. It wasn't that I had never been kissed but that someone so well spoken had never kissed me. I closed my eyes and leaned forward, head tilted, lips parted. He breathed into me and tasted of peaches and summer and schoolgirl crushes. He tasted of possibilities. He stroked my cheek with his thumb. The space between my legs throbbed. I shifted on the car seat. His hand slid down my shoulder. I tensed just the littlest bit. His tongue probed my mouth. I tucked no into my cheek and saved it for later.

∽◦∾

A few weeks before the wedding, there was another night, another car, and another guy. This time I was in Southern California visiting Grandma Hicks. His name was Chuck. I remembered his name. Although his family hadn't lived in our neighborhood when we lived on Marburn, they were very good friends of Mother and Dad's. Mother always had a crush on the father: the Italian Stallion. I sat in a parked car outside Grandma's house with his son, Italian Stallion Jr. He was the spitting image of his father: six feet tall, broad-shouldered, dark eyes, olive skin. He oozed sex. He was perfect. He was twenty.

That night, after a day of basking in the sun at Malibu Beach, I sported a hot California tan, feeling sultry, alluring, and sexy. I glowed.

My pretty tan will make me ravishing tonight!

This time there was no talking. Chuck leaned across the seat and pressed his lips into me, his tongue into me, and his chest into me. He flattened me against the car door. His passion scared me. I became overwhelmed, unsure, certain Dad, David, Grandma Hicks, and Daisy would be monumentally disappointed in my behavior this evening,

I chose her because she said no.

"No" perched on the edge of my tongue like a high diver, poised, tense, and ready. But there was a problem—a big problem. No could hurt someone's feelings, and I knew how much that stung.

Chuck's arms slinked around my body, touching, probing, groping. His hands found my breasts—my big, beautiful bust. He rubbed and cupped and squeezed. Desire like I never knew swelled inside me. I sucked in my breath and wondered if Mother was ever in a parked car with Chuck's father, if his hands were ever on her breasts and if she wanted him with the same intensity as I wanted Chuck. This thought derailed me a bit—first that Mother might have ever made out with his father and second that there was any part of me that was like her. Anxiety formed a fist in my stomach.

I pushed Chuck away. He fixed me with those deep, chocolate eyes and curled his lips back into a smile. He thought I was being coy, playing hard to get. He dove in again. Unbuttoned my sweater. Kneaded my breasts. He was rough, hungry. One hand meandered down yonder toward my happy mountain.

∽◦∾

It wasn't the first time someone had been down there.

His name was Peter. He was seventeen. I was fourteen. He stuck his hand down my pants.

"Why are you doing that?" I asked.

"Because I'm going to marry you, and that's what we will do when we are married."

Well, that made sense. I didn't rush to pull his hand out.

∽◦∾

Chuck's hand was forceful, knowing. I was on fire. I was heaving. He was heaving.

"I want you," he whispered.

His touch, his desire, poured into me, filled up years of longing to be touched, to be held, and to be wanted. I crouched on the edge of a cliff, wanting to spread my arms wide, to let go, to jump, to fly.

Suddenly, I was ten. Mother was slinking up against Dr. Paskowitz, caressing him, her purpled nipples pressing into him.

Then, I was eleven. Mother was telling me about the ecstasy of a man's hardness as I bled into my panties for the first time.

The memories crowded me. I tried to nudge them away. I felt disgusted with myself and with my own natural, sexual desires. *What if they discover who I really am? Dad, David, Grandma, and Barbara's family? What if they find out I really want sex, that I want a man to drive his hardness into me, and that I don't want to say no?*

I concentrated on Chuck's tongue in my mouth to push away the dark terror that billowed in my chest. Then I felt it: his hardness pressing against me.

Mother's voice echoed in my head: *It's pure ecstasy, Sharon. You'll love it. There's nothing better.*

Panic set in. I wrestled my desire to the ground and grabbed Chuck's wrist.

"No, please, stop," I squeaked. Then again, more forcefully. "No!" I pushed his hands away. He pulled back, disbelief and shock etched across his face. I fumbled with the buttons on my sweater. "I'm sorry," I whispered, and then I bolted from the car.

∾○∽

I doubled over in the bathroom with agony. Grief squeezed, crushed, and overwhelmed me. Outside, family and friends mingled and celebrated. There was food and drinking and dancing. It was David and Barbara's rehearsal dinner.

I knew I should be happy, thrilled, bursting with joy. Instead, my throat convulsed. Reality, sharp as a scalpel, sliced me. David was off to a new life. A better life. A life away from crazy, a life of happy and normal, a life that didn't involve men in white coats and trips to mental hospitals and shock treatments. A life I wanted for myself.

My experiences that summer—living with Barbara's family, making out with intelligent, ambitious men in parked cars, using my body as bait—had opened a new world to me, a world in which I had some fun: pure, unadulterated, uncomplicated fun. And now it was over.

David was leaving me.

Grandma was in the bathroom with me. She rubbed my back, like she had when I was a little girl. She cooed softly in my ear, kissed me gently on the crown of my head. She understood. This comforted me, and I sniffled and gulped a few shallow breaths. I looked at myself in the mirror. Black rivers of mascara trailed down my cheeks. My eyes were puffy and swollen. I wrapped my arms around myself, trying to hold myself together.

The next day, David was married. The day after that, I left with Mother and Dad. Back to Hawaii. Back to the chaos. Back to a boyfriend who spoke in incomplete sentences. Back to a life that, once again, swallowed me whole. Normal, always the tease, followed me to the airport, winked at me, and waved good-bye.

I RETURNED HOME TO MY senior year and a life that no longer fit. Tom had waited for me all summer. It used to be cute. The way he wanted me. The way he needed me. The way he was nothing without me. It was no longer cute but desperate, choking, and suffocating.

Still, we dated. We went to the movies. We held hands. We kissed. He wrapped his arms around me and buried me into his chest. He tucked me into his heart to keep me there forever.

My life felt like a stretched-out sweater: misshapen and sagging in all the wrong places. I had tasted normal, and now normal was what I wanted. I clutched it in my fist and swore I would have it again. College was the answer. In college I would find a husband and get my MRS degree and marry normal, just like David did.

I took the SATs. I practically failed them. I took them again. I did worse. My senior counselor told me to forget about college: "You are not college material. Concentrate on a trade, work in retail, or become a secretary. You just aren't smart enough for college."

November rolled around. Mother was getting worse. She had edges. Her crazy permeated the air. I smelled it the way I smelled the rain coming. Fat gray clouds of it tumbled together, hovering over Dad and me, threatening a downpour.

My senior class voted me "Most Ideal." The student body voted me homecoming queen—the first homecoming queen at Roosevelt High School. I was elated: a bright spot in a life streaked with darkness.

When I told Dad, he patted me on the back, saying, "Congratulations, Susie. I am proud of you!"

When I told Mother, she was preoccupied. Agitated. In her own world. I supposed there was a part of me that hoped she would embrace this, celebrate with me, at least come and watch me the way she watched David when he played basketball and football. She was always the loudest, proudest parent in the stands for David. No matter how hard I tried, I could not win her attention. I couldn't win her favor. Not even if I was chosen queen. Resignation introduced itself and shook my hand.

⌀∞⌀

And then we were at the upscale department store when Mother raged and disrobed in front of the shoppers while I hid in the clothes rack. She was mad because they had refused to make her fuck necklace. She paraded down the escalator, totally naked, jiggling, giggling, and swearing at the saleslady, the guards, and the customers. I was chosen as homecoming queen and "Most Ideal," and Mother was traipsing naked at an upscale Honolulu department store. I clenched my fists to my chest in disbelief and devastation. *Now* she chose to be naked in public. Not only did she expose herself, but she also exposed our insane, loony tune life with her.

At the mental hospital, Dad and I shuffled quickly down the white hospital hallways through the double doors into the waiting room. We walked through another set of double doors, another hallway, and headed for the secured ward. The walls vibrated with insanity: a man in a tattered robe, stood in the corner, talking to himself, nibbling on his fingers, shouting and stabbing the air with his forefinger; a woman sat at a table playing with a deck of cards singing to herself in between little outbursts of plaintive wailing and crying; a wild man walked toward me, banging his head with his fist. Best not to look them in the eyes—not to have any contact. Madness inhabited every corner of this place. It brushed up against me, caressed my cheek, stopped in front of me, and demanded my attention.

We finally reached the secured ward. As usual, I didn't know what to expect. We found Mother sitting on the edge of her bed, rocking back and forth, mumbling to herself, and scratching her arms (an adverse reaction to the medication). Her eyes were empty, lifeless, and soulless.

I was devastated. Once again, she was not any better. Dad sat on the bed next to her and slipped his arm around her shoulder. Disappointment covered him like a shroud. He always hoped she would be better, always hoped that when we came here, she would greet him, take him in her arms, comfort him, and tell him everything was okay, now that she was cured. But it never happened. And so, he sat next to her, smoothing back her hair while I stood against the wall watching, hard knots of resentment forming in my stomach.

After a few minutes, Mother looked at Dad. Her eyes were sharp-edged. "You shithead. This is your fault. Get me out of here. Get me out of here now!"

Dad pulled back. "It's going to be okay, Carolyn," he said, his voice soothing. He tried to rub her scratched arm. She jerked away. She turned toward the wall, turned her back to him.

"Leave me alone," she murmured. "I want a divorce."

Dad concealed his hurt. "I love you, Carolyn."

〜〜〜

Roosevelt High School scored another touchdown. The crowd roared, clapped their hands, and stomped their feet. Money changed hands under the bleachers of the Honolulu Stadium. The air buzzed. The fans were wild: another city championship for three years, and best yet, beating our rival, Punahou School.

I waited nervously with the homecoming court beneath the wooden bleachers that led to the locker rooms. It was almost halftime. The girls in the homecoming court were fidgeting and swishing their layers of crinolines, their faces split wide with smiles, flushed with excitement.

My stomach morphed into hard stone. I couldn't focus. I blinked, but it didn't help, so I blinked again. And still the world looked like a Picasso painting from the cubist period: everything disjointed and not aligned. *What is wrong with me?* Finally I was not invisible, yet to be invisible was the thing I wanted at that moment. A double-edged sword. My desire to be seen and not seen at the same time was each a desperate act of self-preservation.

Another touchdown. Another roar. Another wave of numbness washed over me. I felt like I was sleepwalking underwater. Faces twisted and contorted into great big clown smiles. Conversations distorted, out of sync with mouths that curved around invisible words. I closed my eyes. The sun shining on the football field was too bright. Images of Mother's naked body on the escalator toppled me. I was spinning. Reeling. Falling into a dark hole. Down. Down. Down.

I clenched my jaw to restrict the flow of tears. All I wanted was some attention from her—some acknowledgment. I wanted to know, for once, that I mattered to her. Would it have been so hard to hold it together long enough to cheer for me as homecoming queen? A small sob escaped. Then I heard the clatter of football cleats as the team brushed past me and into the locker room. Hands pushed, shoved, and guided us to the stadium field, into the sunlight. The crowd roared its approval. Pat Tyler, the first runner-up, stepped forward in her beautiful strapless dress, her skirt flowing from her tiny waist, buoyed up by millions of crinolines. She flashed a gleaming smile and waved. The crowd cheered. I stood next to Pat in an ugly, mousy, brown sarong that was twisted around my waist and chest. (With Mother's hospitalization, there had been no time to buy a special dress for me.) My cheeks flushed hot with embarrassment. I felt exposed. Ridiculous.

Right there in Honolulu Stadium, sitting in a horse and carriage by myself, staring at a horse's ass as it trotted around the field in front of thousands of roaring, cheering football fans, I disappeared by degrees into nothingness.

WHITTIER COLLEGE ACCEPTED ME ON probation, which astonished me since I had only made Cs at Roosevelt High School and practically failed the college entrance exam twice. But Dad wrote a killer entrance essay stressing my desire to reconnect to my Quaker heritage. He knew that Whittier College was named after the Quaker poet and abolitionist John Greenleaf Whittier. He also knew that Elias Hicks was a famous Quaker preacher and his cousin, Edward, was a famous Quaker painter. Those who agreed with Elias Hicks were generally called Hicksites. Though Mother claimed the Nowells were descended from the kings of England, it was the Hicks' heritage that launched me toward my mission: to get my MRS degree by nineteen.

Part of me was excited to go—to put some distance between Mother and me, to unstitch myself from her quicksilver moods, to have a little adventure of my own. And then there was the part of me that would have preferred to grow roots like the bamboo and cling tightly to the red dirt of Hawaii. Dreaming of, wishing for, and craving adventure was one thing. Actually living it was an entirely different story. The small details twisted me in knots: *How am I going to get from the airport to the college? How do I open a bank account? How do I write a check? What happens if I run out of money? What if I don't make any friends? What if I fail to find a husband?* I had never lived on my own before, never lived away from the surety of Dad. His steady predictability comforted me. *What shall I do without that?*

∞

Before I went to college that summer, my high school friend Judy died. She was bright and bubbly, just starting her life like the rest of us in the Roosevelt High School graduating class of 1958. It was unexpected. The ovarian cancer whittled her away little by little, and by the time the doctors discovered the giant tumor, it was too late.

Before her funeral, I went to Tom's house. I hadn't broken up with him yet; it was not the right time. His mother's death a month earlier was also unexpected. She was an effortlessly sweet woman, soft like a wool blanket and just as comforting. Tom and his brother were her whole world and she, theirs. I thought it cruel to leave him when he needed me most, when he needed to curl up in my arms and shiver with grief. Besides, he buried his mother with a picture of me cradled in her arms, linking us to eternity. It didn't seem fair to tell him then that I didn't love him anymore.

Tom and I sat on his couch, dazed and numb. Two deaths in six weeks. It didn't seem possible. We curled around each other, our faces slippery with tears, trying to make sense of it all.

Then he was in me.

Penetrating. Pumping. Thrusting. Driving.

Our fingers laced together, our bodies a confused tangle of desire and grief. We didn't plan it. It just happened. I had an insatiable hunger to physically connect with another human being. The deaths emptied me, leaving behind a fragile shell of what used to be, and I wanted to fill it up somehow. Even if it meant filling it up with someone I didn't love.

He was on top of me, straining inside me, claiming my virginity. For the first time, I felt alive, filled, and connected. Dad's voice rung in my ears: *Don't get caught with the goods, Susie.* Tom pulled out, ejaculating across my stomach. I washed off his warm, sticky sperm, pulled on my panties, and together we drove to Judy's funeral. We said nothing.

Tom and I sat in the third pew, surrounded by mourners. Judy's lifeless body lay stiff and rigid in the coffin at the front of the church. Tom slid his hand over mine and filled the spaces between my fingers, the way he had filled my emptiness an hour earlier. The pastor spun condolences, comforts, and words of hope for all of us. I sat there, stone-faced, still feeling Tom throbbing inside me.

There were many choices at Whittier, especially since I had shocked the faculty and student body by dancing Tahitian at the general assembly. Dancing was not allowed at the Quaker college, but I didn't think of it as dancing but an educational experience, even if the dance was exuberant, vibrant, and primal. I wore a very skimpy bra top with my green cellophane grass skirt that sat just below my bellybutton. My flat belly and sultry hips vibrated with each movement. Back and forth. Round and round. Shimmy. Fast. Slow. Fast. Slow. Inviting. Sensual. Seductive.

It's how you're supposed to dance Tahitian.

It's cultural. Educational.

After that, I became very popular with the football players.

Finding a husband was a little trickier than I thought. I met Bill: perfect, smart, athletic, and ambitious. A take-charge kind of guy. He smelled of money. His dad owned his own contracting business. Dad and Mother would be proud. Bill had the means and the drive to work hard.

One afternoon we drove to his house in the San Fernando Valley. It was a beautiful home, exactly like the kind I wanted to live in one day. No one was home. We went to his bedroom and plopped on his bed. Bill's hands roamed all over me, and part of me wondered if he really liked me or if he had a different idea about the kind of girl I was. He kept pushing my hips from side to side and kissing my bellybutton. Apparently not everyone appreciated the cultural significance of Tahitian.

Bill's hands wandered under my blouse, and I knew exactly what he wanted. He thrilled and terrified me at the same time. I wore my promise to myself to *be nothing like Mother* as an accessory. I wore it wherever I went; every time I lost control, I panicked. I didn't want anyone to think I was crazy because crazy meant shock treatments, mental hospitals, and no civil rights. However, Bill set me on fire. When he pressed me with his hard body, I threw caution to the wind. I kissed him deeply and pressed back. Bill slid his hands into my panties. We were so into each other on his maroon tartan bedspread that it took a moment for us to realize that his bedroom door was opened. We both froze when we saw his Mother watching us. Bill quickly shielded me with his body.

"I'm home," his mother said simply and then closed the door.

I wanted to hightail it, but Bill's mom invited me to stay for dinner. We sat around their huge dining room table. His mother wore a permanent scowl on her face. Apparently she didn't tell Bill's dad because he pleasantly yakked and yakked all the way through dinner. Bill stared at his plate. I wondered if my embarrassment had tattooed the word *slut* on my forehead.

Bill stopped calling me.

My roommate, Dixie, wanted me to meet her high school classmate. He didn't go to Whittier. I liked him already. Not that the guys at Whittier were not promising prospects. It was just that, well, I had a bit of a reputation since dancing Tahitian at the assembly. Apparently a lot of the boys thought I was "that" kind of girl. My chance of finding a husband on time was collapsing around me.

I didn't really know much about Dixie's friend, Ronald, except that he went to Cal Berkeley, that he wanted to be a dentist, and that he hadn't seen me dance at school and so didn't think I was a slut. He sounded promising. Ronald and I dated for a few months. He was everything a girl could want in a husband: clean cut, polished, a fraternity man. And those eyelashes! It was the eyelashes that got me. Our little girls would look stunning with those gorgeous, blonde eyelashes framing sparkling blue eyes.

I went home for the summer to tell my parents.

꒰ꔛ꒱

"Mother, Dad, I finally found the man I want to marry. His name is Ronald. He is a pre-dental student."

At the mention of pre-dental, Dad cheered: "A professional son-in-law. The first professional in the family."

"We'll have to wait seven years to get married, until Ronald graduates from dental school. We're only sophomores in college now."

Dad frowned. "Why wait to marry? You can get married in a year. A year is long enough to get to know someone."

"But Ronald goes to school at Berkeley. That's in Northern California. When will we see each other?"

Dad shook his head.

"Listen, Susie. You invite Ronald here so we can meet him. If you and Ronald want to get married, I'll pay for all your expenses. I mean everything. All your living and college expenses for you and Ronald for as long as it takes, including Ronald's dental school. We want to make sure Ronald becomes a professional man."

Dad squeezed my shoulder.

"You will never have to worry about money. My little girl will never have to struggle."

I wrapped my arms around him.

"How does that sound, Susie?"

It sounded like he had bought me a husband. But I didn't complain. I would finally build a life of my own, one that didn't involve fuck necklaces or trips to mental institutions or Mother running naked in department stores. A life that Dad wanted for me—for himself.

⌒⌒⌒

Dad was so proud of me he couldn't stop smiling. My stomach did flip-flops, backward somersaults, and handsprings. I wasn't sure I wanted to do this. I was too young. I was only nineteen. I needed more time. I should have told Dad, but everything was planned. It was disastrous to even consider canceling now. All those guests! All the food! Impossible. We had passed the point of no return.

I turned to Mother. "Is this a good idea?" Normally I wouldn't dare ask her, but as her daughter I desperately wanted the guidance and comfort of my mother.

Just a few days earlier I had showed her my diaphragm. I hoped she would show me how to use it properly and compliment me on the woman I had become. Instead, she laughed. "It's so small, Sharon!" She showed me hers, which was a lot bigger. "Now this is a real diaphragm, for a real woman!" Even as I felt any last vestiges of hope that we would connect as mother and daughter disintegrate like ash, all I could think was, *Holy shit! What does she have, a cavern?*

⌒⌒⌒

Mother fluffed the edges of my dress and straightened my veil.

"It'll be fine, Sharon. Ronald's a good man. He has ambition, drive. He's perfect. Don't worry. Everything will be fine."

I wasn't convinced.

"Is that why you married Dad? Because he had ambition?"

"I married your father because he had his own car. It was the middle of the Depression. I was miserable at home. He was my ticket out of there." Then she leaned forward and said in a low voice directly in my ear: "And. He. Ate. My. Pussy. I figured anyone who did that must really love me."

She enunciated each word slowly. That told me she was on the edge of manic flight—probably not today, maybe not tomorrow, but soon. By that time, Mother and Dad would be home in Hawaii and I would be a newlywed with a husband to tend.

Mother slipped my arm through Dad's elbow. Dad patted my hand.

I thought I was going to cry.

Dad winked at me.

I stifled my tears as the church doors swung open.

If you want to make God laugh,
tell him about your plans.

—Woody Allen

Part Two

1960–1981
California

EVEN THOUGH I HAD BEEN POPPED, I climbed into my marital bed faking innocence. Ronald expected a virgin, and a virgin I would be. Well, it wasn't all pretending. Even though I had already had sex, I didn't understand the pleasure part of it. There was penetration, some moving about, and then it was done. It was nothing like the ecstasy Mother promised. As long as I could remember, the joy of sex, the ecstatic release of orgasm, had been lobbed around the family dinner table like a grenade: a topic of conversation to shock dinner guests, to prickle the thin-skinned, and (I thought) to enhance David's sexual prowess. I knew a good girl chose a husband to choose a life, not to be sexually ecstatic like the three of them flippantly discussed.

If Ronald asked why I didn't bleed or why it didn't hurt when he slid into me, I'd tell him what Mother told me: "I was born without a hymen." However, I suspected it had broken when I landed badly on the center bar of David's bike when I was around eight years old. Either story protected my reputation as a virgin, a good girl.

Ronald and I lay next to one another; the air thickened with awkward inexperience, sheets pulled up to our chins. I pointed and flexed my toes. Ronald coughed. We looked at each other and exchanged shaky smiles. Then Ronald climbed on top of me. I hiked up my white lace honeymoon negligee and spread my legs. Ronald fumbled around, slipped once, and then managed to slide inside me. As he pumped, I lay ramrod straight as I imagined good, chaste, inexperienced virgins must do their first time. I stared at the ceiling. He stared at the wall above the bed. Then he gasped and pressed me into the bed. I patted his back. He pulled out, rolled off me and off the bed, and took a shower. I douched, just like his mother had told me I should. *You have to get all that nasty sperm out, Sharon. It's garbage!* Ronald flossed and brushed his teeth. We crawled back into bed, turned off the lights, and lay in the dark next to one another—strangers.

∽∞∾

71

"Sharon, get dressed. We've been invited to the neighbor's for cocktails. I met them down at the pool. This is so great!"

Dad paid the rent for our one-bedroom apartment across the street from Long Beach State University where Ronald and I transferred for our junior and senior years. Ronald majored in zoology, and I majored in philosophy. I had fallen in love with philosophy the previous summer when I took philosophy classes at the University of Hawaii. Philosophy comforted me as I learned that all humans have the same quests about life and death, mind and body. I was not alone. I heard Dad's voice: *Susie, we are all the same; only our cultures make us appear different. People all over the world have the same basic needs. They love, have hopes, and want the best for their families. No difference.*

Ronald was impressed because the couple was older, twenty something. I didn't care. I was in bed all afternoon, my arms wrapped around my midsection because it was that time of the month.

"I'd really rather stay home, honey."

Ronald's face tightened.

"I don't feel very good," I continued. "I've got cramps."

I shrugged him an apology and then dragged myself out of bed and into the kitchen to boil water for tea. A part of me wished Ronald would offer to make the tea for me—that maybe he would crawl into bed with me and rub gentle circles across my belly until the cramps went away. I hoped that he would take care of me the way Dad took care of Mother. At nineteen, I was still young and naïve enough to believe this was how marriage worked: when the wife was ill, the husband dropped everything to take care of her.

Still, as I stood next to the counter waiting for the water to boil, I thought myself lucky. I had landed a great husband. Besides, Dad wanted me to choose with my head, not my heart, to choose a man with drive and ambition. Ronald was going places. He was smart. And we looked good together: Ronald with his blond, Aryan good looks and me with my dark hair and eyes and lithe figure. We were the poster children for the perfect American couple.

Suddenly Ronald rushed into the kitchen, his face purple with rage. I jolted and stumbled backward, landing on the cold linoleum kitchen floor, my head next to my brand new state-of-the-art white Frigidaire. The words, "You shithead!" rolled around in my head. Unfortunately, they never made it to my mouth.

"What do you mean you'd rather stay home?"

Ronald stood over me, glaring at me. His average five-foot-eight stature towered over me; he looked like an ugly giant, not the perfect husband I had married two weeks earlier. I looked up at him in stunned disbelief and then rolled over on my side to pull my legs into me.

"How am I supposed to tell them no after I've already told them yes? Huh? Answer me!"

The force of his anger scared me.

The teakettle whistled a single piercing note, slicing through happily ever after. All that practice of curling up into a little ball in the closet when I was three years old finally came in handy. It really helped when the force of your husband's anger found you on the floor because you didn't feel like having cocktails with the neighbors.

"I don't want to hear about any cramps. Get up. We're going!"

He turned and left.

I lay there on the cold kitchen floor for a moment, shell-shocked. My mind scrambled to understand what had just happened. *Did I do something wrong? Is there something wrong with Ronald? Is he sick? Is he crazy?* Suddenly everything took on a surreal quality. I floated, drifted, engulfed in the vertigo of disbelief.

I heard the thrum of the shower.

I peeled myself from the linoleum floor and silenced the screeching of the kettle. I glanced around the kitchen, trying to find something to right my world, to stop the pitching and rolling. My heart pounded against my ribs. I stumbled to the front door and ran into the street in my bathrobe with no shoes. I ran until I couldn't run any further. I dropped to a curb. I cinched the belt of my bathrobe. Through my tears, I looked around. I didn't know where I was or how I had gotten there.

❦

"Sharon. Where have you been?"

It was an hour later, I thought. I was not sure. Time seemed to have slowed and then stopped altogether, like a photograph. But this picture wouldn't make it into our family album. I somehow had wandered home. Ronald looked pale. Worried. I was not sure if he was worried about my safety or if I might leave him. Then how would he pay for dental school?

"Where did you go?" he asked.

"I don't know. I'm not really sure. I just ... went for a walk."

"I am so sorry, honey," he whispered in my ear.

I didn't react. I was numb.

Marriages take time and compromise. This I knew. Besides, I had done what I was supposed to do, what was expected of me. I had found a husband with professional aspirations to take care of me and to provide for me. We would have money; we would have status, definitely a life of privilege. The life I wanted. The life that signified I was good and worthwhile and that I mattered. The life that would please Dad, which allowed him not to worry about me. The life that he bought for me. At the very least, it was a life away from Mother, away from her chaos. A chance at normal teased me to stay. Everything would be all right. I needed to work a little harder at it. Be more understanding. Be less self-centered.

⋘⊙⋙

IN JUNE 1962, RONALD AND I both graduated from college. Mother and Dad flew over to celebrate our college graduation. They arrived during the week of final exams. Mother busied herself with planning a graduation party for us at the hotel where they were staying. From the moment I saw her, I knew she was on an upswing. She was frenetic, urgent. Everything irritated her. Her eyes flitted and zoomed. Conversations were disjointed, broken, and unintelligible. I was distraught. I couldn't think, and anxiety formed a fist in my stomach. I failed my easiest final exam.

Even though I was on edge about Mother, I was giddy at seeing Dad. I missed him every day. I missed our little team, just the two of us. And even though I didn't really want him to know that Ronald had a temper, there was a piece of me that wished he would see it in my eyes, that he would know, somehow, and rescue me.

I shared with Dad about going to graduate school, about my love of philosophy and how I got mostly all As in my philosophy courses. Washington University in St. Louis had accepted me for the master's program in philosophy. Ronald was going to St. Louis University Dental School. It was perfect. Dad was patient. He listened. He waited. He drew his brows together in bewilderment.

"I don't understand, Susie. Why are you going to graduate school?"

His question took me by surprise. Hadn't he heard a word I said? I tried again. "Because I want to teach philosophy. I want to be a professor."

"Why? You will never have to work. I'll support you until Ronald has his dental practice, and then he'll support you. You're twenty-one already, Susie. When are you having children?"

I blinked back my disappointment. My heart plummeted to the floor. *Is that all he's really ever wanted for me? To be someone's wife? To pop out a couple of kids? Does he think that's all I can do?* Self-esteem hissed out of me like a deflating balloon. It suddenly occurred to me that not all closets have four walls. I felt light-headed, claustrophobic. I started to protest. *I object!* But there was no judge, no jury, no one to hear my case. To press the issue was to risk upsetting Dad, and I absolutely could not do that. Any hint of pain in Dad's face unraveled me. Instead, I pasted on a smile.

"Sure, Dad." My voice was the wrong pitch, filled with tears. "Time to have babies."

⌐⚬ⵘᵔ

The party was in a small cabana adjacent to my parents' hotel. Mother packed the guest list with her old friends from Marburn Avenue. I realized this was her showcase. Her party. She spun through the room, twirled through the guests, waved her hand magnanimously, and thanked everyone for coming. Ronald and I might as well have been wallpaper, decorations, ice sculptures next to the punch bowl. I stood in the corner and grimaced, praying the night would end soon so Ronald and his parents wouldn't grasp the reality and extent of her illness.

"This pill will save the world!" She twisted through the crowd with little clear brown-capped capsules nestled in her palms. She threw them in people's faces. Her newest discovery. Amphetamines. The wonder drug. "It's so wonderful. It makes everything beautiful, clear, perfect. This little pill is the answer to peace. Everything is so fucking clear! I am going to call President Kennedy. He needs to take this pill too. It's fucking brilliant! All world leaders must take this pill. The clarity! The vibrancy! The freedom! There's nothing else like it in the world!"

The guests laughed, shook their heads, and enjoyed the show. To them, she was just Carolyn: flamboyant, entertaining, and seductive. They didn't know. They didn't see it in her eyes or hear it in her speech—the warnings that this might turn ugly.

Her mania whittled away at me and reminded me that next to her, I was unimportant, insignificant, nothing. She whirled through the guests, laughing, shouting, and snorting with delight. Ronald shot me a look: *Is everything okay?* I nodded. Even as panic twisted inside me, I didn't know how he would react if she decided to strip or told him she wanted to fuck him.

I sprang into action. I joined the fun and pretended this was all normal. This was how we partied. I told jokes. I spun gales of laughter. I mingled. I danced.

Suddenly, Mother stopped in the middle of the room. Her face darkened. I froze.

"I'm thirsty! Bring me a drink!" She yelled for Bailey's Irish Cream.

For some reason, this sudden request for alcohol frightened me. Usually her manic highs were like an engine revving up. They escalated and then reached a sort of tipping point where she went soaring off the edge. I was prepared for that. Alcohol with these pills was an unknown quantity. I had no idea what they would do to her, no idea what to expect. I glanced at Dad. Concern etched across his face. She was unraveling faster, twisting, twirling, a kaleidoscopic frenzy.

Mother drained the glass. Then another. She slammed it down on one of the tables. She laughed. Dad tried to slip his arm around Mother's waist to calm her. She pushed him away. She tensed. She glared at him. She glanced around the room. Dread pulsated in my ears.

"Party's over," she announced loudly. Then with a flamboyant wave of her hands, she said, "Everyone go home now."

The guests exchanged glances.

No one said anything.

And then everyone left.

THE NEXT MORNING DAD CAME to our apartment. Mother had locked him out of the hotel room for good. Dad looked exhausted, defeated. Once again, her insanity propelled our lives forward. Like a tired, worn-out habit, Dad and I fell into step beside each other. We planned to get her help. That meant the men in white coats.

I called Mother in her hotel room.

"Sharon, I'm divorcing your dad. I can't stand the son of a bitch. Kicked him out on his ass!" She paused as though to create suspense. She giggled. She sounded like a little girl.

"I took the biggest shit ever!" she boasted. "I filled the toilet over and over again. It was overflowing with shit!" Proud of herself. Proud of her shit.

I had no response to this. What was I supposed to say? Congratulations on your great big shit?

"It feels so great, Sharon. To shit out all that anger and tension. It's all from being married to your dad, you know. Son-of-a-bitch. Dumping Harold is dumping shit. A whole big toilet bowl of shit!"

I sighed. "I'm coming over to see you, Mother."

"No. Absolutely not. I don't want you here. You'll bring your father, and I don't want to see that shithead. He's pathetic. You do know that, don't you, Sharon? He's absolutely pathetic. He can't even take a shit without my permission!"

"Mother, I'm not asking. I'm telling you. I'm coming over to see you."

"And I told you no, Sharon. I'm calling President Kennedy. To tell him about these pills. He absolutely must take these pills! Oh, and I'm calling everyone I know to tell them about the divorce. Wow, Sharon! I feel so fucking free! A whole lifetime of shit down the toilet! And the flies on the wall agree with me. They think I'm right, that I'm doing the right thing. I know because they are fluttering their wings. It's how they talk to me. They like me because I'm the only one who understands them. I am the only one who understands how they communicate. Fuck, I feel so good!"

I heard the sandpaper scraping of an emery board in the background. She was filing her nails while she was talking to the flies on the wall. I pressed my ear to the phone again.

"How long do you plan to stay in the hotel room, Mother?"

"Oh, I don't know. Doesn't matter. Forever, maybe. I have everything I need right here. A phone. My address book. Friends to call. My flies. They have names. I've named them all. They really like their names. They told me so. And the maids bring me everything I need. Oh, Sharon, isn't this all so wonderful? This is what I've been wanting for years, needing for years. To be free of that bastard. He drains me. He doesn't love me. He needs me. An endless, sucking need. He thinks need is love. He has no fucking clue what love is."

She sighed and scraped her nails some more. "You do know the difference between need and love, don't you, Sharon?"

Before I could answer, she continued: "I really do feel so fucking fantastic, Sharon. Your father is a complete asshole. Can't believe it took me this long to get rid of him."

"I'd like to visit you, Mother," I said, trying to bring the conversation back around. Stopping her rants was a bit like trying to stop a freight train coming at you full speed. I glanced at my watch. "I'm coming over."

"Don't you dare, Sharon! I don't want you here. I don't trust you. You're too much like your father. I don't want anyone around me that reminds me of him. You are not a Nowell. You aren't good enough for that. You're trailer-trash Hicks. Stay away."

She slammed the phone down.

Frustration roiled inside me. Twenty minutes later, I knocked on her hotel door.

"Mother, let me in."

"No! Go away! Leave me alone!"

"I want to see you."

"No, you don't. You have your dad with you. I know you do. Leave me alone. I don't want to see either one of you. I'm done with both of you!"

I pressed my forehead to the door, flattened my palm against it.

"I'm alone, Mother. Let me in."

There was a pause. A beat. And then, "Are you really alone?" Her voice was muffled and timid.

"Yes, Mother. I promise. I'm alone. I just want to be with you." The lie burned as it slid through my teeth.

She opened the door a crack.

I smiled at her.

She smiled back.

The men in white coats barreled past me, and with lightning speed, they grabbed Mother, wrestled her to the bed, and put her in a straightjacket. Then they strapped her to the gurney.

She spit at me. "Fuck you, you shithead! Just when everything is so fucking clear, you ruin it!"

Her words pierced me. My heart beat against my ribs, trying to get out, to get away. It pulsed with shame at what I had done.

"You'll be sorry, you little shithead. Always your daddy's little girl. I'll get you."

The men in white coats wheeled her away.

Dad and I followed the ambulance to Long Beach Memorial Hospital. We admitted her. She raged and spewed hate at us. Orderlies took her to the secured ward, where she would have round-the-clock protection and medication.

I heard someone say, "We will help her. She will be fine. Everything will be okay."

I had my doubts.

The door to the secured ward hissed shut, locking her in. Dad and I went down the long, sterile corridor toward the exit, black ribbons of betrayal trailing behind me.

THE NEXT DAY MY MIND tripped over what had happened, my heart blackened with shame. Logically I knew there wasn't anything else for us to do. She needed help. Still, the force of her anger rang in my head: You'll be sorry, you little shithead. Always your daddy's little girl. I'll get you.

Ronald didn't say much. I paid little attention to him. My focus was on taking care of Dad and making sure his needs were met during this time of crisis. Ronald tried to be supportive, to be a good husband. He asked about my day, if there was anything I needed, if there was anything he could do. I shrugged him off, dismissed him.

I unlocked the front door of our apartment and nudged it open with my foot; my arms were filled with bags of groceries. No one was home, and I was grateful for a few hours to myself. I was barely into the apartment when I saw them.

Hundreds of red rose petals were scattered throughout the apartment.

She had been here.

In our apartment.

It wasn't possible. She was locked away at Long Beach Memorial in the secured ward; I had seen the black iron bars on the windows and the doors. My throat closed, and the room started to spin. I dropped the groceries and bolted out the front door.

I tore down the stairs, two at a time, and burst into the manager's unit. Terror clawed at my chest. She hated roses. To her, they meant death. When she was seven, her father had died of food poisoning. His wretchedly large body was displayed in their parlor for over a week. Roses were scattered over the rotting corpse to cover the smell. Mother hid under the house.

And now there were roses scattered throughout my living room. I couldn't feel my knees. I doubled over, clutched my stomach, and hyperventilated. I knew I wasn't being logical. She had never physically hurt me. Then again, I had never betrayed her like this.

The apartment manager stared at me. "Can I help you, Sharon?"

I pried myself upright to catch my breath. My lungs were on fire.

"Was anyone in our apartment today?"

"Why, yes. She said she's your mother, so I let her in. Is she still there?" He was ridiculously calm.

By now, adrenaline, fear, and panic had twisted together, and I was shaking uncontrollably. "Don't you *ever* let anyone in our apartment without our permission!" The force in my voice surprised me. I was feeling a little out of control, and I didn't like it. I composed myself and looked the manager in the eye. "Do you know what you've done?" I wanted to cry.

The manager, stunned, shook his head dumbly. I turned away from him and raced back upstairs to our apartment. I went down on my hands and knees, frantically scooped up rose petals, and tossed them in the trash.

I called Dad immediately at Uncle Louie's house. He rushed to our apartment.

"How did she get out?" he asked.

His insane wife was somewhere in Southern California with no ID or money, wearing only a muumuu, no bra, never panties, and no shoes, her moral compass completely impaired. There was no telling what she'd do or where she'd go. She was, quite literally, out of her mind. Dr. Paskowitz's words crossed over an eleven-year divide: *she doesn't know she's sick.* This was the first time she'd escaped, the first time Dad hadn't known her whereabouts, and the first time control of the situation had slipped through his fingers.

"We'll find her, Dad," I whispered. "Don't worry."

He squeezed my shoulder. He leaned on me. He needed me.

Dad called the hospital. He kept his voice calm and steady, indicating he was the one who held it all together—the one who would swoop in to rescue Mother, just like he always had. I was in complete admiration and adoration of his strength, his ability to stay so controlled in the midst of the chaos. And even while I tried to help Dad, to be a comfort to him, I knew this was different than true strength—the strength to keep trying in spite of it all.

Mother had tricked the night guard into opening the door. She convinced him that her family was framing her. He helped her escape. The hospital was sorry.

Dad called the police. He called the morgues, hospitals, relatives, friends, anyone, and everyone. Nothing. No one had seen her. The afternoon dragged on, folded into the next day and the next. Still nothing. Dad and I twined ever more tightly around one another. Ronald slipped in and out of the shadows. I was aware of him only peripherally. I imagined he tried to help, tried to offer comfort, and probably even scoured the neighborhood in our car looking for her. I don't remember.

Where could she be? Is she still manic? Did the hospital drug her? Is she depressed? Is she lost? Scared? Is she wandering aimlessly through the streets of Southern California, homeless, dirty, hungry? Sleeping in a cardboard box? Under a bridge? And then: *Is she dead?* It was this last thought that stuck around for a bit, filling my mind with wonder. *What would it be like if she were dead?* The enormity of it consumed me—not just the fact that I would no longer have a mother but that the way of life as I knew it would instantaneously grind to a halt and flip completely upside-down, like Alice's Wonderland.

On the fourth day of her escape, I sat on the couch curled into Dad's side, worrying the edges of a throw pillow. Dad's eyes were ringed with worry, and his body bent with helplessness. Hospitalizations kept Mother safe from herself and others. Her wandering the streets alone scared him, and there was nothing to be done except sit there, shackled to the phone, waiting for it to ring. Waiting. And waiting.

And then it rang.

Dad yanked the receiver from its cradle. Uncle Roy, Dad's brother, was calling from Oregon. I sat up and tucked my legs underneath me. Dad's shoulders curled forward. He clamped his hand over his eyes.

"Oh, thank goodness," he murmured. "Thank goodness."

His voice was filled with tears. The hard knot of tension inside me unfurled at Dad's relief. As he talked, he wrote some information on a notepad and hung up the phone. He slumped forward, head on his knees, relieved, exhausted. She had been found. She was safe.

She was at a motel in the San Fernando Valley. For my entire life, I would marvel at Mother's resourcefulness during her manic benders. I still didn't know how she managed to convince the motel manager to allow a bare-footed, unkempt, clearly deranged woman with no money to rent a room for four days.

Yet, when Mother decided to call Uncle Roy, a retired policeman, in Oregon to tell him about the divorce, to brag about it, to tell him how Dad was ruining her life, didn't she know he would call Dad? I could hear what she must have said: *Every time I start to feel good and see things clearly, your fucking brother commits me! Fucking asshole!* Uncle Roy would listen and wisely agree. Then he would ask her where she was staying. Then Uncle Roy called Dad.

Somewhere in here, Mother's older brother, Gordon, had visited her at her motel. He confessed that he had molested her when she was little. (She instantly forgave him—no big deal when you're manic.) He played his ukulele; the two of them sang and danced, a party for two. While Dad and I turned inside out with worry, it never occurred to Uncle Gordon to call Dad because he never thought Mother was sick. He never did. He thought, like Uncle Ernie, that she was just having fun.

Once again, Dad and I sprang into action. Dad called Uncle Louie in Sunland. He called David in Fresno. Another plan hatched. Another net cast. Another trap set to catch her, ensnare her, tie her up, and tie her down for her own good. There was a party. Bait. Mother loved parties. David made the call because he hadn't betrayed her—yet.

"Mother, it's David. Uncle Roy called to tell me where you are staying. Barbara and I are in Southern California. We would love to see you. We'll drive over."

"David! So good to hear your voice! Yes, come over. Come over right away. I've left your father. That fucker was having me committed for having a little fun. You know how he is. Always trying to spoil my fun. He thinks I'm sick! Can you imagine? I'm not sick. I'm great. In fact, now that I'm getting rid of him, I couldn't be any fucking better!"

"Yes, Mother. Yes, I understand. We'll talk about it when I get there. I'll see you soon. Don't go anywhere. I'm coming over right now."

She giggled. "Hooray! See you soon, son."

David arrived at the motel and knocked on her door. She opened the door. She was messy. Dirty. She wore a blonde wig that sat crookedly on her head. Her eyes were wild, insane, devoid of reality. She had no shoes. Her bare feet were filthy, crusted in the dirt and grime of the city. She grabbed David in her arms and kissed him on the cheek. Her tangle of words and thoughts spilled forth—

jumbled, disconnected, and unintelligible. Mother and David got in his car and drove to the party at Uncle Louie's home in Sunland. At the party, she danced, sang, and beat everyone over the head with details of her divorce. Then she got in the car again, this time with David, Barbara, and Uncle Louie. She banged her hand on the window as the car pulled away from Uncle Louie's house.

"Where are we going?" she asked.

"We're going out to eat," Uncle Louie answered. He didn't mind being part of the deception. Uncle Louie always sided with Dad. Besides, as a Los Angeles City Fire Captain, Uncle Louie rescued people. That was what he did.

Mother pouted. "I don't want to go out to eat." She stuck out her lower lip. "I want to go back to the party." She crossed her arms over her chest in a huff.

"You'll love where we're going, Sis," assured Uncle Louie. "Besides, we want to talk to you about the divorce. My house is just too noisy."

At this, Mother perked up.

"Well, good." She patted her brother on the shoulder.

Soon after, the car stopped. Mother straightened her blonde wig. She got out of the car, looked around, and pursed her lips. She frowned when her eyes ran the length of an imposing gray building.

"Where the fuck are we?" she shouted as she realized they were not at a restaurant. She started backpedaling. David grabbed her by the elbow.

"We're at the hospital, Mother. Los Angeles County Hospital. You need help."

Her lips curled back over her teeth. She growled: "You shithead! You fucking shithead! Not you too!" She wrenched away from David and flattened herself against the car. She was a caged animal, desperate for a way out. David and Uncle Louie positioned themselves so she couldn't bolt.

Mother screamed: "First my husband, then my daughter. Now my son and brother. All shitheads!"

She tried to run. David grabbed her. Then the white coats grabbed her. She spied Dad and me. The air grew thick with helplessness, with hopelessness. I watched the white coats strap Mother to a gurney. Again.

"You shithead!" she shrieked. "You're all shitheads!"

When they wheeled her into the hospital, we followed. We sat in the waiting room while Mother lay strapped to the gurney, a torrent of profanities pouring down on all of us. A doctor came with more white coats.

Mother twisted her head, the only part of her body she could really move at this point. The blonde wig tilted sideways. "You shithead," she spit at the doctor. "Are you the main shithead in this fucking place?"

The doctor nodded and took Mother's pulse.

"Great. Are you the one I need to fuck to get out of here? I'm finally divorcing this shithead over here," she nodded in Dad's direction, "and you shitheads think I'm sick. If you only knew how fucking clear everything is. Fuck you!"

The blonde wig bobbed precariously off center.

She really looked funny. Her arms and legs were strapped so tightly to the gurney that she could only wiggle her hands and wrists. She flapped them about. "Shithead!" Flap. "Shithead!" Flap. Flap. "Shithead!" Flap, flap, flap. She strained her neck toward the ceiling. The wig slipped so that it hung over her face, tufts of it flipped up every time she yelled "shithead." Perhaps it was impolite to laugh and to find humor in the middle of Mother's mental chaos. But what were the other options? The comic relief made it somewhat bearable, like maybe it wasn't real but only someone's twisted idea for a comedy sketch and any minute now the small group in the waiting room would burst forth in applause and Mother would hop off the gurney to take a bow. *I'll be here all week. Don't forget to tip your waitress.*

Laughter filled the waiting room. Mother was no longer angry but instead was delighted she had an audience. "What a bunch of shitheads you all are. All of you." Like a seasoned comedienne, she paused to gauge the onlookers' reaction. More laughter encouraged her to continue: "A person can't feel good without everyone saying she's sick. Give me a fucking break!" Another pause, more laughter. She was on a roll. "Shit! Heads! Shitheads! Shitheads! Shitheads!" She tossed her head and laughed, pleased with her performance.

The doctors took a few more vitals. The wig fell off. Suddenly Mother, irate, her face the color of a tomato, looked directly at me, her green eyes flashing hate. "I'll get you," she hissed. Suddenly, it wasn't so funny.

LOS ANGELES COUNTY HOSPITAL was dismally gray: the sky, the walls, and the cement walks that snaked around the property. I felt like I had just walked into a cement basement. A gray closet. A tomb. I stuck close to Dad as we walked through the corridors to visit Mother. Other patients sneaked against the walls, in the shadows, along the floor, whispering, shouting, mumbling, and banging some part of their bodies on some immovable object.

When the orderly opened the door to Mother's room, she screamed at us to leave. She showered us with "shitheads." She threw a tantrum and climbed into the corner of the bed, where she perched and cursed us for spoiling her fun. Mother tucked her knees under her hospital gown. She crooked her finger at me. I didn't move. I didn't trust her. Instead, I stared at her. Her eyes got dark.

"I like this little girl here," she whispered. "She's twelve. She talks and talks and talks in a big room where they make us go every day. I'm the only one who ever listens to her. Because I think she's perfect."

Mother's words poked me in the ribs. I wondered if she had any idea how much I longed for her to sit and listen to me, to take the slightest interest in me, to tell me she thought I was perfect. Jealousy prickled along my spine. Mother shifted her position on the bed. Her legs dangled over the edge, and her foot madly tapped the linoleum floor.

"The stupid shithead nurses tell me—order me—to stop listening to her. But I don't. Why should I? I keep talking to her, and she keeps talking to me." She furrowed her brow, cocked her head to the side, laced her fingers together, and set her hands gently in her lap. As if in deep thought, her eyes drifted off to a corner of the room. "She calls me Mother Mary," Mother whispered. "She loves me. She loves me, and I love her."

Dad and I looked at one another. Mother sat in silence, her eyes closed. I looked at my watch. Time was interminably slow in mental hospitals. Then her head snapped up, eyes blazing. She pulled her knees to her chest and rocked back and forth. She fixed her eyes on me.

"Do you know what they did to me?" Her voice suddenly sounded deep and guttural.

It startled me. I shook my head.

"They yelled at me. For talking to her. They grabbed me by the hair and dragged me down this hallway and threw me into this cell! They locked the door!"

Mother uncurled her legs and bolted from the bed. I flattened myself against the wall. Dad stood up and stared at her, his eyes and mouth turned down at the corners, shoulders slumped forward. Mother sidled up to Dad, walked her fingers up his chest, and smiled at him.

"Do you know what I do?" she asked. "Hmmm?" She set her hands on her hips. Dad remained stone-faced.

"When they give me a pill, I hold it in my cheek until they leave. Then, when they're gone, I wrap it in a tissue and throw it away." Her face grew hard. "Those fuckers," she snapped. "Think they're so smart."

She whirled away from Dad and flopped on the bed. She sucked in a deep breath and blew it out through her mouth. She drummed her fingers on the mattress. She pinched her lips in her fingers. I looked at my watch again. We had been there for less than ten minutes. Mother looked up and flicked her eyes between Dad and me.

"Why are you still here?" she asked.

Dad looked at me, his brows arched. I knew this meant he was ready to go. Finally.

The next day, Mother fluttered about the room. "Isn't life just grand? Glorious! Exquisite! My delightful husband." She kissed him deeply on the lips. Dad stood there, rigid. Mother twirled over to me and held my face in her hands. "My beautiful daughter!" She looked deeply into my eyes. For a second, I believed she meant it.

Mother showed us a wall in her room smeared in black.

"Look what I did! I painted this picture." She lightly ran her hands over the smooth stucco. "It was such a plain wall," she lamented. "So plain. So I made a picture. I found some burnt matches and drew Gloria and me. You remember Gloria, don't you?" Dad and I nodded stiffly. "Well, look. I drew a couch. See? There's Gloria sitting on the couch, and I'm lying with my head in her lap. She's plucking my eyebrows." Mother beamed like a child showing off her artwork.

I squinted my eyes at the charcoal mess on the wall. All I saw were lines and smears and smudges. Chaos. Disorder. Like she emptied the contents of her brain onto the wall.

"When we were girls, Gloria wanted to shape my eyebrows, but she totally plucked one out!" Mother doubled over, her body wracked with hysterics. "Boy, was I surprised not to have an eyebrow! Bald as a baby's ass!" Then she flipped and became serious. "I miss Gloria. Do you like my picture? I like it very much. I think it's very good."

On the third day, Dad and I attended a commitment hearing. It was not just the courtroom that was paneled in dark wood but also the seats and tables—everything dark, somber, and serious. The judge appeared in his black robe. He sat behind a dark, elevated desk that was imposing and intimidating. I felt small and insignificant sitting in this dark courtroom across from the judge on high, as though I was the one who had done something wrong, as though I was on trial.

A few minutes later, Mother was escorted into the courtroom, flanked on either side by a male orderly. The three of them sat across from the judge, who peered at them—at us—from behind his mighty wooden desk.

Mother looked subdued, lethargic, and spent; there was no fight left in her. She looked as though she had been shocked again; her eyes were vacant and out of focus. This time I would not be the one she clung to; I would not be the one to introduce her back to the world, back to herself. And there was a part of me that was suddenly protective of Mother. *What do these people know of her? Do they know she is an excellent cook? Do they know she can hear a song once and play it perfectly on the piano? Do they know she sews her own clothes? Do they know she has family?*

Three psychiatrists had examined her and testified that she was unable to care for herself, a danger to herself and to society. The diagnosis: manic-depressive disorder with schizophrenic tendencies. The judge slammed his dark gavel on his dark desk. The sound of wood on wood solidified the diagnosis. It was now indisputable. It was now official. She had been publically declared insane.

"Where do you want to commit her?" asked the judge.

Dad stood and cleared his throat: "Westwood Hospital."

WESTHOOD HOSPITAL was a private psychiatric hospital just north of Los Angeles. William Randolph Hearst originally built it as an estate for his movie star sweetheart, Marion Davies. As a hospital, it became a palace of healing. Walls of stone stretched an entire city block surrounding it. In the middle was a beautiful open courtyard, welcoming and peaceful. It had a gentleness and a serenity that stood in stark contrast to the gunmetal despair of LA County Hospital.

Dad and I walked through the courtyard, and the constant clench of tension inside me released a little. Everything was crisper here. Clearer. The colors were more vibrant. Even the air was cleaner somehow. I drew in a long breath and held it in my lungs. It tasted of hope. It tasted of wholeness. It tasted of freedom.

Dr. Hellinger, Mother's psychiatrist at Westwood, told us he could help her, cure her, and make her well. He would be able to give Dad his wife, and he would be able to give me my mom. That was how I remembered it anyway. Doctors were very careful not to offer any guarantees, and it was unlikely Dr. Hellinger ever made any promises. Still, I heard promises. He did say he was going to try psychoanalysis—a new word for me. I was hopeful. I took a deep breath. *Wouldn't it be wonderful if she doesn't have any more shock treatments or medications that make her vomit?* The word *psychoanalysis* gave me new hope. With the doctor's help we would rescue Mother, kick her madness to the curb once and for all, and finally start living the lives we all wanted. We were determined.

While Dad saw Dr. Hellinger for updates, I visited Mother. She still didn't want to see Dad—still insisted she wanted a divorce. But I understood that this was just part of her illness. She didn't really mean it. She just couldn't think straight. She didn't really want to leave him. Not after everything he did for her. Not after he loved her so fiercely, so relentlessly.

I left Dad with Dr. Hellinger and buoyant with optimism, trotted down the hallway, through the sunny courtyard, and to the secured ward where Mother was locked up with twenty-four-hour private nurse care. She didn't ask about me, but that was okay; I knew she would. Soon.

She said, "Dr. Hellinger asks me if I would like some company during the day. A personal aide. Someone to talk to. But this man is old, must be sixty or seventy, and so big. He likes to show me off in the exercise yard. Likes to watch me play basketball without any underwear and tells me to reach way up to make a basket. He is proud of my breasts. He takes credit for them."

"Takes credit for your breasts? How does he do that?"

She snapped loudly: *"In his head.* To the different, whatta-ya-call-'em in the hospitals?"

"Orderlies."

"Yeah. To the different orderlies." Then loudly and succinctly, separating each word, she repeated, "He. Takes. Credit. For. My. Breasts."

Then she whispered: "I do have a nice shape, and he exercises the hell out of me. He is really okay but so old. All he does is sit by me, not even talk. Just be there. Sometimes he talks to the other orderlies about football and my breasts. If he doesn't like something I do, he locks me up in my room. I am telling the doctor I don't like him."

Then, she quickly changed moods again. She hissed: "Your dad keeps sucking my teat. All he does is suck and suck, sucks all the life and energy out of me. Keep him away from me, Sharon."

When she talked about Dad like this, I became a thousand shades of discomfort. Because I knew Dad was a good man, a good husband. Consistently she told me not to confuse need with love, but what if she couldn't tell the difference? Bottom line—she was wrong. Dad was a saint. He loved her. She'd see that soon, when the meds kicked in, when Dr. Hellinger put the fractured pieces of her brain back together. She would remember then that she loved Dad as much as he loved her.

On another visit, she was cheerful: "Sharon, honey, come in. Look at my pictures." She showed me her paintings of wild colors, and maybe one picture had a flower. "Aren't they good? Very good? I make them for the doctor. I painted some the other day for the doctor called comedy and sadness."

"Mother, do you mean tragedy? Comedy and tragedy?"

"Oh yeah, that's it. I outlined the faces with ribbons and decorated the faces with beads. I'm so proud of my oil paintings.

At this place, I feel very creative. And the best part is not seeing your dad if I don't want to."

I tried to change the subject: "Mother, you seem happy here."

"Oh yes, I am not thinking about leaving at all. No plans. No plans at all in my mind."

Then she started to cry. "I am so hurt by the treatment I have had in the past. The doctor is so nice here. I don't want to leave."

And, then … another visit changed our lives.

"Sharon, guess what?" She paused and giggled. She wiggled her foot. Arched her eyebrows.

"What, Mother?" I hated it when she acted like this. She was a teenager, a child.

"Last night, I got caught." She giggled.

She continually puzzled me.

She sighed, exasperated with my slowness.

"I got caught having sex with my night nurse! He really cares about me. I think he is about my age. I'm forty-four, right? Anyway, last night, he just jumped into bed with me. Of course, I let him. Someone walking around with a flashlight checks the rooms every night. He's just a young nurse. He catches my night nurse on top of me." She started to giggle again. "Heck, he didn't even have a chance to come. We were just getting started. He felt so good inside me. As he pulls away and gets off me, he says, 'Oh my God, what have I done?'"

"Mother, he must have been sorry."

Mother shouted, "Better believe it!"

Then softer: "They fired him this morning. I will miss him."

She quickly changed pace. "Let me show you my latest painting."

As I left her that day to meet Dad in the foyer of the hospital, my mind twisted around the probability that Mother really had slept with her night nurse, and it left a taste like stale vomit in my mouth. When I saw Dad, I saw it etched into his forty-six-year-old, lined face. He knew. It was true.

"They gave your mother a pill to prevent pregnancy," he said, his voice cracking. "Dr. Hellinger is very sorry. The night nurse has been fired. It won't happen again. He wants to continue treatment. He says this is only a minor setback." The words spilled from Dad's mouth like stones. He looked at me with empty eyes. Dad shook his head.

"When Dr. Hellinger told me about the night nurse sleeping with your mother, I no longer felt she was my wife. I felt nothing for her. I can't do this anymore. I am sorry, Susie. I can divorce her, but what will you and David do? How do children divorce a parent? I will always be here for you. I just don't want be married to your mother. I will make sure that she is well taken care of financially. I am sorry, Susie. "

I didn't question or talk to Dad at that moment. He was totally exhausted. Whipped. Done.

IN THAT SUMMER OF AUGUST 1962, Ronald and I climbed into our new Pontiac that Dad had bought us for our trip to St. Louis. We packed it with our belongings, our life in California. Ronald shifted the car into drive, and we pulled into the street. Dad, who came to bid us farewell, slowly disappeared in the rearview mirror. I wondered if my life up to that point would also slowly disappear.

I looked over at Ronald, my husband—the man I was meant to count on, to lean on. The man who was meant to take care of me, to make sure I never had to struggle. *Is he going to be a suitable team captain? Is he going to drive the ship of our lives with the same grace and stability and confidence as Dad?* I had my doubts. Still, as the tires hummed over the asphalt, I wanted to reach out to my husband, to touch him, to crawl into his side and relax into him. I wanted to explain to him the pain, the turmoil, and the confusion I felt: how my inability to save my family was gnawing at my core like a giant sewer rat; how I wish I could have done better. But I didn't. I couldn't. *How can he possibly understand?*

We drove for days; the road ahead unfolded before us, carving out the distance like a gash. We made our way out of California and into Nevada, through the barren desert. The heat melted the air around us. The thing about driving cross-country was it gave you lots of time to think. Too much. My thoughts stampeded, scrambling one over the other into a state of frenzy, clamoring for attention.

My mind arched and twisted around the divorce, the fact that Dad was quitting, upending all our lives because Mother had slept with her night nurse. It didn't make sense. He knew better. He knew that hyper-sexuality was part of the deal: an uncontrollable urge to fuck. It was one of the things he liked best about her—that she was never satiated. Always wanted more. She was a match for his own intense sexual desires. And now he was punishing her for it. Punishing her for being crazy. What had made him change? What had flipped his switch? And now she was my responsibility. Well,

David's and mine. Still, as Ronald and I hurtled down the road, this new, unwanted responsibility for Mother felt like a bomb strapped to my leg.

I balled my hands into fists. Anger nudged at me. I pushed it away. Ronald rolled down the window. Hot, dry air whipped through the car. The heat was oppressive. It burned my eyes, my throat. I needed to be more understanding. Dad was doing the best he could. He was wracked with guilt at breaking up our family, his perfect family: a beautiful, talented wife, a son first and then a daughter. The American dream—shattered by an innocent fuck.

Guilt buzzed in my ear. I swatted at it. The tires hummed on the road. They whispered: *Good daughters don't get angry with their sainted fathers. Good daughters don't leave their fathers behind.*

Ronald and I crossed the Colorado state line. The sky darkened, and fat drops of rain splattered the windshield. As we climbed through the Rocky Mountains toward Denver, the two-lane road became slick beneath the tires. Ronald accelerated into a bend in the road. Suddenly bright high-beam headlights swept across the lanes, blinding us. Ronald wrenched the steering wheel to the right to avoid hitting the oncoming car. The car skidded. I gripped the door handle. Ronald gripped the steering wheel, white-knuckled. My heart leapt into my throat. Rain beat the windshield. Ronald pulled the steering wheel to the left. We skidded some more and careened toward a cliff. I closed my eyes. Death slipped a cold hand over my shoulder. Ronald slammed the brakes; the Pontiac fishtailed.

As Ronald and I hurtled toward certain death, one question sunk its teeth into me and demanded an answer: *how can I die if I'd never really been alive?* I made a quick promise to myself: *If I survive this, then I will live my life for me. I will become the woman I know I can become. No more making myself small and invisible.* The cliff loomed large through the sheeting rain. I pushed myself into the seat, closed my eyes, and braced myself for the weightlessness of flight.

Impossibly, the car stopped with the front passenger-side wheel spinning off the edge of the cliff. Ronald and I sat, trembling, hearts cracking against our ribs. Death pouted in the back seat. Rain clattered on the roof. Our breath fogged the windows in short, spasmodic bursts. Ronald and I climbed gingerly out of the driver's side of the car. The rain felt like tears on my skin.

Later that night, Ronald and I made love. Madly. Ferociously. Hungrily. We clasped each other, buried ourselves in each other, and touched each other in all the right places, seeing each other for the first time. We fumbled and tangled ourselves. We tried to climb inside one another, rubbing, twisting, and connecting. I was slick with passion, rocking back and forth, eyes closed, back arched, melting into the ecstasy of the heat between my legs. Electric pleasure shot through me. I tingled and gasped. I exploded. I was alive.

∽∘∾

"You can't quit, Sharon." Dr. Hahn shook his head. "You've just started the program."

In spring of 1963, I was sitting in Dr. Hahn's office. I told him I was leaving the graduate program in philosophy. He was not pleased. Neither was I. But I had no choice.

"Our understanding was that you were a serious scholar. And you've demonstrated excellence in your studies thus far. To quit now ..." Dr. Hahn shrugged his shoulders as his words trailed off. I became intensely interested in the speckled linoleum floor.

I wanted to explain to him that it wasn't my fault and that I had done everything I was supposed to do. Sometimes life worked in direct opposition to the things we might want.

I cleared my throat. "I understand everything you're saying, Dr. Hahn. And I am a serious scholar. It is just that, well ..."

It was just that I couldn't get out of bed.

It was just that I couldn't stop vomiting.

It was just that I was pregnant.

It was an accident. A mishap. The diaphragm didn't work. The spermicidal jelly didn't work. Who knows how these things happened? With my morning sickness, I vomited most of the time. Sometimes I sat on the toilet and vomited in the bathtub at the same time. Any smell and every smell sent me careening into the bathroom. I didn't tell Dr. Hahn these things, of course, although given that he took himself very seriously, I would be mildly interested in how he'd react to that level of detail.

Dr. Hahn sat in his swivel chair, and he stared at me as though if he stared at me long enough I might change my mind. I rubbed my hand over my belly.

Dr. Hahn sucked in a deep breath and then sighed. "Okay, then." He shrugged his shoulders. I shrugged my shoulders. I got up to leave. I thanked him for his faith in me, in my abilities as a student, in my potential as a professor, as an intellectual equal. He shook my hand and opened his office door.

"If you change your mind, you're always welcome to come back," he said.

I nodded a thank you.

"We need women like you to become professors," he said. "So the men can do the research."

~~∞~~

My hormones were all over the place, from euphoria to despondency. I spent three months in bed while the life growing inside me turned me inside out. Physically. Emotionally. The Woman-I-Was-Supposed-To-Be told me this was the right thing, this was the right next step—that once I had my baby I wouldn't miss the loss of my career, that I would find unending joy in my family, that marriage wasn't really about love but about a lifestyle. Life was a heavily invested game of Capture the Flag, and if I performed my tasks well, then I could sleep better at night knowing I was a good woman, a woman to be proud, and a woman other women would envy. I could be the woman Mother never could be. The Woman-I-Was-Supposed-To-Be had some very good points.

And then there was the Woman-I-Wanted-To-Be, who constantly jabbed her finger in my side and reminded me that life was more than being an ornament on someone else's tree. That I had brains in addition to beauty and I should not be satisfied with dissolving and morphing around the men in my life.

The days unfolded with regularity and precision, just the way Ronald liked it. He got up. He cooked bacon. He made coffee. The smells drove me to my knees. I hunched over the toilet, heaving and coughing. I stayed home. I cleaned a little. I vomited. I vomited some more. I read Tolstoy's *Anna Karenina*—the book assigned to me in the class I had recently dropped. I lay on the couch and watched television. I vomited. Ronald came home with bags of groceries. I fixed dinner. I vomited.

During that first year of dental school, Ronald smelled of formaldehyde from dissecting corpses. He scrubbed his hands at the kitchen sink, but the smell never went away. I headed for the bathroom and heaved and sputtered from the pungent smell of the formaldehyde.

To his credit, Ronald tried. He asked me how I was feeling. He offered to help with cleaning and cooking. Still, we didn't move toward one another. The connection we felt during our near-death sex—the one and only time I'd had an orgasm—didn't take. Our lives, as ever, ran like parallel lines, a constant gap between us.

When I was four months along, I could feel life kicking. Little butterfly flutters inside me. I started to plump out, rounding with the shape of my first child. Ronald strutted around like a puffed-up rooster. The proud poppa. His hands rubbed my growing stomach at every turn. His life was unfolding according to plan.

The doctor poked and prodded. He weighed me. I gained too much. I was a pound overweight. He yelled at me and prescribed amphetamines. He told me it was fine to take the pills, nothing to worry about; the placenta protected the baby from everything I ate or drank. I didn't believe him. Somehow, I knew it was wrong. Somehow I knew everything I did affected my baby. Still, I took one pill. My heart raced. I felt out of control, like Mother. I threw the pills down the toilet. I ate healthy—vegetarian. I kept my weight in check. I paid attention to the needs of my baby even before birth. I was a good mother.

DAD DIVORCED MOTHER IN FEBRUARY of 1963. He appointed Uncle Louie, David, and me as trustees of her trust. The income from her trust would take care of her for the rest of her life. After her death, the assets would be split between David and me. All Dad wanted from the divorce settlement was control of his construction company, Hicks Homes. He felt he could always make money, but Mother was unable to work, so he left her income from all of their personal property. During the same week he divorced Mother in Reno, he married his childhood friend, Kathy. Dad showed Kathy his financials as owner of Hicks Homes. He wanted Kathy to know he would take care of her—just like he told Mother. Just like he told me.

The summer of 1963, Ronald and I made the long drive from St. Louis to California to visit our parents. Mother had recently been released from Westwood Hospital and was living with Aunt Mackie and Uncle Louie in Sunland. Dad and Kathy were leaving California soon for Hawaii.

∾

"You've got to get your mother out of here," fumed Uncle Louie. "She's driving Mackie crazy."

I could tell by Uncle Louie's voice that he had reached his limit too.

I drove to their home to see Mother. It had been a year since I had seen her—since she had slept with her night nurse, since Dad had jumped ship. I was jittery—half-excited, half-afraid—to see her. I didn't know her condition, her treatment, and her medications. Uncle Louie wanted her "out of here." What was I supposed to do? I didn't even live in California. I was pregnant, just visiting for a few months and then going back to St. Louis.

"Oh, Sharon," Mother said when she saw me.

She pinned herself against me. She cried. She squeezed me tighter. I was momentarily stunned at this display. It was impossible—improbable at the very least—that she was happy to see me. I squeezed back tentatively, and my swelling womb pushed up against hers. My child nestled against the space where she had carried me for nine months. We were, in that instant, however clumsily, connected: mother, daughter, and grandchild.

Suddenly, Mother began to sob uncontrollably. I was little startled and confused. I didn't know if those were tears of depression or joy about my pregnancy or unexpressed love for me, a tsunami of delayed affection and warmth and intimacy. I pulled back and wiped my hand across her cheek, which was slicked with tears.

"It's okay, Mother. It's okay."

She choked on her tears, knocked my hand away, knitted her brow, and screwed her lips. Then she looked at my distended belly.

"Oh, what? You think you're special because you're pregnant? Well, you're not. It's not always about you, Sharon."

Her words slapped me. *When has it ever been about me?*

Mother flopped onto the couch and started sobbing again. "The divorce! It's so unfair!"

The divorce? Of course, what was I thinking? It was all about her. She whined about the terms of the divorce being unfair, about how her own son had tricked her into signing the papers, about how she was sick and how could Harold, how could her son, take advantage of her in that way?

"After everything I gave to that man! He's nothing without me! Can't even take a shit without me!"

My head spun with her complaints. I was out of practice. I had forgotten what a whirling tornado of self-centeredness she was. Immediately, I felt like a helpless child again, caught in the middle of her storm, no shelter in sight. My knees went numb. My heart bucked in my chest, and that familiar knot in my stomach surfaced. I wanted to hide. To escape.

"Sharon," she said sitting up on the couch. "I want you to arrange a meeting. I want to meet with your dad."

I shook my head. He'd never go for it. I knew he didn't want to see her, and I didn't want to get caught in the middle.

Mother held her hand up, signaling me to wait. "I just want to talk to him. I never had any say in the divorce. There was no discussion. Just papers to sign. I just want to talk to him about it."

She sniffled. I shook my head again: not doing it. This time, I was going to tell her no—a definitive, clear no.

Mother sat up straighter. There were no more tears, no soft weepiness. Instantly she became sword-like: sharp and hard-edged. She stared at me, into me, through me, her eyes steeled and cold. I stiffened. For my entire life I would never be able to adjust to the sharp, unpredictable turns of her moods: the way they lassoed me and brought me to my knees.

"You have to, Sharon. Your dad listens to you. He trusts you. Arrange the meeting."

The truth was, I thought she might be right this time. Was it fair to divorce a mentally ill woman who was in the hospital for treatment? I thought she had a right to say her piece. This was the 1960s and the rise of civil rights for all people. I wondered if the mentally ill would be given their civil rights too, or would they continue to be strapped down against their will, taken to mental hospitals, zapped with electric shock treatments, and doused with meds?

Still, to arrange the meeting, I would need to lie to Dad, and I didn't think I could live with myself for doing that. I clenched the word no between my teeth while Mother continued her rage, throwing guilt-tipped darts. No skittered to the back of my throat. I swallowed and gagged. Then I surrendered. I arranged a meeting for the next day. I lied to Dad. I told him that I needed to talk to him alone and could he please meet me at Ronald's folks' house?

Dad arrived on time. I hugged him tightly, an apology, a silent plea for forgiveness. He was so happy to see me and gave me a big bear hug.

"How are you and the baby, Susie?"

I said nothing and led him into the kitchen. Dad flinched when he saw Mother sitting at the kitchen table. When she smiled, his face tightened, and he looked me a question, an accusation. Mother patted the seat next to her. Dad scraped back the chair at the other end of the table, sat, and folded his arms tightly across his chest. I sat between them, a buffer, a pawn. Picked clean. Used well. Stretched between the poles of my parents' righteous indignation.

"Okay, Sharon," Dad said, glaring at Mother, the edge in his voice reserved for my betrayal and me. "You arranged this. You sit here and listen. Really listen to your Mother."

Mother squirmed in her seat, her hands flat against the tabletop, poised for battle.

"Not once will she ask me what I want," Dad continued, nodding in Mother's general direction. "Not once will she be concerned about me and what will make me happy. She is narcissistic. Doesn't care about anyone but herself. You just watch." He never took his eyes off her.

She stared him down. Mother's anger came thick and fast. "You shithead!" She slapped her hand on the table.

I jumped.

"I always wanted to divorce you but on my terms, when I wanted! You are nothing without me! Goddamn you! You are nothing! I made you. You cannot even shit without my permission. I will tell you when we will get a divorce."

Mother's rage hung as black as pitch in the space between them.

Dad leaned back in his chair, eyes fixed on Mother, twenty-eight years of disappointment stretched taut across his face. "We're already divorced, Carolyn."

"I know that, you dumbass." She leaned forward and folded her hands on the table. "Listen carefully, Harold. I want an accounting of all our assets. I know what you're worth, and I want my fair share. The next time you hear from me, it will be from my attorney. You screwed me in the divorce, and now I'm suing you, you asshole."

The movement was involuntary, the way my neck snapped toward Mother. It wasn't her anger that drew me, not even the fact that she was suing my father. That was to be expected. But she was not only interested in the financial gain; she was also interested in her day in court. She wanted to be validated. She wanted to be acknowledged for being "the woman behind the man" who built a successful company.

The determination in her voice, the lucidity, captured my attention. She wasn't manic or depressed. She was clear-headed. Sober. Decisive. Vindictive. Fat, black bubbles of anger roiled inside me. I had long suspected that she faked her illness, using it as an excuse to behave in hurtful and inappropriate ways. Using it to explain away her lack of affection or attention toward me. Sitting there in my in-laws' kitchen, listening to her threats she was making with calculated vengeance, I thought my suspicions had been right all along: she wasn't really sick.

I told Dad it was time to go. He agreed, and we walked to the front door together, leaving Mother wrestling with her rage in the kitchen. I reached for Dad to give him a hug. He put his hands on my shoulders and smiled at me weakly, sadly.

"Susie, please understand that it is not easy to divorce a sick woman. If her trust ever runs short of money, just let me know. Did you notice that she never even asked about me? That is what my life has been like for the past twenty-eight years. I have finally found some happiness with Kathy."

He sighed. "I feel badly that David and you have to police her now, that you have to shoulder that burden, but ..." He shrugged his shoulders. "I don't know what else to do."

I didn't know either. Other than to do what I always did. I assured Dad that it was okay. That David and I didn't mind. That it was his turn to enjoy life. Everything would be just fine. Dad ducked into his car, pulled out of the driveway, and gave a little wave. I rubbed little circles over my stomach. I watched his car disappear. As I turned to go into the house where Mother was pouting like a petulant child, I couldn't help thinking that this was all just a little bit unfair for everyone.

UNCLE LOUIE PUT MOTHER ON a plane home to Hawaii. Ronald and I drove back to a house Dad bought us in Clayton, a suburb of St. Louis. I forgot about Mother and her lawsuit and concentrated on my life at hand. I found it comforting: a life of expectations, simply because there weren't too many moving parts. Life, for the most part, was calm. Not perfect. But calm. Okay, maybe not totally calm. Predictable. And I could live with that.

∽⚬∼

On September 28, 1963, I gave birth to a baby girl: Cynthia Lynn. Cyndy was exquisite, perfect. I loved her immediately. I kissed her wrinkled, pink forehead and cradled her in my arms. I whispered, "I love you" a thousand times a day, and I wished I could tattoo those words to her brain, to her heart, to make sure she never forgot. I left soft butterfly kisses on her tiny belly and nibbled at her fat, pink toes. An unbreakable bond soared through my being. I pressed her to my chest so she could hear my heartbeat and know she was safe.

Her pediatrician told me not to say no to her before she was two years old. He said her little brain couldn't register the word no. When Dad visited with Kathy, he said, "Bullshit." Mother said nothing. Since she was home in Hawaii, I had little contact with her. She couldn't focus enough to arrange a visit.

Cyndy grew more beautiful every day. And since her birth, Cyndy screamed. She was fierce and determined. Her little face purpled with frustration, hands clenched into tiny fists. I tried to help her be quiet: I walked her, I rocked her, I sung to her. I was patient, calm, and stable, working hard to quell the surges and swells of panic that told me I was doing this wrong.

∽⚬∼

Grandma Hicks visited from Oregon when Cyndy was one. I paraded my family in front of her—my professional husband, my beautiful baby girl. I wore them like badges of honor, proof that I was good and worthwhile. *See, Grandma? I did it. I have the good life. The right life. The life Dad has always wanted for me—the white picket fence with squeaky-clean husband. Do you see?*

The four of us rode a crowded paddleboat down the Mississippi. The river's muddied waters slapped rhythmically against the side of the boat. Grandma cooed and fussed over Cyndy, her yellowing eyes misty with the pleasure of her great granddaughter. Ronald stood with his hands jammed into his coat pockets, huddled and pinched against the cold air whipping off the water. Cyndy sucked madly on her sterilized pacifier. She waved her hands, conducting an invisible orchestra from inside her stroller. Grandma and I grinned from our hearts in admiration of Cyndy. Things were good.

And then Cyndy started to snuffle and twitch. A small cry escaped. Then another. And another. I watched in horror as Cyndy screwed and contorted her face in an escalating fit of discomfort. I rubbed her belly and silently willed her to calm down. *Please, oh, please. Calm down!* I looked at Ronald. He narrowed his eyes, a warning: *Don't embarrass me, Sharon.* Adrenaline pulsated through me. The paddleboat chugged along. Grandma smiled, oblivious to the impending disaster.

"Quite the little fusser, isn't she?" Grandma said. "Takes after your mother." She joked. I knew she was joking. She had to be joking.

Suddenly, Cyndy spit out her pacifier. She drew in a huge gulp of air. Her scream ripped through the St. Louis afternoon, shredding the illusion of perfect, happy family. Ronald was apoplectic. He dug his fingers into my arm.

"What did you do to her?" he demanded. "Now see what you've done? Everyone is staring at us!"

I glanced around at the deck full of passengers. Some stared; most did not. Still, Ronald imagined his image was on the line in front of this group of strangers. His one-year-old daughter was not perfectly in control of herself. This logically led to the conclusion that his wife was unable to control said daughter, which, of course meant Ronald was not able to control his wife, as every good husband should.

Ronald scooped up Cyndy's pacifier from the boat deck and thrust it in my face. "Her pacifier is now dirty, Sharon," he seethed. "What will she do for the rest of the trip without her pacifier? Huh? Tell me!"

I was tempted to tell him she could suck her thumb, but that would make things worse. I didn't think I could stand another lecture on the unsanitary horror of thumb sucking and the ensuing astronomical orthodontic costs required to fix the damage.

Ronald put his face in front of mine. "Do something," he said through clenched teeth. "She is embarrassing me, and so are you."

He stomped off to the other side of the deck. I was mortified, ashamed. I looked at Grandma. Her face was a mix of confusion and pity. I wanted desperately for her to be proud of me, of my family.

She grabbed my elbow. "What is the matter with Ronald?"

Her question knocked me off balance.

"Nothing is wrong with Ronald, Grandma." I forced the words through a smile and hid the five-fingered bruise Ronald had given me. "Everything is okay. Everything is just fine."

I crawled inside the lie and pulled it shut over my head.

Nine months later, on June 3, 1965, I had another beautiful daughter: Julie Lynn. I now had two precious girls with Ronald's blond, curly hair and long eyelashes.

I poured myself into the role of the perfect wife, to fit our lives into the image of perfect family. I kept the house well stocked in the manner of a good hostess. I was prepared for the occasional visitor, the unexpected dinner guests Ronald bought home. We had bottles of vodka, gin, bourbon, and scotch and mixes for martinis, vodka gimlets, and scotch and soda. A ceramic cigarette case was placed on the coffee table in the living room. Every end table had an ashtray. There was wine—Chablis, chardonnay, merlot, white with fish, red with meat. And after dinner there were liqueurs—brandy, cognac.

I threw parties to make my husband look good. I was bright and bubbly, the perfect hostess. When the guests left, Ronald was furious with me for laughing too loudly, dancing too wildly, talking to a man for too long.

He apologized profusely, pledging not to be jealous. According to Dad, the best way to keep a man happy was to drain him sexually. *I'll screw his fucking brains out. That should help! Maybe.*

At one of our dental student parties, Lavina told other wives how she sat on her husband's face. And wiggled around. About how much he enjoyed it. I listened in rapt attention. Enthralled. Perplexed. *How does he breathe?* I looked over at Ronald, standing in the corner: stiff, rigid, and unable to get comfortable. I imagined sitting on his face, the flick of his tongue, the race of my pulse, and the explosion of delight. I would smother him. I would laugh and howl and wipe the tears from my eyes. Afterward, of course, he would want to floss his teeth.

∞

June 1966. Ronald graduated from dental school. Both of us received awards: Most Improved Student for Ronald and Most Supportive Wife for me. I was the only nonstudent to receive an award and the first to receive this particular honor. Ronald slipped his arm around me, pecked me on the cheek, and posed for the camera, his arms filled with trophies.

At the graduation party, Buddy, a handsome, unmarried dental student, caught my eye. He was sophisticated and charming. He possessed a magnetism that made the space between my legs throb with hunger. Something dangerous about him awakened a powerful animal lust within me. He cornered me, scotch in hand. He told me Ronald would never make any money—that he was too slow, too meticulous, too much a perfectionist. He told me Ronald was not the man for me. That I deserved better. I thought he might be right.

∞

Ronald landed a job with the Veteran's Administration in Los Angeles, California.

We packed our bags and headed west. We rented a cute little house in Sherman Oaks with a white picket fence. The days settled into a predictable rhythm—cooking, cleaning, straightening the house, and obsessively making sure everything was in its proper place, sterilized, perfect. The girls and I took trips to the park to ride the swings and merry-go-rounds. We watched Captain Kangaroo and Mr. Rogers. I did the shopping, cleaning, laundry, meals; I washed the dishes, bathed the girls, tucked them into bed, and had sex with Ronald or not. And I liked our life of routine, of predictability. So what if Ronald and I didn't match in matters of the heart? So what if our sex was rigid and mechanical? He had controlled his temper. Although I didn't really love Ronald—and since the first outburst six years ago, had absolutely no respect for him as a husband or a man—strangely, I didn't resent him. Because of him I had my daughters, my two fair-haired angels. Because of him I had the right house in the right neighborhood with the right picket fence and the right friends with whom we barbequed on Saturdays. We were rich in the currency of social acceptance. We had "made it." Wasn't that the goal all along?

I settled myself into my papier-mâché marriage, into my papier-mâché life. We were a happy family. Okay, maybe not happy but normal. Regular. Just like everyone else. And there was something to be said for that—something to be said for days that simply melted into one another, days that just sort of slipped by, unnoticed, unremarkable in their comings and goings. I embraced my life of regularity and routine. Of conformity. I clutched it, white-knuckled, nails dug deep.

DAD HAD A STROKE IN November 1966. He was only fifty years old. The news hit me with such force that I couldn't remember how to breathe. I flew to Hawaii immediately and joined Kathy, Grandma, and David at Dad's bedside at Queens Hospital. I didn't recognize my father. He was pale and drawn, ashen. He looked shriveled under the fluorescent hospital lights, his head wrapped in a bandage from the emergency brain surgery where doctors had carved out a tumor from the side of his head the size of a lemon.

The doctor hurled a flurry of words at us: carcinoma, just in time, good prognosis, we got it all. We nodded.

The doctor asked: "Was your father ever hit in the head? Did he ever have a head injury?"

Because we couldn't remember a head injury, I called Mother, hoping she would remember.

She laughed. "Serves him right! He's getting what he deserves! Ha!"

She hung up on me. I took a deep breath and called her again because the doctors needed to know. She told me when they had sailed to Maui about six years earlier, he was hit on the head by a mast on their boat. She was unaware of Dad being hit because she was below. It was only when she went topside; she found him unconscious on the deck. She had no idea how long he remained unconscious before she found him. She didn't ask about him or apologize for her callousness.

The men of his company, Hicks Homes, and the subcontractors, visited with their wives. They brought an endless stream of flowers, cards, and well wishes, their faces drawn tight with anxiety. They loved Dad—called him "the Old Man," a term of high endearment and respect in Japanese culture.

Four months later, Dad and Kathy visited Ronald and me in Sherman Oaks. Dad and Kathy were optimistic about his full recovery. Dad was cancer free, and although his emotions might wobble and list unpredictably, his reasoning was intact.

And yet, despite his assurances in a letter I had received from him recently that he was getting stronger every day, that he would return to his old self in no time because with Kathy he finally had begun to live, something had irreparably changed in my dad. There was an uncertainty about him, a hesitation in his movements, in his speech. He was quiet and still, lacking the vivacity, the tenacity, and the self-assuredness that had forever cast him as a superhero in my eyes. He didn't trust himself. His lack of emotional control had him flummoxed, and it embarrassed him. He restrained himself from speaking, afraid of saying or doing things incorrectly. Movement required thought. If he forgot to concentrate on it, he listed toward the left when he walked. There was a brokenness about him that left little stress fractures on my heart. Still, they believed he was getting better.

I made meatloaf for dinner when they came to visit. Dad sat at the kitchen table, watching me. Our conversations were careful, a little stilted, slow. I showed off for him like a trained seal. I mixed the ground beef with eggs, oats, tomato sauce, and herbs. I squeezed and kneaded it between my fingers. I pounded it into shape. I slid it in the oven. I peeled potatoes, boiled them, and mashed them. Sautéed the vegetables. Set the table, poured the drinks, and served the food

During dinner, Dad told Ronald his sex life with Kathy was still going strong. Then he began playing with something in his mouth. With shaking fingers, he dug around his tongue. He pulled out a piece of waxed paper. Dad's face twisted into confusion. He held it in front of him, twisted it around in the air, and stared at it with the intensity of a jeweler inspecting a gem for flaws. Then he turned a few shades of green and vomited. I blanched. In my excitement to show him my skill in the kitchen, I had mistakenly mixed waxed paper into the meatloaf. My perfect dinner was ruined. Dad crawled from his chair and shuffled to the bathroom. I was horrified. I thought I had killed my dad. Kathy ran after him, supported him with her hand at the small of his back, and rubbed his shoulders while he threw up. I came undone and pressed my hands to my forehead, helpless, mortified. *What have I done?* More violent vomiting. Vomiting up blood.

The ambulance arrived; white coats strapped Dad down to the gurney. The siren ripped through the California night as they whisked Dad to the hospital in Burbank: a Catholic hospital, St. Joseph's.

Another stroke. Another surgery. Another tumor removed, this one from the other side of his brain, also the size of a lemon. I didn't understand. The doctors in Hawaii had said Dad was fine, that he would recover, that there was no more cancer. Clearly they were wrong.

It was a misdiagnosis. It began in Reno four years earlier at a corner clinic—the day Kathy and Dad got married. The clinic doctor had removed a black mole from his shoulder and told Dad it was benign and he would be fine. They were wrong. Little knots of anger bunched up in my throat. *Why did he go to a corner clinic? He knew better!* Dad's carelessness left me feeling breathless, like I'd been punched in the gut.

And then again in Hawaii. The first stroke. The first tumor. Another misdiagnosis. This time doctors said it was a carcinoma. They said he would be fine.

My father was not fine.

My father was dying.

He had only days to live.

Over the next seven days, everything appeared kaleidoscopic, spinning and falling into dizzying, fractured circles. I watched the melanoma whittle my father down, rob him of his strength, his vitality, his hope. He became a slip of a man. As illogical as it sounded, I realized for the first time, as I stared at my dad lying in his hospital bed, disappearing by degrees, that he was mortal and that no matter how badly I wanted to—have always wanted to—I couldn't save him. This thought exploded through me like a wrecking ball.

Dr. Amerongen, Dad's neurosurgeon, was furious with the doctors who had misdiagnosed Dad. He told us he was the same age as Dad and he would want to know if he was going to die. He said that knowing death was on the horizon could change everything (like maybe Dad would want to change his will) and not knowing the truth was as good as robbing Dad of his life. He offered to testify on our behalf if we wanted to sue.

Ronald shook his head. "We will not sue. It is unethical. It is not professionally courteous. Doctors do not sue doctors."

I was livid. I glared at Ronald. What right did he have to make such a decision? Kathy decided it was best to follow Ronald's advice since he was a man who knew what was best. After all, he was a doctor too—a doctor of dental surgery. There was nothing I could do. Because she was Dad's wife, Kathy made all the final decisions regarding Dad. Four years of marriage trumped twenty-six years of being a doting daughter.

When I called Mother to tell her Dad had a few days to live, she was beside herself with glee. "Serves him right for wanting to give me a lobotomy all those years ago! He's getting what he deserves, in the brain."

She hung up. I stumbled back into Dad's hospital room, curled up in a chair, and swore I would never see her again.

Dad slipped in and out of consciousness. Grandma, Kathy, and I held vigil. We took turns sitting with Dad, holding his hand, and telling him how much we loved him. From time to time, Dad's eyes opened and flicked slowly back and forth between us, the three women he loved most, as though he were trying to gather and hold us close. And then his gaze slipped past us and landed on a cross hanging on the wall opposite his bed. His eyes grew as round as saucers. Kathy and Grandma watched Dad anxiously. They were both desperately Christian and couldn't reconcile Dad's impending death with his atheism. For Dad, there was no afterlife—no sweet reunion with loved ones on the other side. There was only this life and after that … nothing.

In that moment, I wanted to believe in a heaven, like Kathy and Grandma, where rivers of crystals and jewels wound through streets paved with gold, where luminescent angels fluttered about with golden halos and iridescent wings, where I might once again feel the warmth of my dad's embrace and drink in the twinkle in his eyes.

Inexplicably, Dad yelled, "Jeeeesus Chrrriiiist!"

Grandma and Kathy exchanged quick glances, their eyebrows arched in disbelief, each seeking confirmation in the other that they both heard what they thought they had heard. Instantly, they both squealed with relief.

Grandma clapped her hands. "Praise Jesus! My son finally accepts Jesus as his savior! Hallelujah! Now I will see him again in heaven!"

She dropped to her knees, palms pressed toward the ceiling. Kathy sobbed softly, quietly, and deeply—grateful. They heard salvation.

I heard, "You've got to be fucking kidding me! I'm going to die in a Christian hospital?" A tiny smile dashed across my lips.

A few days later, Dad's breathing was quick and shallow, his heartbeat soft and thin. I wasn't ready for him to leave me.

He looked up at me.

"Am I dying, Susie?"

"Yes, Dad. Yes, you are dying," I said, slowly and softly.

I knew he would want the truth.

He nodded, thoughtfully, digesting the idea.

Then he asked another question: "Are you having any fun yet?"

The question startled me. I didn't know fun was an option. For a moment, I wondered if he knew about Ronald, about his temper. I wondered if he could see it in my eyes. I wanted to ask him, "What do you mean by fun?"

Instead I replied, "Sure, Dad."

For the second time in my life, I lied to Dad. I wanted to cry. He nodded his head again, satisfied. He closed his eyes. I folded his hand into mine. He couldn't go. Not yet. Not ever. I had never known life without Dad. What would I do without him?

Dad's eyes flickered open again. He seemed surprised to see me standing there. He swallowed thickly. "Susie, I want you to know I am dying a happy man because of Kathy. And I want you to know, Susie," I could barely hear him. I leaned in closer. "You are the only one in the family who never disappointed me."

And then he was gone.

～∞～

It was the day after Dad's funeral in Hawaii—or at least I thought it was the next day. It is difficult to remember such things during times of trauma and loss. Time seemed to expand, refusing to line up in neat little orderly increments like minutes and hours and days. Anyway, the next day, Kathy, David, and I met with the trustees of Dad's estate. As sole owner of Hicks Construction Company, Dad had divided the ownership of the company into thirds—one-third to Kathy, one-third to David's four children (divided equally), and one-third to me. David had requested that Dad leave his one-third to his children and not to him directly.

At the meeting, an attorney did all the talking. He was cold and harsh—rude. He told us to return to California. There were explicit instructions in Dad's will that his family had nothing to do with the business. The attorney continued, "There is nothing for you here. We don't want any trouble. You should be thankful for what you get."

David and Kathy were stone-faced. I was bristling. *Surely Dad wouldn't approve of this. He wouldn't approve of his family, his loved ones, being treated like this, iced out of the company—would he?*

"We are in control," the attorney warned. "We will make all the decisions."

David and Kathy stood.

I stood.

They shook the attorney's hand.

"Thank you," said David.

Kathy nodded her consent.

I stood there, slack-jawed. I didn't understand what had just happened.

DAD HAD DIED A MONTH earlier. I stumbled blindly through the days, dazed, hollowed out, feeling like an amputee. Dad was a phantom limb, the ache of loss acute and persistent. I spent much of my time clutching my girls to my chest, wanting to keep them safe, to keep them near me; suddenly I was terrified I might lose them too.

Ronald and I attended a dental convention at the Ambassador Hotel in Los Angeles. I wandered after him, well-dressed, well put together, tripping over the shackles of compliance that had tangled around my ankles. I drank like a fish, spilling wine down my throat. I refused dinner. On the way home, grief over Dad's death buried itself in me like a hatchet. Split me open. Scraped me raw. I couldn't think. I couldn't breathe. I rested my head against the car window, the city lights smearing by and despair flowing from me in great black rivers.

Ronald drove into the driveway. I staggered into the house. Our recently divorced next-door neighbor, who had graciously offered to babysit the girls, asked me what was wrong. I was mute. I shook my head. Words couldn't contain my agony. Ronald, thick with liquor, stomped off to the bedroom. I pasted on a smile to cover the black tracks of mascara.

"Thanks for watching the girls," I said, my voice blunt and flat.

He hugged me. He knew I was hurting. "It's going to be okay. If you need me, I'm just next door."

I thanked him again and showed him to the door. I went to the bedroom to get into my pajamas. My bones suddenly felt too heavy. I didn't see Ronald; I thought he must be in the bathroom brushing and flossing his teeth. Then I saw him in the shadows of the bedroom, hands on his hips, face purple with rage.

"You would *never* cry over me like that if I died!" Ronald seethed. He was trembling, daring me to disagree with him.

I said nothing. What was there to say? Dad had always told me, "Susie, you can't reason with the unreasonable." Suddenly I became cold sober. I pulled back the covers, crawled into bed, turned my back to him, and curled into myself.

The next morning Ronald left for work—a chasm of silence between us. When the front door clicked shut, something in me snapped. It was then that I knew that Ronald would never change. I would always be dancing around his moods. This was who he was, who he had always been, who he would always be. Something primal yawned open inside me, whispered that it was now or never, told me I didn't have to take his shit anymore, that I had done my duty, paid my dues. Besides, Dad's death freed me to walk away. Dad would never know that my marriage was a failure.

It happened swiftly, smoothly, like milk pouring into a glass. I packed bags for the girls and me. We took a cab to the Los Angeles International Airport and hopped a plane to Uncle Roy and Grandma in Oregon. Once we were there, I called Ronald.

"I'm getting a divorce." There was an eerie calmness to my voice.

"Please, Sharon. I'm sorry. I should have comforted you. I know you miss your dad. Please don't leave me."

"Ronald, it's too late."

I EMERGED FROM MY DIVORCE exhausted yet triumphant. I hoisted my newfound freedom above my head, drunk on my own newly discovered power and independence. I rushed headlong into my new adventure of single motherhood, awakening my dormant dream of becoming a philosophy professor, unfurling my long-muted voice, relentless in my determination to be somebody. And I swore off men—cross-my-heart-hope-to-die-stick-a-needle-in-my-eye—because men were toxic and would impede my unwavering march toward my inner personal growth.

Well, no. Not exactly. Like an animal held captive for too long, I stepped outside my cage, drew in one deep, satisfying breath, and ran straight back in, locking the door shut behind me for ten years.

The divorce was mostly uneventful. We had no assets since Dad had sold the house in St. Louis and we were renting in Sherman Oaks. The judge ordered Ronald to pay child support of $345 a month for each daughter until they became eighteen. Then Ronald was also ordered to pay for the girls' college expenses when the time came, which was fair since Dad paid for six years of Ronald's college, including dental school, so he wouldn't be mired in debt when he graduated. Ronald and I agreed to share custody of the girls. They would live with me; he had visitation every other weekend.

Wham, bam, thank you, ma'am. I was a divorcee.

∽∘∾

I worked as a legal secretary for an attorney in Los Angeles. I put my girls in a daycare that looked like fun for them. I was besotted with independent womanhood. I skipped through the days, rosy-cheeked, eyes aglow, shoulders thrown back, head held high. Every once in a while I gave a little leap and clicked my heels together just for the fun of it.

I started dating the next-door neighbor, just for kicks. He was the polar opposite of Ronald: athletic, brown hair, brown eyes, and scraggly little mustache. I wasn't entirely sure if he had graduated from high school. He told me he worked at an insurance company, but I never knew what his job was. He could have worked in the mailroom for all I knew. He stood five-foot-four—maybe five-five if he bounced up and down on his toes, which he had a habit of doing. Still, he was simple, uncomplicated. He was the kind of guy who spent his free time working out at Muscle Beach in Venice.

An attorney at the office where I worked in Los Angeles attracted me. He was ridiculously gorgeous, knew it, and flaunted it at every turn. He was the original pretty boy in a Patrick Swayze sort of way. He was hot—stick-your-finger-in-your-mouth-and-press-it-to-your-ass, sizzling hot. He asked me out. I batted my eyes, looked away coyly, blushed, and then declined the invitation.

"I'm dating someone," I said.

Patrick was not deterred.

He followed me around the office like a bulldog hot on the trail of a female in heat. He followed me into the law library, draped himself across my desk, flashed his oh-so-sexy smile, and asked me out again. I cleared my throat, crossed my legs to temper the throbbing between them, and politely declined.

"I'm so sorry, but I'm seeing someone," I breathed. "My next-door neighbor."

Patrick strolled over to the high-rise window next to my desk and pointed down to a bench in the courtyard below, where the next-door neighbor was sitting, waiting for me to join him for lunch.

"Him?" Patrick asked, looking back at me, amusement swimming in his pool-blue eyes.

I got up and stood next to him, following his finger with my eyes.

"Yes, that's him," I said.

A smile twitched across Patrick's face. He looked at me and then looked back out the window. My head, at this moment, was next to Patrick's bicep, and I wondered, briefly, what it would feel like to wrap my arm around it, what it would feel like to have that muscled arm wrapped around me, holding me tight, keeping me safe.

Truthfully, I was still hoping for a knight in shining armor—someone to rescue me from a life of single motherhood. It was not that I didn't enjoy being a single mom, but it was harder than I thought. The previous week, when I had gone to pick my girls up from daycare, I had been slammed with guilt because I didn't recognize them. I couldn't pick them out in the crowd of toddlers scurrying about the playroom. When I finally found them, I thought, *I'm missing their childhoods, missing their growing up.* Their faces had changed so much, were filling out. Pretty soon I wouldn't know them at all anymore. I knelt on the carpet right then and there, scooped Cyndy and Julie into my arms, and whispered an apology into their ears. I traced their faces with my fingers, as if to burn them into my memory so I would never not recognize them again. Then the daycare director informed me that I had to keep the girls home for at least a week. They had the mumps.

I looked out the window again, with Patrick staring down at the next-door neighbor. The noon sun heated the space between us. He slipped a muscled arm around my shoulder. I wilted and saw stars.

"Be right back," he whispered. Then he turned on his heel, bounded down the stairs, crossed the courtyard, introduced himself to the next-door neighbor, and shook his hand. Then he said something and pointed to the window where I stood looking down at them like Rapunzel trapped in the tower. The two of them walked to the entrance of the building. I was aghast, mortified, appalled.

A few minutes later, Patrick sauntered into the office; the next-door neighbor trailed him like a piece of toilet paper stuck to a shoe. I sucked in my breath to keep from squealing. My face flushed hot with embarrassment. Next to Patrick Swayze, the neighbor looked like a rumpled little troll. I smiled nervously and picked at my stockings. *What should I do? Grab the sexy, educated Adonis and dump the stammering troll?* But I didn't. I dated the next-door neighbor. After all, he was convenient, and it wasn't like we were going to get married.

And then we did.

Less than a year after divorcing Ronald, I was, impossibly, pregnant. I didn't know exactly how it had happened. I was pretty sure it wasn't my fault. I ran down the checklist of birth control steps. Diaphragm? Check. Spermicidal jelly? Check. Allegedly sterile neighbor? Check. Still, the pregnancy test came back positive. Dad had warned me not to get caught with the goods. Next-door neighbor was elated. He wanted kids. He told me he loved me. I did the right thing and married him.

Five months later in a Unitarian Church, I shifted my weight. I slung my arm under my protruding belly. I vowed, "This baby will now have a father." I patted my belly, held my head high, and waddled down the aisle to the tune of Simon and Garfunkel's "Feelin' Groovy." *Slow down, you move too fast.*

It was a mistake.

It wasn't the song I had picked.

Someone had screwed up.

∽◦∽

Four months later and a week away from my delivery date, my distended belly was almost unbearable. I smoothed my hands over stretched skin; life kicked outward, and the weight of my decision to marry my next-door neighbor weighed heavily.

It was late afternoon. Dusk muted the bright colors of day, softened the day's sharp edges, and sighed as evening began. Cyndy was five. Julie was three. They quietly played in their bedroom. I was tired. These last few weeks were always the hardest: ankles and fingers swelled, back and knees hurt, couldn't get comfortable. I hauled my sizeable self up the stairs of our Hollywood Hills home to lie down, to close my eyes just for a second.

Joe had followed me into the bedroom, grabbed me by the shoulders and shoved me down on the bed.

I retreated and crossed my arms over my stomach, an instinct.

"Stupid fucking bitch!" he seethed.

I twisted my face toward him and narrowed my eyes. Panic took hold. It was too soon, too early to deliver. Cyndy and Julie had come two weeks after my due date. I really wasn't expecting to deliver for another three weeks.

He straddled me and raised his hand.

I yelled, "You bastard. Get me to the hospital. The baby's coming."

After twenty-four hours in labor, I lay in my hospital bed, white sheets and white walls everywhere. The nurse handed me my son. I cradled him in my arms. He was perfect. His eyes were bright and alert, and they latched onto mine. Baby Joe was beautiful.

∽◦∽

Life unfolded as a series of dos and don'ts, a catalogue of allowances. My second husband became Big Daddy. He was the man of the house. I did as he said, or there would be trouble. It was important for me to keep the peace for my children. So I tap danced trying to make it all perfect, believing that if I had the house in perfect order, our lives in perfect order, then maybe he wouldn't get mad and would therefore treat the kids and me kindly.

I did not stop to figure out how history had repeated itself: another angry son-of-a-bitch husband. Instead, I did what I did best: I threw myself into it, spun lies and donned blinders, set another stage of smoke and mirrors. I became a magician, a master of illusion. The only reality was the one I chose to create, the one I chose to see. I was so good at conjuring false happiness; I convinced myself this could work. I convinced myself it had to work. I couldn't face the fact that I had failed twice to secure the perfect life Dad dreamed for me.

I wiped the toilets and the sinks and shined the chrome—no smudges, no streaks. I hung the towels correctly, same length, equidistant, no wrinkles, no stains. I hung the toilet paper correctly, raked the shag carpet, mopped the floor, cleaned the windows, bathed the kids, cooked dinner, filled the candy dish, and plopped the kids in the corner with one toy each. "Hush now, be quiet, no talking, no laughing, no noise." I combed my hair, put on lipstick, and smiled: "Hello, dear, how was your day?" Big Daddy ignored me, poured himself a scotch. Then another and another and another. He tromped upstairs and sat behind his giant oak desk in his study that my inheritance had bought.

I was not allowed to wear high heels, too much make-up, gym tights, clothes that showed my slender figure, or sheer bras that showed my nipples. I was not allowed to take classes, go to the gym, work out, see a male gynecologist, tell a joke, spend my own money, talk on the phone, talk to another man for too long, or buy any clothes or groceries without Big Daddy's preapproval of the type to purchase or amount to spend. I was not allowed to cuddle my son, pepper him with kisses, or tell him I loved him.

"You'll make him a sissy! Stop that! He is *my* son!" Big Daddy said.

I walked a tightrope with an umbrella clenched between my teeth, high above an amazed and bewildered crowd, and no safety net in sight. Big Daddy periodically told me he would kill me if I ever left him.

I was terrified for my safety and for the safety of my girls.

This was not the life I wanted.

A fantasy of escape morphed into a plan.

Soon, I told myself. Very soon.

And then.

I was pregnant.

Again.

I was inconsolable. Despair, pure and clean, sliced through me, flayed me open. All hope was lost. With this fourth pregnancy, there was no way out of this cataclysmic disaster that was my life. Leaving seemed impossible. I would be a single mother with a philosophy degree and four children. I would be divorced a second time inside of two years.

I stumbled through the first few months of my pregnancy, sick, dazed, and desperate for some miracle, any miracle, salvation of any kind. Big Daddy continued to rule the house, our lives, with an iron fist, a handled half-gallon jug of scotch gripped in his fingers and a crystal-cut tumbler full of ice. He drank, got drunk, and passed out; I left him on the floor. We all liked it better when Big Daddy was drunk. He slowed down and mellowed out. Scotch smoothed out his edges. Shut him up. It relaxed the mean in him. I kept the house well stocked with scotch.

∽∘∾

I knew from the second Guy was born that he was special—that he was a gift sent to soothe the cuts and bruises of my battered life. He was absolution for all my bad choices. I might have made a deal with the devil—married the devil, in fact—but I would have the last laugh. I saw it in Guy's nose, his forehead, and the way his gray-green eyes lit up when he looked at me, the way they were filled with curiosity and compassion and humor. I pressed my son to my chest, and as he latched on to my breast, I flipped Big Daddy the bird behind his back. Guy looked exactly like my dad.

IN LATE 1970 WE MOVED from Hollywood Hills to the Chevy Chase area of Glendale; from a small two-bedroom to a large four-bedroom home that I purchased with my inheritance money. Big Daddy still worked for the insurance company on Wilshire Boulevard. I was not allowed to go to his office. He told me his job was important, vital, and indispensable, but I never discovered what he did at the office. I never saw a paycheck. Each month I gave my monthly checks and any additional bonuses from my inheritance to Big Daddy. He paid the bills. We lived extravagantly: large house, large yard, two cars, a pool, a Jacuzzi, a condo in Palm Springs, vacations galore. To Big Daddy, image was everything. To keep the peace, I let our friends think our life of privilege was all because of Big Daddy, that he was the breadwinner—that he was the reason we lived so well.

He drank, he yelled, he demanded, he pounded his chest and strutted around the house, the proud cock. I watched the front door each evening, hoping he wouldn't walk through, hoping he would be killed in a car crash, struck by lightning, or gunned down in a random robbery at the liquor store where he bought his alcohol. And even as every rational, defensive part of me shrieked in protest, there was always that one niggling little voice that whispered: *Why don't I leave?*

I started each day with a clean slate: a burgeoning opportunity to muscle my life into the shape I wanted it to take. I woke the kids, fed them, clothed them, made their lunches, threw all the kids in the car, and drove the girls to school. Later I had a cup of coffee, played with the boys, cleaned the house, and picked up the girls. I helped with homework, bathed the kids, picked up their toys, started dinner, and raked the carpet. (Big Daddy did not want to see little footprints on the living room carpet.) When Big Daddy came home, he poured himself a scotch. I cleared the table and washed the dishes. Big Daddy poured more scotch. I tucked the kids safely into bed and collapsed into my own bed, exhausted.

I got up the next morning, dressed myself in denial, painted my face with a smile, and mascaraed my way to happiness. I joined thirteen community organizations, including: the PTA (Mother called it Pussy, Tits, and Ass), Junior League, tennis club, book club, volunteer for the Glendale Symphony, the LA Philharmonic, March of Dimes, and the Veteran's Hospital. I decorated my life with purpose, slapped on a fresh coat of staying busy being a mom (not a mother), and playing a wife.

We had good friends: Karen and Jim, John and Shirley, Barbara and Bud, Joyce and David, Joan and Don, Sandy and Dick. We had excellent parties, we played tennis, and we had a gourmet club that met monthly. My friend Karen made me a T-shirt—a cross-eyed turkey with the words "Perfect Sharon" printed at the top.

I had a fabulous, excellent life.

Except for when Big Daddy was around. Except for when he bullied the children and me. I was doing my best to keep the peace—to craft a perfect family and the perfect life. I had long since abandoned the idea that I could divorce Big Daddy—that leaving to save my children and myself was the best course of action. I swept that idea up with the dust bunnies and tossed it out like yesterday's garbage.

Even though it was the 1970s and the Women's Liberation movement was gaining momentum, I clung ferociously to the image of the "good wife" of the 1950s, the one whose job was to make sure the home was a place of peace, order, and tranquility—a place where my husband could renew himself in body and spirit. I had been raised to believe that successful women were dependent on their husbands, in need of a man's protection and acceptance. My value was limited to and determined by how well I carried out my man's every order, how well I agreed with him on everything. Of course, I carried the additional burden of my fierce determination to be nothing like Mother. That was the salve I applied to my wounds: no matter how bad it got, at least I was nothing like her. I was in control. I had it all together. I wasn't crazy.

∽∽

Julie was ten. Big Daddy had ordered her to mop the floor. Beforehand, he had placed a string in the corner under the cabinets, and she missed it. He ordered her to mop the floor again—and then again until she found the string. At dinnertime Big Daddy passed a plate of rolls around the table, first to his son Joe and then to the rest of us. When the plate reached Julie, Big Daddy jerked it away. "None for you! You are too fat!" He laughed, intoxicated with his own power. Then Julie snuck some chocolate ice cream. Big Daddy yelled at her, called her "fatty" and "piggy," and made disgusting snorting, snuffling noises through this nose. "You are so fat! No ice cream for you, Julie!"

Julie looked at Big Daddy, her eyes great big blue pools of feigned innocence, and said, "But I haven't been eating any ice cream."

Big Daddy huffed and told her to go look in the mirror. Julie shuffled over to look in the mirror hanging in the hallway; she saw her chin was streaked with chocolate. Her face fell. Her eyes soaked with tears. She was caught.

"Go to your room!" barked Big Daddy. "And don't come out for the rest of the day!"

My heart cracked and bled. In private, I told him he was a bastard. He called me a bitch in front of my children.

In the backyard, Big Daddy called out, "Come here, son!" Both boys tore across the yard to their dad's outstretched arms. Joe, age four, got there first. Big Daddy swept him into a great big hug. Guy, age two, piled into his leg a few seconds later. Big Daddy kicked him away. "Not you. I said 'son.'" Guy stared up at his father, eyes as round as saucers. His lower lip trembled. Then he ran to me and crawled into my lap. I held him tight. Big Daddy laughed an evil, derisive laugh. "What a sissy." Then he tumbled to the ground with Joe and pinned him on his back with tickles.

When you want something badly enough, you thread lies through a loom of denial: *It will get better. It's not as bad as you think. The kids are just fine.*

∾∘∾

During these years, there were encounters with Mother. They varied in their intensity, their insanity. I sent for her, arranged her flights—not because I had forgotten her callousness surrounding Dad's death but because I needed her with me. She was a buffer between Big Daddy and me. When Mother visited, Big Daddy was not as nasty, and I felt safer. Mother, the kids, and I would tromp through the hills behind our house, laughing and singing at the top of our lungs to a good marching song. Usually we sang "The Battle Hymn of the Republic," written by Julia Ward Howe.

I clung to the hope that Mother and I would be able to cobble together some sort of mother-daughter relationship in which she would be a soft place for me to fall, in which I could talk my life to pieces with her and draw her affection—her approval—around me like a blanket. Unfortunately, despite my most fervent wishing, it didn't happen.

Mother was tight-lipped around Big Daddy. But she told me she thought I lost my mind—divorcing professional, squeaky-clean Ronald after having two daughters and then getting pregnant by the bully next-door neighbor, marrying him, and having one baby and then another. Before I was thirty years old and within seven years, I had four children and two husbands. She thought I might have set some kind of record.

⌖

The earthquake hit at six o'clock in the morning on February 9, 1971, in the San Fernando Valley near Sylmar with a magnitude of 6.6. There were four strong aftershocks with a magnitude of 5. The earthquake killed sixty-five people and caused more than a half-billion dollars in damage, including hospitals, schools, freeway interchanges, homes, landslides, and the lower Van Norman Dam. We lived about seventeen miles from the epicenter of the earthquake. Luckily, we had minimal damage: only one kitchen window was broken and glasses and dishes slid from their cabinets, crashing to the floor. We did escape physical harm. The boys quickly ran to our bedroom for shelter. I found Mother sitting on the shag carpet in the girls' bedroom, bathed in a pool of yellowed lamplight, cuddling them, comforting them, and whispering that everything would be fine. She smoothed their hair back, kissed them delicately on the cheek, and pulled them tightly to her. For as long as I could remember, Mother was distant, cold, and unavailable to me, but I stood there watching her comfort my daughters.

She looked up at me and sighed. "Why on earth do you want to live here? Nothing like this *ever* happens in Hawaii!"

I nodded my head.

"I'd much rather be living in a shack on the beach in Hawaii than in this expensive, overdone house in faulty California!"

She turned from me, gathering my daughters closer.

Faulty California. Indeed.

⌖

Big Daddy, the four kids, and I returned from a tense family vacation in Arizona in the summer of 1976. I was exhausted, worn thin by the needs and demands of four kids and an infantile husband. We collapsed into the house. The phone rang. It was Uncle Louie.

"Sharon, your mother was arrested at Marina del Rey where the *Sharolyn* is moored. "

THE *SHAROLYN* WAS A SIXTY-FOOT schooner, my father's biggest toy. I remembered him floating a model of it in the bathtub in our house on Kalanianaole when I was a teenager. He laughed out loud when the Sharolyn was launched in 1959 because he had figured the draft to the inch; he had known exactly the distance from the waterline to the bottom of the keel. He was a man who enjoyed precision the way alcoholics enjoy that first, deep swallow of scotch.

The name *Sharolyn* was an amalgam of Mother's (Carolyn) and my names—Dad's two favorite women bound together on the stern of a ship. When I was eighteen, he commissioned a life-size polished mahogany wood carving of me as the figurehead. The face was mine; the nude body was mine. I liked to think this was because he counted on me to lead him through rough waters and stormy seas.

When Dad died, a scant eight years after the Sharolyn was completed, his estate sold her. A few years later, Uncle Louie and Aunt Mackie purchased her, bringing her back into the family where she belonged. She was now moored in Marina del Rey, south of Los Angeles.

∽o∾

Sunday

I pressed the phone to my ear, sinking slowly into the news, knowing Mother was manic again and in California.

"What do you mean she was arrested?"

"She was trespassing on the *Sharolyn*. She trashed it, Sharon. Threw our belongings overboard into the marina."

I took a deep breath and released it. I was not equipped to deal with this. I had ten loads of laundry, four hungry kids, and a husband who needed to get drunk.

Big Daddy, in his infinite impatience, yelled at me, "Who is it, Sharon? I'm hungry, dammit! Where's my lunch?"

The kids tore circles around me as I cradled the phone between my ear and my shoulder.

"It's Uncle Louie. Mother is in town and may need our help."

Big Daddy pointed his finger in my face. "*You* are *not* getting involved. You already have a family to take care of! Me! I don't want her in this house! End of story!" He opened the pantry door to grab his scotch. He went to the cupboard for a crystal glass and then to the refrigerator to drop ice cubes into a glass—one, two, three, four. The scotch flowed, three fingers. He sipped, sighed, and then became silent.

I rolled my eyes.

"Some of those items are irreplaceable, Sharon. There's more. You might want to sit down."

My head started to spin. I slid onto the kitchen stool.

"She also went on other boats in the marina and threw the owners' belongings overboard. Then she threw dockworkers' cables into the marina. She was arrested. Fortunately, no one's pressing any charges. That's not the worst of it, though."

There's more? I pinched the bridge of my nose between my thumb and forefinger. My mind limped around in a circle, flopped down, tried to get comfortable.

"There was a second arrest. And for this one, they're pressing charges because your mother"—note that he said, "your mother," not "my sister"—"was naked [shocking], and she undressed a small boy. She played with him on the dock with a hose in an obscene manner. She said she was trying to reach all his holes with water to make sure he was clean."

Any energy I had left hissed out of me like a deflated balloon. I was wiped clean—emptied out.

"What are we going to do, Sharon?"

I had no idea what *we* were going to do. I knew Mother had manic episodes in the fourteen years since her hospitalization at Westwood. David became her policeman during those years. He managed her person and estate with relative ease, I thought. He flew to Hawaii to help Mother when she was committed or jailed. He did all her accounting and paid her bills. I knew that had been a source of great annoyance for Barbara, who incessantly reminded David that he had a family to tend in California, and why couldn't someone else handle Mother's affairs? And I thought she had a point. For whatever reason, it didn't occur to me to tell Uncle Louie to handle it himself. It was his schooner, after all, and his sister.

But I knew it might be my turn now. After all, my life was already insane. What was one more thing?

"I don't know what we're going to do, Uncle Louie. But don't worry about it. I'll take care of it."

It happened that fast.

In the blink of an eye.

I dove headlong back into Mother's chaos.

❦

Other facts were as follows: When the police arrived to arrest Mother, she was naked, she resisted, and she danced around on the dock. They threw a blanket over her and locked her in the backseat of the patrol car. While on the freeway during rush hour, Mother threw the blanket off and pressed her breasts and somehow her perfectly manicured bush to the window. She nearly caused a traffic accident. More than once. There was a wire screen separating her from the officers in the front seat. They couldn't reach her. She laughed, taunted, and teased. She pressed her nipples through the screen—for the entire twenty-five miles it took to get to Norwalk Metropolitan Hospital.

❦

Monday

I called David. We decided to move her to Westwood Hospital, and when she felt better ("well" had been abandoned as a viable outcome; the goal was simply "better," "functional"), she would return home to Hawaii. Now I had to get Mother to agree.

I called Mother at Norwalk. I asked her whether she wanted to go home to Hawaii or back to Westwood Hospital. I wasn't really offering her a choice; I just knew it would be easier if she felt like she had made the decision.

"Fuck you, you little shithead!" she snapped. "I'm tired of people bugging me. Especially you! I'm having fun here at Norwalk. I'm helping people straighten out their problems. When I get out of here, I'm going back to the *Sharolyn*."

"You can't, Mother. Uncle Louie doesn't want you aboard the *Sharolyn*. It's his boat now."

"Fine. Then I'll go to their house."

"Uncle Louie doesn't want you there either."

"Then I'll come to your house."

"You can't. Big Daddy won't allow it."

"Then I'll go to David's house."

"You can't go there either, Mother."

There was a pause.

The phone went dead.

I wondered how long I had until the next storm. I dumped a load of laundry in the washing machine and made lunch. I dusted, vacuumed, scrubbed toilets, and filled the crystal candy dish in the living room with Andes mints because the green wrapping matched the color of the living room carpet.

Two hours passed.

The phone rang.

Mother sobbed. "Sharon, I want to go home." It was a ploy, a trick, a deception. The tears weren't real but merely useful—a cleverly wielded tool of manipulation. I wasn't impressed. I stuck to the plan.

"How about going to Westwood Hospital first for a little rest? Then you can go home."

The wound in her voice healed immediately.

"Oh, yes, please, dear. Yes. I would like that very much. Please transfer me right away."

I called Westwood Hospital and asked for Dr. Hellinger, who had been Mother's doctor fourteen years earlier. He was on vacation. I talked to Dr. Rendinell. I asked him to open a bed for Mother for the next morning. I called the ambulance service to arrange a 9:00 a.m. pickup at Norwalk Metropolitan Hospital. I called Norwalk to inform them of the transfer. I called Westwood to let them know Mother would be arriving at 10:00 a.m.

I hung up the phone.

I collapsed in a heap, relieved.

In the evening, I plopped the kids in the bathtub, one after another, picked up toys, cooked dinner, washed dishes, dried dishes, and put dishes away. Big Daddy hid upstairs in his study, drowning himself in scotch. At least he was out of the way.

I drove to Sunland to get Mother's things from Uncle Louie's house—things she left aboard the *Sharolyn*. There were three cardboard boxes of food and two suitcases containing a robe, a nightgown, one long muumuu, one short muumuu, a sweater, and a shawl. No panties, no bra, no shoes. There were cosmetics and a backgammon set. There was a plane ticket to Hawaii and some checks—no jewelry.

"Where is her jewelry?" I asked Uncle Louie.

"I'm keeping it until she pays for all the damages to the *Sharolyn* and the loss of our belongings that she threw overboard."

He handed me a list and a bill for thirteen hundred dollars in damages and lost property. I thanked him and folded the list and bill in my purse. I raced home, tucked the kids into bed, and cleaned the kitchen.

Big Daddy was sitting in the den nursing his umpteenth scotch.

"You are to have nothing to do with that woman," he slurred. "I forbid it!

I ignored him and crawled upstairs; I fell into bed, into a dark and restless sleep.

I had been home from vacation for less than thirty-six hours.

~~~

Tuesday

I swam up from the depths of sleep, not wanting to get up, some fragment of memory tugging me toward the surface. *Mother is being transferred today.* The thought jolted me awake. I peeled myself out of bed, got dressed, fed the kids, dressed the kids, made the beds, cleaned the house, cleaned the dishes, picked up toys, and raked the carpet; everything was perfectly in its perfect place. I didn't want any complaints from Big Daddy. I didn't want to give him any excuse to call me a bitch. No matter what, the house had to be in perfect order. I arranged with my friends to take care of my kids. I drove my yellow, wood-paneled deluxe station wagon with the license plate that read "Mrs. K" to Westwood, a forty-five-minute drive through Los Angeles.

The ambulance finally arrived two hours late. When I saw Mother, my heart stopped. I almost didn't recognize her at fifty-eight years old. She had gained about fifty pounds since I had seen her last, and her coffee-colored hair had turned a salty gray. A twinge of sadness twisted inside me. She was always so proud of her lithe figure, her perfect proportions, and her beauty. I was always so proud of her beauty.

She was manic, with a white sheet draped around her neck like a sarong, adorned in expensive rings, bracelets, and necklaces. She was queen of the Islands! She waved and blew kisses. She bent her wrist to me—an invitation to kiss her ring. I wondered, absently, how she was able to hang on to her jewelry.

I asked Mother for her jewelry, told her I would keep it safe for her. One ring was stuck on her swollen finger. The doctor soaped her finger to remove the ring. She batted her eyes at him. I tucked Mother's jewelry in my purse. I told the doctor lithium made Mother vomit. I handed him a bag full of Mother's clothes and toiletries.

I told Mother I was leaving.

"Fuck off!" she yelled.

~∞~

Wednesday

Next day was same routine. I straightened the house, arranged care for the kids, and dashed to the hospital. Mother bounced on her bed. She told me nothing was wrong with her—that the rest of the world was fucked. She galloped around the room. She had super powers. She could fly. She could see into people's minds. She could see the truth they were hiding from themselves and the world. She claimed to be "Dona Ana," the eternal female life force from George Bernard Shaw's *Man and Superman*. She could bend men to her will. She wanted to fuck the orderly.

I met with Dr. Rendinell. He told me he could only hold her for seventy-two hours and that he would release her on Friday. Dr. Rendinell's words landed hard and heavy, knocking the breath from me. This meant Mother would be released in less than two days. The room spun; I was suddenly dizzy, shaken, terrified. She was manic, delusional, a danger to herself and others, a time bomb waiting to explode.

I left Westwood with a foreboding heart. I sat in Los Angeles freeway traffic for hours. Then I gathered the kids from my friends and slumped through the front door. There were phone calls to make. There were bills to be paid: to ambulance companies, to Mother's friends for exorbitant phone bills, stolen items, missing items, a $500 purchase of yards and yards of material for sarongs.

~∞~

Thursday
I called Dr. Rendinell to plead for a commitment. He was sorry, but he didn't commit patients. I called LA County Hospital to inquire about commitment proceedings and was told that Mother could be held for fourteen days with only the doctor's signature. Dr. Rendinell refused.

"Seek conservatorship," he said.

I made an appointment for the next morning at 9:00 a.m. with an attorney to begin conservatorship. I called the sheriff for arrest reports needed for conservatorship. Denied. I called the hospital for her medical records needed for conservatorship. Denied. "We only release records to current doctors or conservators," they said. Fine. Great. Got it.

Friday
I met with an attorney. Yes, conservatorship was the best way to go. Wonderful. Not so fast. There was glitch—it would take thirty days. Thirty days? I couldn't wait thirty days. It was too long. She needed help now! Try again. Better news: I could get immediate conservatorship in one day.

Dr. Rendinell called. He'd changed his mind. He issued a fourteen-day hold on Mother—a miracle. Mother was secure, safe at Westwood—for now.

Later that night, I got a phone call: "Get me the fuck out of here! I don't want a fourteen-day hold! Fix it, Sharon!"

And then again, an hour later: "I can't do this anymore, Sharon. I can't take this medication. It's killing me. Call the doctor. Tell him I don't want to take it anymore. Please, Sharon. You fix this."

Saturday
Early in the morning, I got another call. "Come get me, Sharon. I want to go home. I'll be good. I promise. I just want to go home."

I bought her a plane ticket home, hustled the kids in car, tore down the freeway, picked Mother up at the hospital, paid the hospital bill while Mother signed herself out AMA (against medical advice), and dashed to Los Angeles International Airport.

"I want to fly first class, Sharon," Mother announced as we walked toward her gate, my children skipping after us.

"I only bought you a regular-fare ticket, Mother."

"That's unsatisfactory!" she snapped. "You just have to learn how to get what you want in life, Sharon. I can get anything I want. Just watch me."

My stomach tightened. I just wanted her to get on the plane and go home. I wanted to go back to my regular life, which, after this past week, looked pretty damn good. Mother behaved at the ticket gate. She behaved during the boarding process. On the other hand, I was two heartbeats away from an aneurysm. The anticipation of what she might (or might not) do overwhelmed me. The fact that she could control herself enough to get what she wanted pissed me off.

I asked if I could board with her, explaining that she had been recently released from the hospital. (I failed to mention that it was a mental hospital.) Mother marched onto the airplane. I ambled after her and swallowed the fear that had taken residence in my gut. Suddenly, Mother tripped and fell to the ground. A flight attendant rushed to her side and helped Mother to her feet. Mother limped, yelled, and complained that she would sue the airline.

Lawsuit was Mother's third-favorite word.

The flustered flight attendant asked what she could do to make it better. I was suddenly seized by the impulse to clap in appreciation of Mother's performance. *Give this woman an Oscar!* I crossed my arms over my chest instead. Mother winked at me and then looked at the flight attendant, her face pinched in mock pain.

"Oh, dear," said Mother to the flummoxed flight attendant. "Perhaps a seat in first class? Where I can stretch out my leg? Yes, I think that would help."

Mother slipped her arm inside the flight attendant's elbow, flashed me her cat-that-ate-the-canary grin, and limped toward first class like a wounded animal.

I found my four children pressed against the waiting area window watching planes land and take off. I waited for Mother's plane to leave. I wanted to watch her go. While I waited, I ran down the list of menial tasks that must be accomplished when I got home, mentally touching each of them, as if to remind myself that my life, while uneasy at times, had solidity, weight, and a sort of constancy to it that I found comforting. Big Daddy, while admittedly an asshole, was just plain mean, not crazy. I'd rather deal with mean.

As Mother's plane pulled into the sky, relief washed through me, and tension drained from me in great big bucketfuls. The chaos was over, for now. Still, I knew it would happen again—that she would come unannounced, a tempest of madness, uprooting, destroying, ravaging, caring nothing for the devastation she left behind.

I THREW MYSELF BACK INTO my life of reckless compliance. I believed in cause and effect and embraced it with renewed fervor. If I kept the house clean, organized, and perfect, then my life would be clean, organized, and perfect. I knew I could do this like I had when I was little. Mother had said, "A clean and orderly house is a clean and orderly life."

I pressed on.

I was the original soccer mom, driving my kids around town to soccer games, Pop Warner Football, T-ball and little league, piano lessons, and school carnivals. I volunteered for the Republican State Central Committee, Republican conventions, worked with assemblymen and senators, and attended political parties with the Reagans. A big hitter for the Republican Party liked me. He cornered me at a party and told me I reminded him of a beautiful bird in a gilded cage—that he couldn't understand why I had married a dullard. He said that he would want me for a wife, but he was already married. I blushed and I laughed delicately. I stared at Big Daddy standing in the corner, nursing a scotch—ignorant, unsophisticated, a bore. He embarrassed me. We did look ridiculous together.

Still, I pressed on.

I started working out at a women-only gym. Big Daddy allowed it, although he was not happy about it and insisted on screening everything I wore. He found leotards obscene and forbid me to wear them. I settled for shorts, an over-sized T-shirt, leg warmers, Reeboks, and a terrycloth headband. I went three times a week. I started to feel good—really good. Stronger. The fuzziness in my head dissipated. I felt less and less like I was sleepwalking underwater. The parts of me that had withered and atrophied over the years being married to Big Daddy started to develop, take on shape and size and strength.

I read Wayne Dyer's *Your Erroneous Zones*. His chapters on guilt and worry empowered me. I learned they were useless emotions. I highlighted, underlined, and annotated in the margins. I drank in his words with the fervor of one who'd been lost in the desert for years. I feasted on the ambrosia of New Age thinking that told me I was powerful and I had choices, even as a woman.

Big Daddy was furious. He tore the book apart and threw the pieces in my face.

"Don't ever think you are leaving me!" he snarled. "This book is shit! I will kill you first!"

I lifted my eyes, prepared an argument, and then changed my mind and walked away to wait for the knot in my stomach to unclench.

◦⚬◦

Big Daddy invited his two brothers, Fred and Eric, over for dinner. The three of them together were like a keg of dynamite, the competition between them a lit fuse. Big Daddy wanted to show off: his house, his obedient wife and children, and his elaborate lifestyle. I wasn't in the mood to argue. *You can't reason with the unreasonable.* Dad's words echoed in my head. And Big Daddy was one unreasonable son of a bitch. I spent all day in the kitchen. I cooked roasted squab with homemade raspberry sauce, roasted potatoes, homemade rolls, and homemade chocolate cream pie. (I learned from Mother how to prepare a beautiful dinner.) I set the table with fresh flowers, linen, sterling silver, Waterford crystal, and our best china (wedding gifts from when I married Ronald; these Big Daddy had chosen not to destroy). I fed the kids, bathed them, and got them out of the way. I dressed in my favorite party dress. I was on stage, expected to perform in this circus.

Dinner unfolded without incident, without compliment. I was gracious and kind. "Let me refill your wine glass. May I get you anything else?"

Big Daddy ignored me. I spent most of my time in the kitchen, as dutiful, quiet, and invisible as all good wives should be. I looked at the clock every fifteen minutes and wondered why time insisted on passing at such a glacial pace.

After dinner, with the four of us sitting around the dining room table, the conversation turned to the origin of their last name.

"Is it German or Austrian?" Fred asked.

"Must be Austrian," said Eric. "From the Hapsburgs, royalty."

"And does it have an s at the end or not?" Big Daddy asked.

A semi-friendly debate began whether or not there was an s on the end of their name—as if this was of monumental importance. Big Daddy slammed back another scotch. The three of them circled round and round this question of the existence of an s and lobbed it back and forth across the table. Their fingers formed steeples beneath their chins, and they stared at the question with intense consideration.

I was bored with the wannabe-Hapsburgs, tired of this whole charade. This had to be the dumbest conversation anyone had ever started. A hot irritation burped within me. I stood to clear the table. Big Daddy pinned my wrist to the tabletop, narrowed his eyes as a warning. He had not asked me to clear the table yet. I was being rude by getting up in the middle of their very serious discussion.

I sat down, rubbing the sting out of my wrist. Irritation rose like red-hot magma, burning the inside of my throat, my mouth; I swallowed it down so hard it hurt.

And then Fred said: "So, what the hell does the s stand for?"

Holy fucking shit.

It happened so fast that I wasn't even totally aware of what I was doing. It was like an out-of-body experience. One minute I was sitting at the table, and the next I had thrown my chair back and leaped up from the table.

"Shitheads! S stands for shitheads! You are all a bunch of fucking shitheads!"

Silence.

A beat.

I picked up my plate, pushed in my chair, and sauntered off to the kitchen; my words hung in the air like great billows of black smoke. I rinsed my plate in the sink. The rush of water and the clinking of china were the only sounds punctuating the silence. Smug satisfaction danced on my lips.

❧

And then I learned Big Daddy was having an affair. He was screwing some bimbo at work. We had invited friends over for his birthday. I answered the door for our party guests, and there she was. I had never met her or seen a picture of her, but I instantly knew. I told her she was not welcome in my home, in my doorway, on my front walk. I slammed the door in her face. I confronted Big Daddy. He mumbled and looked down at his shoes. He cleared his throat. He picked at a thread on his shirt. Even though my ego was bruised *(How dare he cheat on me! I am perfect!),* giddiness began to bubble up inside me. Understanding crept in like a Polaroid coming into focus: Big Daddy had just given me a way out.

Why did it take an affair to end our marriage? Why weren't the years of Big Daddy's tyranny enough? It wasn't that easy. For starters, it was my second marriage. It was easy to blame the failure of my first marriage on Ronald—the drinking and the temper tantrums. But how would I explain a second divorce? How would I explain failing twice?

There came a point where I started to think that perhaps I was the problem. After all, I was the common denominator. So I tried harder to make it work. I turned myself inside out trying to prove that I was, in fact, not the problem but rather I was the solution, because to face the possibility that there was something irrevocably wrong with me was unthinkable. Added to that were a million other excuses: my kids needed a father; no one in the neighborhood was getting divorced; I didn't want to disappoint my family—"Sharon screwed up again"; and bottom line, to the outside world, we looked like the perfect American family. Who was I to shatter that illusion?

More to the point, though, there was comfort in the known, the familiar—the devil I knew versus the devil I didn't. I fell into a rhythm, predicting the cycles, finding a sick sort of validation in it all because certainly if I wasn't there to pick up the pieces, then it all got shot to hell. I was necessary and needed and had it under control. Only I wasn't and I didn't and the only person I was really fooling was me. Then the bimbo showed up on my doorstep one night and the façade cracked and splintered. I was left holding the shards of my broken life, turning them over and over in my hands and wondering if I could have made it work if only I'd been just a little more perfect.

❧

Big Daddy had repeatedly threatened to kill me if I ever left him. I had every reason to believe he was telling the truth, so I secretly found an attorney who recommended a psychiatrist who specialized in bullies.

It was August of 1977, nine years after I tottered down the aisle, my belly plump and rounded with my third child. Nine years. Nine years of tucking and folding myself into the shape I believed I was supposed to hold as a good wife and mother. Nine years of trying to carve out that white picket fence that was supposed to keep me safe.

I sat in the psychiatrist's office, surrounded by books and potted plants that were in various stages of dying. It struck me as appropriate given the circumstances. The summer sun angled through the office window, across the brown leather couch on which I sat, and it warmed my knees. Some sort of music designed to soothe the emotionally afflicted played in the background. Copies of *Newsweek* and *Time* littered the top of the coffee table. I wondered, momentarily who would be interested in reading about world events in a psychiatrist's office. Did it help to compare the sad state of one's life to the sad state of the world? Absolutely. On more than one occasion over the past decade, I had reframed my marriage by reading many books about the wives of King Henry VIII: two were beheaded, two abandoned, one died shortly after childbirth, and only one outlived the king. When I looked at it through that lens, I figured I didn't have it so bad. My huge, newly decorated house on the hill was not the Tower of London.

Dr. Stone was warm-eyed and soft and patient. His voice felt like a soft, cotton blanket wrapping around me. Dr. Stone listened and took notes. Then he told me to make a list. He called it the Ben Franklin test, which basically involved me drawing a line down the middle of the page and listing all the reasons to stay on one side and all the reasons to leave on the other. I told him I had done that already and handed him my list. I had two reasons to stay: he was the father to my two boys and we had good sex. (The sex was still amazing because it had a *fuck you, you're going to miss me when I'm gone* quality for me.)

Dr. Stone said, "You don't know what good sex is, Sharon. You can't know what good sex is until you've had it with someone you love."

Love. I had no idea what he meant. I chose a husband to choose a life.

Dr. Stone and I agreed that my two reasons for staying were not strong enough to remain in a tyrannical relationship. We agreed that I had already made my decision and that I would be happier eating McDonald's and staying in a little apartment with my kids than eating roasted squab and living in a grand two-story house in the hills of Glendale.

"It's time, Sharon," he said as he leaned forward over his desk.

Dr. Stone instructed me not to confront Big Daddy.

"I know how to deal with bullies, Sharon, and that's what your husband is. A bully. You just get him to my office next week. I'll take care of the rest."

I stood and shook Dr. Stone's hand. His handshake was firm and strong. Relief spilled into me like water filling a glass.

∾◦∾

Big Daddy and I sat across from Dr. Stone in stiff-backed wooden chairs. I had told Big Daddy that the purpose of our meeting was to fix our crumbling marriage; he was hell-bent on playing the part of the cooperative husband. He sat, shoulders slumped, feet crossed at the ankles, hands folded in his lap, a posture of penitence.

Such bullshit.

Stone wasn't falling for it.

Dr. Stone said without preamble, "Sharon is getting a divorce."

Divorce. The word filled the room, pressed into the corners.

Big Daddy glared at me through narrowed eyes. He shook his head and puffed out his chest. "She can't. I won't let her." The pitch in his voice was wrong. It was too high—like he was trying too hard. Like he already knew he couldn't win.

Stone leaned back. His face showed no emotion. He was in total control. I was in awe. "I have news for you. It takes two people to make a marriage work and one to break it up. Sharon is breaking it up. She is divorcing you."

Dr. Stone's words were cool and smooth and round like river rocks. Dr. Stone quickly swiveled toward a large calendar mounted on one of the office walls and pointed. "Let's set a date for you to leave. Two weeks ought to be enough time. How about August twenty-third?"

Stone pinned Big Daddy with his stare.

I swallowed a smile.

Silence hung like a fog, thick and heavy. And then, ever so slowly, Big Daddy deflated like a punctured balloon. He wrapped his hand across his eyes. He drew in a long breath as though through a straw. He nodded his head. Submission.

I was stunned, dizzy with disbelief. I suppressed an urge to leap over the desk and wrap myself around Dr. Stone.

Big Daddy and I walked to the parking lot when it happened. It wasn't intentional. It poured from my being: "I can't be responsible for your happiness. I cannot live with you anymore."

The words felt fragile, like a newly hatched bird that had fallen from its nest. I'm not sure why I said them. I knew the words were pointless and redundant at this stage of the game, but somehow, as the words hung between us in the parking lot adjacent to Dr. Stone's office, I felt as though some part of me had just taken flight.

Big Daddy snickered. "You're the lucky one. I have me twenty-four hours a day. What are you complaining about?"

Huh. Just like I thought. He really was one miserable son-of-a-bitch.

❧

Two weeks later, Big Daddy left like a whipped puppy with his tail between his legs, and I wondered why I had been so afraid of him for so long. Freedom broke over me like a rainstorm, and I danced giddy and gleeful in the puddles. I cut my hair in a pixie, I told jokes, I spent my own money, and I smeared dirt around my kitchen floor and slid through it bare-footed. The kids and I bought a cat, a snake, a hamster, and a frog. We baked cookies, we made messes, we left toys lying around the house, we jumped on the couch, and we left the living room carpet un-raked, littered with candy wrappers. I bought high-heeled shoes, leotards, and bras that showed off my nipples.

MY HOUSE BECAME GRAND CENTRAL Station for T-ball coaches, team players, neighborhood kids, neighborhood meetings, and neighborhood dinners. I cooked and cleaned, but not as frantically as before. I found some comfort in the mess.

I dated one of the T-ball coaches who was recently divorced and lived down the street. BJ. Bobby Joe. Blow Job. He told me I was the best little cocksucker in Glendale. I wondered, *Why just Glendale?*

BJ was tall and slim, lewd and crude; he loved whiskey, women, gambling, and horses. He pissed wherever he felt like it; he ignored messes. He was bold, fearless, and brash.

I was in love.

We went to bars. He kept $30,000 cash in the glove compartment of an old rusted-out beater that didn't lock. I worried.

"Darlin'," he said in his easy Kentucky drawl. "Don't worry. No one will look in a beat-up car for anything. Let's go have some drinks." He slipped his arm around my waist and guided me easily into the bar, past the people spilling out into the streets, as though he was the king and I was his queen.

Before a race at Hollywood Park, BJ bought a horse, a claimer, for ten thousand dollars. (Claimers were horses that anyone could purchase before a race for the right price.) We climbed into the stands. "They're off!" The horses galloped around the track, hooves pummeled the brown earth, heaving, snorting, and sweating. BJ's horse was last by a lot. He smacked the glossy program across his thigh and said, "Fuck!" And then the horse dropped dead right in the middle of the racetrack. BJ laughed. "Well shit!" The track sent him a bill for removing the horse from the track and for disposing of the body. BJ wrote "fuck you" on the bill and sent it back.

I was happy with BJ. With him I felt like I could be myself. I felt free, released from the shackles of marriage and husbands and responsibilities. I was released from being good and proper and perfect. In his eyes, I was great just the way I was, whatever way that might be. He had no expectations, no requirements. He loved me for me.

BJ would bet $20,000 on football in a weekend. He lost. He laughed. In Las Vegas he folded thousands of dollars inside my panties. He told me to take off my bra because he liked to brush his hand up against my breasts while he was betting at the tables. I felt exposed. Naked. Alive. We walked through the slot machines, past the Pai Gow tables, past the Roulette wheel, past the poker tables. I rode the smooth flow of his leisurely Southern gait, his easy, steady style. He settled at one of the tables. He dropped five hundred, then a thousand, and then fifteen hundred. He never flinched. When he winked at me, I went to the bathroom, pulled out a wad of warm cash from my panties, came back, and handed it to him. BJ pulled me to him and kissed me with such force I couldn't feel my knees. He dropped another five hundred.

In our hotel room, I stripped naked and danced for him to the music of the Bee Gees: "More Than a Woman." BJ was delighted, mesmerized. He sat, transfixed, his erection straining against his pants. I spun and twirled and spun and twirled until I felt like I could fly. We fucked each other's brains out. And in the middle of my third orgasm, I thought, *Guess what, Dad? I'm finally having fun.*

My life had a new rhythm. It sparked and crackled like fireworks. Colors seemed brighter, sounds were richer; the world was suddenly crisp and clear. It had edges that were sharper and more defined. Even the air tasted sweeter somehow. Divorcing Big Daddy and being with BJ felt as though someone had pulled back the dark, heavy drapes of conformity and let the sunshine stream in. Shadows were illuminated, and dust motes danced like faeries.

On a Sunday afternoon in August of 1978, the phone rang.

"This is the attorney general's office in Hawaii. I'm calling to inform you that your mother has been arrested and committed to Queen's Hospital. She claims she is the queen of Hawaii and her boyfriend is the king."

Boyfriend? I pressed my lips together. *Not now, Mother. Please not now. I am fighting for custody of Joe and Guy.* Since he had moved out six months earlier, Big Daddy had been stalking me, following me home from the store, turning up in my kitchen, and following me on dates with BJ. He had followed us for a hundred miles down the coast to Del Mar. He followed us for another hundred miles to Rancho Mirage in the desert. In the driveway, Big Daddy twisted my arm and threw me down.

"You will *never* see *my* sons again," he hissed.

I couldn't move. But that was okay. I thought Big Daddy would leave if I didn't move. And he did. A neighbor found me lying on the driveway and took me to the hospital for X-rays. I had a badly bruised tailbone.

⌐∞⌐

"The two of them have been traveling all over the islands, writing bad checks, stealing, acting obscene," the attorney from the attorney general's office said.

He cleared his throat.

I knew there was more. There was always more. Nothing was ever simple when Mother was on a manic trip.

"Go on," I said, my voice hoarse.

"Well, a woman is claiming to be her daughter, and she's taking your mother's blank checks to the hospital for her signature. We don't know who this woman is."

"Uh-huh, go on."

"We have arrested 'the king'. He is in jail. His name is Rudy. He is thirty-eight years old."

Mother was now sixty years old and dating someone my age.

"I think you need to come immediately to protect your mother's belongings."

I nodded into the phone and set it back down on the receiver.

BJ crinkled his forehead. "You all right, darlin'?"

I shook my head.

⌐∞⌐

When I landed in Honolulu, Francois, my childhood friend, picked me up and whisked me off to a local eatery so we could talk, so I could get my bearings. Leroy, another childhood friend, joined us and brought with him Bob, his partner from the Honolulu Police Department. After introductions, I told them about Mother, my voice now warped with exhaustion. Impossibly, Bob knew Mother.

"The crazy naked lady is your mom?"

I sighed. Having a mentally ill parent imbued me with a sort of specialness; no one else I knew had a parent like me. It gave me a little extra something to throw on the table: *Here, top that!*

Bob laughed. "One day, when I was flying the helicopter, dispatch said, 'There is a naked lady on Kalanianaole Highway with a salad bowl over her head.' And then, 'Oh, never mind. It's just Mrs. Hicks again.'"

Francois smiled and looked at me, his eyes softening. He knew. He was there at the anniversary party. And during that same year, when Francois was eleven, Dr. Paskowitz's wife had seduced him. It happened when Francois collected money for his paper route; Mrs. Paskowitz opened the front door in her negligee.

I patted Bob on the arm. "Yes. That's my mother."

Bob offered me a place to stay. He lived on the beach in Hale'iwa, a small surfing town on the North Shore, miles outside of Honolulu. I considered it. Hotels were expensive, and Mother's house was unlivable according to the police, although I didn't know why yet. I told Bob thank you, that I'd like to take him up on his offer. We finished our meal and headed outside into the warm Hawaiian sun. I straddled Bob's motorcycle, the engine vibrating beneath me. I wrapped my arms around his waist, buried my head into the back of his jacket, and hung on as Bob peeled out of the parking lot.

◦⟋⟍◦

At first she didn't recognize me. "Who are you?" she said. "My daughter? Sharon?" Her arms were red from scratching. The medication made her itch. "How did I get here?" she asked, and then, "Why are you here?" The confusion was real. Madness, medications, and electroshock treatment had temporarily fractured Mother's memory. The doctors affirmed that her loss of memory was temporary. Her memory would come back in time; they were just not sure when or how much memory she would regain.

"I have a new love." Mother's voice carried no life, every syllable a chore. "His name is Rudy. You just missed him."

She hiked up her hospital gown, sans underwear. She aired herself. She sighed.

"Rudy's in jail," I said.

Mother shook her head. "No, no, he was just here." She waved her hand around the room. She wrapped her arms around her waist. "Wasn't he?" she inquired of her knees.

"Mother, there is a woman who visits you. She says she is your daughter. She's asking you to sign your blank checks. Who is she?"

Mother's face contorted in confusion.

"What? Oh ... hmmm ..." She tapped the side of her head with her finger, as if the answer was stuck. "I don't know," she said. She stood, stared vacantly out the window for a moment, and then smoothed down the front of her hospital gown. "Nice to see you," she said, and then she shuffled from the room.

✎

There were maggots everywhere: in the toilets, on the kitchen counters, in the stove, on the stove, swimming around in a pan of creamed corn. Dirty dishes, pots, and pans were scattered throughout the house. Doors, floors, screens, and windows were covered with blood and human shit. Dirty diapers were balled up in corners, under couch pillows, and on top of the television set. The mattresses reeked of urine. Apparently several families—relatives and friends of Rudy's—had been living here. At least that's what it looked like. That's what I told myself. Mother would never live like this, especially not when she was manic. In her mania, she cleaned obsessively. The doctors said it was how she cleared the clutter in her mind.

I covered my mouth and nose with the front of my shirt as I surveyed the wreckage of my childhood home: broken windows, broken screens, and broken slats on the floor of the lanai (patio). Each room was filled with huge green trash bags bursting with Mother's belongings. Whatever wasn't in bags was sorted into piles: clothes, jewelry, art, and shoes. Mother's car, locked in the carport, was filled to the roof with silver, paintings, radios, and clothes. I didn't know if Mother was the one who had bagged everything or if Rudy was committing a robbery. My guess was the latter.

Without warning, memories rushed in: Dad and sunsets and blankets of stars. Boyfriends and Christmases and parties and music and friends. The smell of freshly baked bread and pies and cookies. Mother in the kitchen, beautiful, stunning, an apron knotted around her waist, hands punching dough. She was the life of the party, glamorous and vibrant, the satellite around which we all orbited. As I stood in the midst of my broken-down life and her broken-down house, I was seized by bone-crushing grief. *What happened to her? Where has she gone? Is she lost inside her mind, trapped behind a wall of madness, unable to be saved?* I clamped my hand over my mouth to stifle a cry and darted out the back door.

∾

"There's nothing to worry about. Everything's safe."

Bob was with me at the police station. He reassured me, along with another police officer, that no one was going to steal Mother's belongings. I was very concerned. Thousands of dollars' worth of things—some worthless, some expensive, most bought during any one of her manic spending sprees—were bagged and ready for the taking. I couldn't really explain my concern except that I was suddenly feverish with desire to put her house right, to have everything in order, in its place, as though none of this had ever happened.

Again the officer reassured me: "Rudy is in jail. Officers are watching her house."

∾

Bob was a great lover—on his waterbed, on the couch, on the floor, in the shower. Nothing is better than great sex in Hawaii with the wind blowing and the waves crashing on the shore. Is there anything better than being thrown over the shoulder of a gorgeous, muscled policeman and fucked through the chaos? He was a Polynesian knight on a chrome horse. The infatuation I had with sex at this time was probably always there, hidden underneath the veneer of the good girl. Or maybe Grandma was right when she told me men loved divorcees because they had hot pants.

"So, is his dick bigger than mine?" I was on the phone with BJ, checking on the kids. I blushed into the phone, my silence a confession.

"Come on, Sharon," BJ said, "you can't fool me. Tell me the truth now, little darlin'. I want to hear you say it. Come on, you can tell me."

And I knew I could. That was the thing about BJ. I knew I could tell him anything. Nothing shocked him, nothing surprised him, and he loved a good story. He wasn't angry, merely curious, a little competitive, slightly jealous perhaps. It was his free-spiritedness that I loved. He had no rules and gave no criticisms. If I was having fun, then he was happy. Still, I wasn't really in the mood for penis envy, so I didn't answer him.

The next morning, Bob and I arrived at Mother's house armed with gloves, facemasks, Comet, Lysol, and a variety of carpentry tools.

Everything was gone: the green bags, clothes, jewelry, stereos, dishes, paintings, and televisions—anything of value. Her car—gone. Her bank checks—gone. I panicked. The police told me Rudy was in jail. How had this happened? Bob drove me back to the police station. How were we going to recover Mother's things? The officer on duty was sympathetic and kind. His soothing voice softened my edges. He slid a piece of paper across the counter.

"Fill this out. List every item that was stolen. We'll do the best we can."

"I don't know every item that was stolen." I was near tears.

The officer handed me a pen. "I know this is hard," he said, the compassion in his voice slipping over me like silk. "Just do the best you can."

Later, Bob and I stood in Mother's living room, intimidated by the unending maelstrom spread before us. Even with most of her valuables gone, the mess was significant: yards of stained sarongs, rotted food, jars of urine, empty soup cans, bags of scarves, half-used rolls of toilet paper, shit smeared on the screens, broken doors and decks.

And suddenly, inexplicably, as I stood in the midst of all the disorder, the chaos, I wondered if her brain was like this—if this was her illness staring me in the face. Thoughts stacked up one on top of the other, tangled, tripping, rotting, unused in the corner. Piles and piles of thoughts breeding like maggots. Wiggling. Relentless. Unstoppable. *Your outside world reflects your inside world.* Based on this fetid disarray, Mother's inside world was a stinking, putrid cesspool. So why didn't she take her medications? This question had haunted me for my entire life. It was why I believed her illness was a choice. Why live like this when there was another way?

I turned away. It was too much. Too complicated. Too many moving parts. Then I was in the grips of a frantic need to scrub away all the mess, all the chaos, to put everything back in its proper place, back to where it should be. I tossed and stacked and cleaned and polished. I washed and folded clothes. I re-shelved books. I organized pots and pans and dishes and silverware. I scrubbed and scrubbed until everything was right again.

I STOOD IN THE HALLWAY of a Los Angeles court. Actor Lee Marvin was talking to a gaggle of reporters. He was embroiled in a palimony lawsuit.

"Who's going to win, Lee?" asked an eager, bright-eyed young man. He shoved a microphone in Lee Marvin's face.

Lee answered in his customary deep, unemotional drawl: "The one with the best story wins."

It was lunch. I was on break from my divorce trial. It had been three weeks since I had been in Hawaii. Mother was still in Queen's Hospital in Honolulu, padding around in a hospital gown and slippers until she was no longer a danger to herself or others. When she had stabilized, when she could walk a little more steadily, and when she could tell them her name without hesitation, they would release her. And I would not be there. I would not be there to fold her into the car, settle her into her bed, and explain to her why so many of her things were gone.

She would be okay for a while as she re-oriented herself to her house, her neighborhood, and her life. Then she would begin that slow downward slide into dark depression, where she would hover for days, weeks, months until the mania awakened again, grabbed her by the throat, and dragged her up through the darkness into irrational euphoric delusion. She would be arrested for open lewdness, indecent exposure, shoplifting, trespassing, driving recklessly, theft, disorderly conduct—any of the above, all of the above—and I would dump my kids on a neighbor or with BJ, hop a plane to Hawaii, bail her out of jail, visit her in the hospital, pick up the broken pieces, and try to glue her back together again.

This was Big Daddy's defense, the reason he thought he should have custody of the boys and half my inheritance. A psychiatrist from the Center for Legal Psychiatry interviewed us. Big Daddy told the psychiatrist that I was irresponsible and unreliable. He claimed I was neglecting my children. I was always out, never around, always flying off to Hawaii to care for my mentally ill mother. How could I provide a stable home for the boys? He had a good point—a compelling story. What made mine better? Simple: Big Daddy was a cheating, stalking, drinking, tyrannical asshole, and that trumped a mentally ill family member every time.

Of course, I had the better story.

Five days later, the judge granted me primary custody of the boys, the home in Glendale, and the condo in Palm Springs. I changed my name back to Hicks, which felt like a warm bath. I was to pay Big Daddy a lump sum; he was to pay child support of a hundred dollars a month. There was one sticky condition in the divorce decree: I was not allowed to move to another state, mainly Hawaii. I nodded at the judge. "Sure, I promise." I crossed my fingers behind my back.

The law firm of Witt, Agnew & Walsh was located in downtown Glendale. Senior Partner Daniel Walsh hired me to be his legal secretary. He was intrigued with my degree in philosophy, even though I had no idea how to turn on an electric typewriter, use a copy machine, or take dictation. Despite my under-qualification in actual secretarial skills, I was determined and hungry to make it on my own this time, to be someone, to somehow make up for two failed marriages in seventeen years. I learned quickly.

After a few weeks of working for Daniel Walsh, he asked if he could review Dad's trust. "You should ask for the financial statements of the construction company, Sharon," he said, flipping through the trust documents. "You have a right to see them since your trust is one-third owner."

I had never seen a financial statement of the company. Kathy, David, and I had been told not to interfere. We had been told to simply accept our one thousand dollars a month and not ask any questions. The trustees told us that if we interfered, they would quit the company, let it die, and leave us with nothing. We complied. We obeyed. We accepted whatever they told us. A thousand a month was better than nothing. A thousand a month was currently saving my ass.

Daniel shook his head and set the trust papers on my desk.

"I would look into it, Sharon. They could be stealing from you."

For a while, everything was perfect. Chaos curled up under the house and slept. All the pieces of my life fell into place: gainfully employed, team mom, loving and devoted mom, lover and beloved. My life, for once, wasn't pretend. As I snuggled with BJ, I thought, *So this is happiness.*

And then, impossibly, inexplicably, inexcusably, I was pregnant. Again. By BJ. A neighbor. Again. *What is wrong with me?*

Actually, I was thrilled. I loved being pregnant, violent morning sickness notwithstanding. But a fifth child? BJ wanted me to have an abortion.

"Please, Sharon!"

An abortion. How could I? How could he ask me to do this? How could I terminate a life inside me? It was not a religious thing but a "life is sacred" thing. I couldn't even kill earthworms, for Pete's sake.

Three and a half months later, I had an abortion. It nearly killed me. The pain was unbearable, gauze stuck deep inside me, like sandpaper, scraping me raw. I screamed. I groped. I clutched and clawed at my empty womb. *My baby! You killed my baby! How could you let me do this? It is a boy. A beautiful, talented, little brown-haired son.* I just knew it. In my dreams, he teased and taunted and condemned me to hell. Agony and guilt coiled around me like twin anacondas and crushed me into oblivion.

Someone, a nurse, a doctor, said, "She is having boyfriend troubles."

Someone else screamed.

It might have been me.

At home in bed, I pulled the covers over my head and hid from my children. I didn't deserve to be seen. I didn't deserve to live. BJ was lying beside me while I sobbed, hysterically, undone by grief. "My son, my son, my son," I moaned, an endless, looping chant.

"Stop it, Sharon!" he yelled. "Fuck! Stop it!"

I couldn't stop. Nothing existed except pain. And then crack! His fist connected with my ribs.

"Shut up!" he screamed. "Just shut the fuck up!"

I curled into the tiniest ball. Pain radiated through my left side like fire. I couldn't draw breath. I couldn't move. BJ rushed me to the hospital. X-rays showed cracked ribs and a collapsed lung.

BJ hovered over me, his face slippery with tears: "I'm sorry, Sharon. I'm so fucking sorry."

I was on pain medication. I wasn't doing well. Depression flattened me, crushed me, pinned me to the ground. I couldn't look at my children. I couldn't remember how to get out of bed. I couldn't remember how to eat, brush my teeth, and tie my shoes. I didn't know whether it was day or night, and I was disinclined to care. I was disappearing by degrees, and that was okay with me. With any luck, I'd be completely gone by Tuesday.

And then I was in a mental hospital. There were faces and hands and questions, so many questions, too many questions, and it was all moving too fast. I couldn't keep up, and I just wanted to rest for a while. They poked and prodded and checked for razors. I told them I wasn't suicidal, but no one listened. More voices and more questions and lots of pinched, concerned faces, and suddenly I was very small and no one could see me and I reached out to tug on the edge of someone's white coat before I disappeared completely. *Please, sir. Please, sir, I just want to rest a while.* And then someone hustled me to a tiny room with a tiny bed and an even tinier window through which I could see a sliver of blue sky. They gave me a pill. They told me everything would be okay and that I should try to get some sleep. I nodded gratefully and dragged my teeny, tiny self into my teeny, tiny bed and dissolved into a black, velvet sleep.

I tried very hard to be mentally ill. I wanted to belong among the certifiably insane, to have no responsibilities except sewing a leather purse and coloring inside the lines and then, only if I wanted. Wasn't that how it worked? You acted crazy and you went to the hospital and you were released from your responsibilities, absolved of your sins. Most people went to church for absolution; I went to the mental hospital. And if I could get a diagnosis—if I could have someone in a white coat with degrees hanging on the wall officially declare that I was sick—then maybe it wasn't my fault. Maybe I wasn't really responsible for killing my child. Maybe I just couldn't help it because I was sick.

I saw Mother do it. It was not that hard. I walked around like a zombie, talked nonsense to the other patients, talked nonsense to myself, stood in line for my medication—red pills, blue pills, green pills, white pills—and stared at the same spot on a blank wall for hours.

In the lounge where patients gathered during the day, another patient, Gerald, sat across from me, tapping his fingers on the cracked Formica tabletop.

"Don't eat the food," he told me.

"Why not?"

"Because it's poisoned."

"How do you know?"

"The aliens told me. They communicate with me through the fillings in my teeth."

I nodded. "Thanks for the advice."

I excused myself and shuffled to my room. I crawled into bed, wrapped the blankets around me like a cocoon, and prayed for death.

It wasn't working. I tried my very best. For three days, I tried my best, but it wasn't working. And the unfortunate truth was that I didn't belong. I told my doctor I wasn't crazy like the rest of them. I was only having boyfriend trouble, and I wanted to go home.

"Yes," he agreed without argument. "You are not crazy. It's best you go home."

I packed my bag. I called BJ to pick me up and take me home. I failed. The one time I had actively tried to be like Mother, that I needed to be like Mother, and I couldn't even fake it. It was harder than it looked.

So I had my tubes tied, nice and tight. Enough of getting pregnant by my neighbors. But the pain didn't go away. Instead, I drowned, pulled down, down, down. The abortion twisted around my ankles like an anchor, and I spiraled into a pitch-black abyss. I popped pills—prescription medications. Pills to sleep, pills for depression, pills for getting me through the day. I tried anything to blunt the pain, to block it out. But I didn't respond well to the drugs. I felt out of control, and I didn't like it. I threw all my pills away.

I was still desperately in love with BJ, and I wanted him. The cracked ribs and the collapsed lung, the abortion, and my brief stint at the mental hospital sat like a steel wall between us—impenetrable. I dated another man who was twelve years younger. He was a beautiful boy, ridiculously handsome, and knew it. He was crazy about me. He told me every time he saw me in my shortest of shorts at the boys' baseball games that he wanted to snuggle his face between my legs. I let him while his wife and kids were out of town and then dumped him. I decided I should focus on me, an unmarried, free woman.

Miraculously, Mother stood at my doorstep.

"Sharon, you're coming home with me for a couple of weeks. I want you to take the *est* training with me. We need to toughen you up, teach you how to get off the roller coaster of life."

I listened carefully. The cadence of her voice was normal—a little edgy, but normal. It was impossible to predict how long her normal period would last, but she wasn't really showing any signs of mania, so I relaxed and considered what she said.

"It will enlighten you, Sharon. You must take control and be responsible for what happens to you."

"What about the kids?" I asked.

"They're fine. Cyndy is sixteen. She can take care of the others. Hell, I was married when I was sixteen. She can manage."

"I don't know, Mother. Can't you just stay here and take care of things for a while? Take care of me?"

"Oh, come on, Sharon. Stop being so weak and afraid all the time. You're not a fucking China doll. Stop being so fragile."

With no strength to argue with her, I submitted. Maybe she was right. Ten days in Hawaii would be good for me. I would have time with Mother, and we could bash men and talk about anything and everything. This would be good for me. For us.

I packed a bag. I clung to Mother like a monkey, and together we flew to Hawaii the next day, just in time for the weekend seminar.

EST TRAINING WAS ABOUT TELLING the truth. Undiluted, unedited, no holds barred, raw honesty. Est stood for Erhard Seminar Training and "it is" in Latin. No excuses. No explanations. No judgments. Tell the truth; accept it for what it is. Then let go. That was the part Mother struggled with—the letting go part.

"I was wronged, Sharon. Terribly wronged. Your father fucked me, your brother fucked me, and now you're fucking me. I know you're stealing from me. Don't think you can get away with it. I know what's going on. All your father's assets should be mine! There wouldn't even be a Hicks Homes if it weren't for me! I *made* that company! I am going to sue you, I am going to sue David, and I am going to sue Kathy. I'll get what's mine. You fucking parasite. You're all a bunch of shitheads!"

For seventeen years, this had been her rant. She wanted a million dollars after the divorce and the widow's share of Dad's estate. She complained endlessly: in Glendale, on the plane, at her house in Hawaii. She never quit, never shut up, always going on about her pain, how she had been wronged, and how I needed to listen to her story. I wanted to scream. *What about me? Just this once, why can't this be about me? I just aborted my child!* The truth, metallic and cold, pressed against me. I had been tricked again. This wasn't a rescue but a kidnapping. It was a ploy aimed at me so I would admit that I continued to suck off her teat, taking all her money. She just wanted her money. She just wanted vindication. She just wanted her day in court.

I couldn't explain to her that her trust protected her from herself. The thing was, when she was manic, she spent money with fuck-you abandon, and then she tried to give away the stuff she had just bought because it cluttered her mind. Money was no object, and stuff had no meaning to her. Hell, she tried to give the house to Rudy. She just couldn't find the deed. Without her trust, without David and me managing her trust, she would be homeless. She didn't understand. Wouldn't understand. Or maybe she just couldn't. That was the thing about her madness; I couldn't tell where it ended and my mother began.

Or maybe I didn't understand. From where I sat, all her bases were covered: no worries, no responsibilities, and no concerns. She was accountable for nothing, to no one. Oh, sure, I knew she was sick. Bats. Mad as a hatter. She couldn't help it. It was not her fault. She didn't ask to be sick. Yeah, well, I didn't ask for her to be sick either.

∽◦∾

I stood in front of three hundred strangers, prepared to share my truth. Mother sat somewhere in the back because all those who had previously taken est sat in the back and couldn't say anything. No sharing. Only listening. Only observing. Good. Now it was my turn to state my case. Three hundred pairs of eyes stared at me in rapt attention.

I cleared my throat.

"I had an abortion, and I feel bad."

No tears. No emotion. Just the facts.

The trainer repeated: "She had an abortion, and she feels bad."

Three hundred heads nodded simultaneously.

Acknowledgment. Validation. Acceptance.

Surprisingly, the twisted knot of grief in my stomach unclenched.

The trainer motioned me toward my seat.

I continued: "When my parents divorced seventeen years ago, a trust was made to protect my mother because of her history of mental illness. My brother and I do not take any fees for acting as her trustees. We do it because it is what our father wanted, because we love our mother. However, she insists on periodically suing us for mismanaging her trust. She accuses us of stealing her money. She calls us parasites and shitheads. She never wins the lawsuits. This only infuriates her more."

I searched the room for Mother. I wanted to gauge her reaction, to see if she was listening. I needed her to hear this. I needed her to hear that David and I were only trying to do what was best for her. I saw only a sea of nodding heads.

I further said, "From her trust, we pay her bills and write her a check from the interest each month for her personal use. This is all in accordance with the parameters of the trust. She gets angry. Furious. She tells me she is very capable of handling her own finances. So I tell her, 'Fine, Mother. You write the checks, you keep track of your money, you decide what to pay.' As trustee, I have to sign the checks. I am the only signatory the bank recognizes. My mother tells me, 'I don't want to do all that. It sounds like work.'"

No anger. No emotion. Just the facts.

It might seem strange that I talked about her at an est training. I could have mentioned my two failed marriages, Dad's death, the fact that my life hadn't exactly turned out the way I hoped, and any number of issues from my sordid life. But I surrendered to her agenda—why she came to California to get me, why she had called David a month earlier and told him she was in the hospital dying and he'd better hurry over to Hawaii before it was too late. She believed that if David and I took est, we would freely acknowledge that we were parasites and shitheads, and we would make reparations. She would feel vindicated, and all would be forgiven. One big, happy family.

I walked on shaky legs back to my seat. The lady next to me gave me an encouraging little pat on my back.

The trainer walked to the center of the stage and looked directly at me. "Recognize that you are in a no-win situation."

A no-win situation. I chewed on the words a bit, sucked and splashed the flavor across my tongue. Yes. Yes. Yes. No way to win. That made sense. Somehow, the futility of it all opened me up. Tension slipped away, and suddenly I was floating above the crowd, backstroking through the bliss of letting go.

This shit really worked.

But Mother did not let go.

Mother refused to speak to me. She spent the next several days obsessively calling the est training office. She demanded equal time to tell her story. She cried. She whined. She pouted. They would not budge. They reiterated: only first-time est training attendees were allowed to share.

❧

Mother was an est-hole. She took every est training offered in Hawaii, not just because of how empowered it made her feel but because she was obsessed with the founder, Werner Erhard. During one of Werner's trips to Hawaii, Mother located him at the Kahala Hilton Hotel. She also found his room number. One night, she stood outside his hotel room banging her fist on the door, screaming, "Let me in! I want to see you! I want to fuck you!" The police arrested her.

Her silent treatment with me didn't last. Mother wanted to regale me with stories about an est sex seminar she had attended years ago.

Mother snickered. "Have you ever felt a dog's tongue, Sharon? It feels like fine sandpaper."

I shook my head. I was not sure what she meant, but that crazed look in her eyes made me nervous.

"I used to put lots of butter." Mother giggled. "Or sometimes peanut butter, all over my vagina, and Timothy licked and licked and licked. Remember Timothy, Sharon? Our Irish setter?"

I felt the color run from my face but kept my face stone still. My recent est seminar had trained me to not react. No emotion. I nodded.

Mother slapped her hand hard on the table.

She looked me dead in the eye. "Why do you think you were outside so much of the time when you were little?"

A low, humming resounded inside my head, a flat line of disgust. Still, I showed no emotion. "And you shared this information at a sex seminar?"

"Of course! And when I did, I created a space for others to share. Sharon, it was so exciting. Others couldn't wait to share about having sex with a donkey, a sheep, a goat, on and on, people shared. You wouldn't believe all the animals named. And I made it happen!" She paused. And then: "Just like I made Hicks Homes happen!"

I tensed. I braced myself for another onslaught, prepared to counter attack with, "It's a no-win situation," wielding the words like a sword.

"You see, Sharon," Mother continued, "I made it safe for others to share. Not only was it safe, but one story also became more bizarre than the other. So much fun. People are so fucking funny."

She leaned forward expectantly. I stared back at her. I didn't know what she wanted me to say. I settled back in my chair and stared past Mother at the bay, trying to digest this new nugget of information. *No wonder Timothy died of a heart attack.*

⌒⌒⌒

A few days later I took another est training seminar on communication. Again I shared. I beamed with pride at my cleverness, the clarity of my articulation. The trainer looked at me and asked, "Why is your voice so sweet and soft? What is going on with you?"

Huh? I didn't understand the question. What's wrong with sweet and soft? I blinked and smiled. I turned a thousand shades of red. My self-righteousness crumbled and fell into a pile of rubble at my feet.

"I sense a great deal of sadness and turmoil behind such sugary sweetness."

I slinked back to my chair and slumped down, puzzled.

Next we were told to sit face to face with the one next to us. My knees touched a very fat lady; our hands flattened against our thighs. We stared directly into each other's eyes. We shared the first thing that came to minds about the other person. Fat was the first thing that came to my mind: disgusting, ugly, undisciplined, weak, fat. The words piled high in my mouth. They startled me, the way they were so mean and unforgiving. I didn't think of myself as mean and unforgiving. I thought of myself as nice and sweet, and what were such awful thoughts doing in my head? The goal in this exercise was to speak the truth. Impossible. What's the point? What's to be gained from such brutal honesty? I shared first.

"You are very much … overweight." I recoiled. I cringed. I waited for the retaliation.

She smiled. "Thank you. Thank you so much. I have always wanted to look like my mom. I admire her so much. She is very heavy too."

I was stunned. I never knew a daughter who wanted to be like her own mother. I slumped back in my chair, amazed.

I SUNBATHED ON MOTHER'S LANAI in my skimpy orange-and-white polka dot bikini listening to the ocean. I felt relaxed for the first time in months. Everything illuminated vibrantly—colors, sounds, smells, and textures. Est had somehow turned up the volume in my mind, reduced the static. I felt alert and alive. High. I breathed in the sweet island air and flopped over on my belly to tan my back, my thighs.

Mother could not or would not let go. She continued to rant that I should turn over the trust, all my money, and all the assets to her. But I didn't care anymore. She could rant and rave all she wanted. There was nothing I could do to make it stop. I understood that now. It was a no-win situation. The trade winds blew cool tickles of soft air across my back. White, cottony clouds drifted lazily across the vast blue sky. I sighed and melted into the bliss.

The doorbell rang and startled me out of my reverie. I hopped up and bounced to the door in my cute bikini. I opened the door and stared directly into the stomach of an enormous Samoan man. I looked up and frowned. His massive body covered the entire space of the doorway. I didn't like his Fu Manchu mustache.

"Can I help you?" I asked, feeling a little underdressed in my bikini.

"I'm here to collect."

"Oh, thanks," I said still sun-drunk. "But we don't have anything to give at this time."

I moved to close the door. His big, beefy hand pushed the door back open. A little hole opened in the pit of my stomach. I crossed my arms over my belly, suddenly feeling very naked.

"I'm here to collect," he repeated. "Mrs. Hicks owes money to Ross Sutherland's Men's Store. I'm here to collect the money."

His words landed like stones. Mother had done it again.

"Sorry, Mrs. Hicks isn't home right now," I lied.

"Who are you?" he demanded.

"I'm a friend," I lied again. "Just visiting for a few days." I cracked a weak smile.

I peeked around his sizeable bulk. In the carport were two more Samoans, cracking their knuckles.

He nodded his head in the direction of the carport. "Where is Mrs. Hicks? That's her car in the carport."

"Her friend picked her up. I think they went to the movies. I don't know when she'll be back."

Please, Mother, stay in your bedroom. I shifted my weight from one foot to the other. I was desperate for a sarong, a towel, a napkin—anything that would provide some sort of cover.

He reached into his pocket; I held my breath. When he pulled out a business card, my heart started beating again. He wrote his name on the card and handed it to me. I took it from his mammoth paw. I recognized his name from the Honolulu news; he was a famous wrestler. Printed on his card were the words:

THE SAMOAN COLLECTOR
We'll even go to heaven or hell to collect.

"You give this to Mrs. Hicks," he ordered. "We'll be back."

Right-o, I thought and then tucked the card into my bikini bottoms.

"Thank you, sir," I said, batting my eyelashes. "I'll make sure she gets it."

I shut the door, locked it, and flattened myself against it, my heart battering against my ribs. I tore into Mother's bedroom, where I found her spread eagle on the bed, not wearing a stitch of clothing.

"Holy shit, Mother." I propped my hand in front of my eyes, as though trying to block out the sun.

"Who was at the door?" She didn't move or cover herself.

I grabbed a sarong that was slung across the chair and wrapped myself.

"Three giant Samoan men, wrestlers," I said, hands on my hips, my breath quick and sharp.

"What did they want?" She was bored with this conversation.

"They say you have an outstanding bill at Ross Sutherland's. What's that about, Mother? That's a men's store."

She waved her hand. She sat up.

"Oh, fuck 'em! That's an old bill. I'm not paying it! I bought those clothes for Rudy and he ripped me off, so fuck 'em. Fuck 'em all!"

IN FEBRUARY OF 1981, MOTHER was arrested three times and charged five times: indecent exposure, open lewdness, criminal trespass in the first degree, reckless driving, and resisting an order to stop. It happened shortly after the est seminar, shortly after I returned to Southern California. Est set her off again, grabbed her by the tail, and swung her toward the moon. She called me boasting of her arrest record. She loved the excitement, the adventure of it all. "You meet the most interesting people in jail," she said a few days before she was taken to Queen's Hospital and committed for three months.

~◦~

Living in California, I felt displaced. I wanted to move home to Hawaii. I planned a quick trip to Hawaii to search for a place to live. Excitement bubbled through my veins like it did when I was getting ready to start fresh. This time it was different. This time it would be different. I didn't know how I knew. I just did. I could feel it in my bones. The life I wanted—the life I craved—was in Hawaii, riding the trade winds, whispering to me, *Go back home, Sharon.*

I dated Dick the week I was home in Hawaii. He was dark and good-looking, an attorney. Daniel Walsh recommended him to me. He said Dick could help me with my father's trust, with investigating Hicks Homes, and Dick could help me find a place to live. During the week, Dick courted me in the style of a gentleman. We went to dinner and took long walks on the beach. We talked about Hicks Homes. Dick expressed concern and said I might have a lawsuit on my hands. He told me he was interested in taking the case.

I returned to Glendale heady with infatuation for Dick. We exchanged letters. Romance and sex dripped from the pages, and promises of love everlasting curled inside ribbons of ink. I didn't know exactly how I felt about Dick. I was not necessarily interested in 'til death do you part. I was still skittish about marriage, about any sort of long-term commitment. And yet, my meandering

165

daydreams swirled and ended with walking down the aisle toward happily ever after, believing that this time, it would finally work. I believed that after all these years holding my breath, waiting for all the pieces of my life to align, waiting for *him* to arrive and magically fill that unnamable, ever-present hole that resided like a pit of quicksand in my gut, I could finally, finally, exhale. I found myself still searching for Mr. Right, the knight to sweep me up onto his muscled steed and ride off into the sunset or preferably into the four-bedroom house with the three-car garage on the ocean. The fantasy of the noble prince and the helpless maiden seduced me. Even though the reality was ridiculously different from the fantasy, like any good seducer, the fantasy continually beckoned, crooking its finger at me, licking its lips, drawing me in and wrapping lies inside cotton candy promises of bliss.

Then Dick sent me a bill for our discussion at dinner. *Excuse me?* The fantasy unspooled like a pulled thread. Livid, I submitted a bill of my own, listing the charges for each of my services: dinner companion, foreplay, missionary position, woman on top, blow jobs, hand jobs. The list was long. The total: expensive. I indicated that the charge for my services exceeded the charge for his and could he *please make sure to remit his payment to me as soon as possible?*

I never heard from Dick again.

Figured.

I was infuriated. I was tired of being fucked over by men—tired of believing in their bullshit, tired of riding the rollercoaster of their games and lies, their promises and betrayals. The thing about Prince Charming and his noble steed were the stories never told. What happened after the prince swept up the princess and the two of them rode into the sunset? No one actually witnessed the prince and his princess living happily ever after.

I counted the days until my feet would touch Hawaiian soil again, until they were stained brick red by the iron-oxide-rich dirt; until the salted waters would tangle my hair and the trade winds would whisk away the residue of failure that clung to my skin; and until I could leave behind the wreckage of my life, put it to rest, scatter its ashes into the wind.

First, though, I had many, many men.

I wish I could say it with a Southern flair, the way Blanche Devereaux did on *The Golden Girls.* She leaned against the doorframe, one arm extended seductively along the frame, and said in that come-fuck-me voice of hers, "I have had many, many, many men."

Okay, she was a slut, but a slut with style.

I made a list, kept a record: John, Jack, Paul, Dan, Jim, Greg, and Karl. And then when I couldn't remember a name (or never knew them in the first place): the man with the broken leg at the bar (can't remember which bar); the piano player at the YMCA—*what will his nimble fingers feel like playing my body?* The three men in Palm Springs—one for breakfast, one for lunch, one for dinner. Whoops, two for dinner.

I bought Zavier Hollander's book *The Best Part of Man.* I studied it; I devoured it. She wrote that nothing could replace the hardness of man. (Mother's words when I was eleven.) Zavier recommended music, "Bolero" by Ravel, because it began slowly (foreplay) and then worked into a frenzied crescendo, music and bodies pressed together, gripping, tearing, ravishing one another into wild musical sexual climax.

I tried Bolero. It worked.

The ridiculously gorgeous man, slick with sweat and exhaustion, looked at me through bleary, spent eyes. "You sure know how to fuck a man, Sharon. Wish I had the energy for another whirl!"

I smiled and pressed rewind.

And then there were the oils and ice cubes and frozen fruits slipped into my vagina. Whipped cream, chocolate syrup, strawberries, and honey. They were all fun, of course, in their own ways, but I preferred natural body scents, musky animal scents, licking, caressing, sharing, the awakening of my body, two bodies twisted and tangled in passion and then the sweet, blissful freedom of release.

I made another list of men I wanted to fuck: an assemblyman, a CEO, a councilman, my psychiatrist, my divorce attorney. I pledged to fuck them silly. Fuck them over. Fuck them all. As I sat across the desk from one of my targets, I crossed my legs slowly so he could see every inch of them, drink them in. I slid my hand down my thigh.

"I'm moving to Hawaii," I said. "And there's something I really want to do before I leave."

Tiny beads of perspiration would suddenly creep across his forehead. He licked his lips and rubbed his chin. "And what is that?"

I leaned forward, my big breasts straining against the fabric of my low-cut dress.

"Go to bed with you. I can't think of a better farewell than sharing the most intimate pleasure possible between a man and a woman."

He coughed. "Wow, I don't get this kind of offer every day."

He wiped his hand across his forehead.

"Sure," he said. "Give me your number. I'll call you."

He shifted in his black leather chair.

He stretched his arm across the desk, hand open, to seal the deal.

He didn't get up.

And so it went, one after the other. None of them declined. Some were married, some opted for more than one round, and one caught his penis in his zipper. All of them were enormously grateful.

I sold my house in the hills of Glendale, had a huge garage sale, and packed my bags and kids. Even though, according to the terms of my divorce, I wasn't allowed to leave the state, I went home to Hawaii.

Be Yourself, Everyone else is taken.

—Oscar Wilde

Part Three

1981–2001
Hawaii

"MOTHER, I WANT TO INTERVIEW you." It was an afternoon in October 1981. Mother was thrilled that I would be writing about her. She had always wanted to write her own story. I was thrilled to have this time with her, these fleeting moments when she seemed to be stripped of her illness, when it was just the two of us. I was learning to savor these moments, to hold them in my mouth, to let the sweetness dissolve over my tongue. I was learning to minimize the grief that inevitably rose when she lost her grip on normal— when the madness took her from me again.

We settled in cushioned chairs on her lanai, and I pressed the red record button on the tape recorder that I set in front of her.

"I feel devastated. And I think anyone, especially a woman, who puts themselves in my place, in my life, would certainly feel the same way."

"Devastated about what?" I thought about the many times she had been committed and had shock treatments, the forced medication, and her arrests.

"What all of you did to me. How the divorce was handled."

I was confused. "You are angry about the divorce?"

"I am not angry; I am hurt."

"What would make you feel better?"

"In the first place, David would have to be willing to talk about it and acknowledge what happened." Tears formed in her eyes. "And of course, you too owe some acknowledgment and some sorrow about that. Some apologies and of course Louie. But just try to ignore it. I can't. I can't. I feel like a hypocrite pretending that everything is okay." She was now crying.

"You feel like a hypocrite when you are with us?"

She nodded through her tears. She dabbed her eyes with tissue, took a deep, slow breath, exhaled, and stopped crying.

"What actually happened that day?" I was still confused about why she was upset about the divorce when that was what she had always wanted.

173

"That day? Louie got me out of Westwood after nine months. I stayed with him and Mackie in Sunland. But it was very difficult for me to get to Westwood Hospital in Los Angeles to continue seeing Dr. Hellinger after my release from the hospital. It is a long drive from Sunland to Westwood, about forty-five minutes. And I was still confused. Not too sharp. It was not easy for me to find my way. David drove from Fresno to Los Angeles to see me. I was so excited. I think, *How neat that he is coming. He can take me to Westwood for my visit to see Dr. Hellinger.* So David drove me.

"I had a regular meeting with Dr. Hellinger, and then on our way home, about a block away from Louie's, David said that he had my divorce papers. I told him I didn't want to handle that now. I didn't want to talk about it now. And he said, 'Dad had the papers done, and they are here,' as he pointed to a big folder in the car. I asked him what the papers said, and he told me not to worry.

"David told me, 'Mother, there is enough here to take care of you. Sharon and I will always make sure you are taken care of. Don't worry.' I thought that I said, 'I would rather be dead than have to depend on you and Sharon.' I mean I just, you know, I don't want to have to depend on anyone. Anyway, why should I depend on anyone? As far as money is concerned.

"David pulled up to this little office in Sunland. We walked into an attorney's office; he was sitting here,"—she pointed to an area in front of her—"David is sitting there,"—she pointed to a space beside her—"and I am sitting here. David already had an appointment and handed the file to the attorney. He studied it over about fifteen minutes, and he looked at me and said, 'Mrs. Hicks, I hope you know what you are doing.'"

Mother bent toward me and continued in a whisper: "The attorney saw that I was signing my life away. David stood up and said, 'Under the circumstances, we feel that this is the right thing to do.' And I signed the divorce papers."

Mother gave a big sigh and then laughed and spoke rapidly. "David says that your father was as nervous as hell." She waved her right index finger and mimicked Dad: "'You take these papers to the attorney and have her sign them. Don't let her see her doctor first.' What a railroad job that was! I didn't even worry about it until I got my wits about me."

"What happened after that?"

"David took me back to Louie's. The divorce didn't affect me. I was just trying to exist day to day."

"Were you on medication?"

"Whatever Dr. Hellinger gave me at that time. The next thing I knew, I arrived in Hawaii and Ed picked me up at the airport. I asked him if I could stay with him and Esther. He said, 'No, because Esther is jealous of you. You can't stay with us. I will take you to the Halekulani Hotel.'

"At this time, our family home left to me in the divorce settlement was being rented. I guess your Dad thought I would be at Westwood a long time. Anyway, I had nothing to go home to. I had no home.

"At the Halekulani, I drank and drank to knock myself out. At the store at the Halekulani, I could get anything I want, mainly booze. I don't remember how many days I was there. Then a knock came on the door, and it was another old friend carrying a red carnation lei on her arm. 'Carolyn, we would love to have you as our houseguest. Please come home with me.'"

Mother cried, "I cannot ... believe ... someone would be ... so nice to me."

She crossed her arms at her chest and swayed back and forth on her chair, heaving sobs. Then she stopped abruptly, dried her eyes, and continued: "After a few days with Irene and Fred, Irene asked to see my divorce papers. Then she turned to me and said, 'It is not fair; you must see an attorney.' I saw the best criminal attorney in Hawaii: Hyman Greenstein. He told me that he would have the divorce set aside, even your dad's new marriage. 'It will go to family court. You will have your share.' I felt so good about that.

"I called your dad to tell him about the lawsuit and the only way that I would drop it is if I could have an accounting and one million dollars. I know that we had three million dollars. At least one-third should be mine. He said that he would contact the accountants, but you know, he never did."

"Then what happened?"

"I get more and more depressed and drank a lot. I had a car that David bought for me—an old Ford jalopy. I woke up, had coffee, toast, and jelly, and then went to the mall. I bought five or ten candy bars for ten cents and then found a movie. In the matinee, I never knew what the movie was about. I actually would eat the candy and sleep. Then I would go to the jewelry store in Aina Haina. Do you remember their jewelry store?"

I nodded.

"Before closing time every day, about an hour before closing time, they had cocktails. I would not drink with them. At home, I would help Irene with dinner for the three of us. Fred always did the dishes. There was no housework to do because they had help. I took their dog, Bo, a toy poodle, for a walk every evening around the neighborhood. Irene and I played cribbage for hours. I was with them for about seven or eight months. Irene was dear but not supportive. She didn't know how to help me emotionally. This was the beginning."

"Beginning of what?"

"I just kept getting worse. I would take four to six aspirin before I would go to bed and a whole handful of sleeping pills. I would drink. I felt horrible. I couldn't relax. My mind kept going and going. If I could just ..." Then she heaved and cried. "This brings up a lot of stuff. I was so depressed because it was so hard for me to concentrate on certain areas. The whole thing was so terrible."

"How old were you?"

"Let's see. It was 1963. Forty-five years old—around your age today. And anyway, I couldn't relax to sleep. I would wake up in the morning, and my bed would be wringing wet. Everything would be soaked—wringing wet. The bed would be too. I didn't want Fred and Irene to know. As soon as I heard them leave for work, I would get up. I know Irene called David for help. A psychiatrist, Dr. (Wild) Bill Cody put me into Queen's Hospital, in the Kekela wing where the mentally ill are. The doctor said if I agreed to stay for three weeks, there would be no shock treatments. I agreed. Hate those shock treatments.

"That is where I met Ed, an attorney. Sharon, I think you knew his son. They lived in Aina Haina. He really looked confused. I could tell by his eyes. He asked me who I was. I told him my name, and he said: 'No, you are my angel.'

"I met another man I really liked named Hal. We spent a lot of time together and made plans for when we were out. I suggested that he make Aloha shirts. He said that he needed capital. I told him that money is no problem. When we got out of the hospital, he flew ahead of me to San Francisco. I got some money from David and Irene and joined him later. I wasn't totally well, but I thought I was.

"I was excited about meeting him in San Francisco. I flew to Los Angeles and borrowed a car from my brother, Ernie. I drove to San Francisco, and there was Hal waiting for me with a beautiful dog—a standard black poodle; her name was Susie. He told me that he had the poodle for years and now wanted me to have her. He was working for a circus in San Francisco. We had a little place together at a motel. I would go to work with him and meet lots of those people. We even drove to Fresno to see David. David was very uncomfortable. He didn't like the looks of this guy. I was high. And what was I doing with a dog?

"Back in San Francisco at the motel room, we got into a fight. I blamed Hal for stealing my movie camera. He got so upset; we had a bad fight, disturbing the peace. He called the police and told them that I was insane. I spent the night in jail with prostitutes. I never heard prostitutes talk before: fuck off and all that prostitute talk. I didn't like it, but it was very interesting. I didn't sleep there because it was too noisy. The next morning we had oatmeal. One girl had on a pretty short fox jacket. I wanted it, and she said I could have it for ten or fifteen dollars. She wanted cigarette money. I bought the coat.

"Don't know how I paid for the coat, because the police take away jewelry, money, etc. I don't know how I arranged to get a bail bondsman or how I paid him. But he came. Got me out. I don't know what I gave him. I remember telling him that I had no place to stay. He said that I could stay with him. I thought, *That is neat.* I was there for two days. Then, here comes David. We went to court. 'My mother's sick.' He took me to a hospital—a private hospital. I think I was there for about three weeks; I don't know.

"Oh, I also remember staying at another place with the poodle. I thought the poodle could swim, so I snuck him outside in the middle of the night, threw him in the deep end, and jumped in to swim with him. He almost drowned me; he started clawing me in the deep end, and I remember the struggle I had with him. I guess it was against the rules. I didn't care, but I did get into trouble."

꙳

I remembered David telling me Mother skipped bail. The bondsman called David for help because the bondsman didn't want to lose his money. Mother got into more trouble at the St. Francis Hotel in San

Francisco. She sang at the piano bar with her poodle on the piano. The pianist asked her to take her poodle off the piano. She refused, so she was arrested. Then the bondsman got a call from Mother from Vallejo, twenty-five miles from San Francisco.

⌒

"Must have been this time that I was taken to Camarillo. Every time you are transferred, you are tied down and thrown into an ambulance. I was there for three months. I had shock treatments six times. When you have shock, you enter a room with cots. There are curtains around each cot, and the doctor and nurses are waiting for you behind the curtains. I did not want to go. They said they were just trying to help me. I remember waking up, gasping for air, and they were giving me oxygen. I did not get out of it too good. The nurses did not respect the doctor. I heard them yelling at the doctor that he went too far this time. And they were pounding my chest.

"Shock is awful. You feel like you are laying on a train track and a train hits you head on. WHAM!

"In San Francisco, I was high. The doctors brought me down. At Camarillo, I was feeling depressed. Sometimes I would work in the cafeteria. It was a horrible place.

"David came for me. I sat in the backseat. He sat in the front seat with his mother-in-law, Daisy. I don't know why she came. I remember sitting in the back seat as we drove to Fresno—to David's house.

"Don't remember how long I was at David's. I would drink. One day David told me to come to work with him and do office work. He handed me a lot of bills to separate. I drank there. Don't remember how I got back to Hawaii.

"Again, I was at Irene and Fred's house. I drank a lot. Irene was upset with my drinking and drove me to a residence in the Kuliouou Valley to stay. She was going to leave me there. There were lots of old people. I said, 'Irene, please do not leave me here. I will promise anything.' 'Don't drink,' she said.

"Anyway, I stayed with her for a while. Then Irene suggested that I live with her sister, Zelda. She had a card shop in Aina Haina Shopping Mall. We got a place together at the Tropicanna, next to the Kahala Mall. Anyway, I knew I couldn't stand Zelda. She was too bossy. Always on me. A real bitch. I couldn't stand her. So she left.

"I lived at the Tropicanna apartments near Kahala Mall for three years. Seems like I caused a lot of commotion there with the children of other owners. The doctor called me and said that I better be careful—it sounded like I was getting high and you know what that means. A real son of a bitch. Never going to him again. He only wants to keep me on medication.

"I went to the Ranch House to play bridge. I couldn't function well but met an Italian girl, Lydia, who became my bridge partner. She introduced me to her husband, Fred. He asked me if I would like some coffee. When he handed me the cup, I held onto his hand in a tender, sexy way. He was hooked. He was mine.

"I think I knew Fred had a problem with drinking because his wife, Lydia, told me. Fred threw up in the toilet: 'Honey, don't let me drink anymore. I'm killing myself.' I refuse to be a policeman, and I told him that I didn't care if he drank; I just wouldn't be around. Fred had a serious liver problem, lots of problems. Okay with me if he kills himself drinking.

"Once, when Jim and Nancy, came over for their honeymoon, I spent the day with them. Ernie's friend KK joined us. Fred was to make stew and rice for us for dinner. But he got so jealous that I was with KK, Jim and Nancy that he threw me on his bed and pounded me on my bust. Boy, did it hurt. Then he knocked out a tooth. I told the dentist, 'My boyfriend knocked my tooth out.' He said, 'Oh hell, what's a tooth among friends?'

"Then I started seeing Sam, a talk show host on night radio. He is so smart. I love hearing his voice. He knew all about my problems with my children and thought that it was horrible that people treat their mother that way. He was on my side. We were going to Europe together. He was wonderful in bed but didn't appeal to me physically. Too bad his wonderful voice didn't match his body. He was tall and very big, I guess, just fat. Didn't want to spend too much time with him.

"David was at my door: 'Mother, Irene says that she is worried about you.' Fred was with David. Sam was upstairs in my bedroom, naked. We were having sex in bed when they arrived, banging on my door. Of course, I answered the door in the nude. My pussy was shaved in a perfect heart, and I was very proud of it. Probably shocked David and Fred.

"Irene told David to see the pictures that I had all around the house. She told him that they were horrifying. The faces in the pictures expressed horror. They were all over my house. David told me he was taking me to the hospital. I told him that I was not going and that he would have to call the police to escort me. He did. The police came. I figured I had to go. Sam was still upstairs, being very quiet, not wanting to be caught.

"We went to Queen's Hospital, or was it Kaneohe? I am confused. When I arrived, I excused myself and went to the bathroom. I would not come out of the stall. Someone came to say, 'Are you ready to come out?' I was sick to my stomach and would not come out willfully. They came and unhinged the door to get me.

"Another time I was at the Ilikai Hotel, staying in a room on one of the top floors overlooking the swimming pool. It was a beautiful room; I was enjoying the view on the lanai. I threw oranges into the swimming pool. I didn't have any clothes on. Some idiot was looking at me with spyglasses. That son of a bitch. I yelled at him, 'What are you looking at me for? You stupid bastard. You should be in your own room fucking your wife.' So now I was disturbing the peace. Someone was knocking on the door. I opened it in the nude. It was a man in a white jacket with a needle ready to inject me. I shut the door and bolted it. 'You leave me alone!'

"The police came and told me that I was going with them. Now I had a sarong on. When I went downstairs with the police, I told them that I was not going to get into the wagon. 'If you are going to take me, you are taking me like this.' I threw my sarong off, and I was naked. You should have seen their faces." Laughing. "They are so stupid. I was roaring with laughter. They threw a blanket over me and threw me in the wagon. When I was in the wagon, I took the blanket off. Fuck 'em.

"The police took me to a holding place. Here comes David and Fred. I guess they took me to Kaneohe. I was confused, not too clear. Fred told me they took me to Kaneohe State Hospital. Fred told me when they drove over the Pali to Kaneohe, he threw out a beer bottle and got arrested.

"Later, Fred moved in with me. I met him in 1965, and he died at the end of 1970. Of course, he wanted to marry me, but I couldn't see any reason to marry. I did marry him just to get his pension from Hawaiian Electric Company and his social security. I had to fight for it, because we were only married for eight months. I think you have to be married for nine months to get social security and pension. Anyway, I fought for it and got it all. After all, I took care of him when he was sick.

"Fred was a real man. He loved to fix up my house, walk on the beach, and pick opihi. He told me so many things—about his grandma who would stroke his penis when he was little. She stroked and stroked the skin back so he didn't need a circumcision. His auntie loved to sleep with him, and she would also stroke and stroke his penis. And Fred liked it too.

"Fred told me about visiting an old lady in Palolo. He was ill, and someone told him to visit this lady. She lived in the back of the valley against the mountain. He had to climb several flights of stairs to her place. She invited him inside and fixed him some tea. He said she healed him. Later he went back to thank her. He drove to the same spot where she lived. *But* there were no stairs, no house, and no old woman—nothing.

"He continually met ghost Hawaiian warriors out night marching. He met them while hiking in the mountains. Fred loved being Hawaiian. He looked like Ernest Hemingway, with dark skin and a white beard. He was very handsome.

"My next-door neighbor, John, was very nice to me. I would take him homemade rolls, and he would come over to help me with things around the house and my car. He invited me to use his gym, and he would leave his gate open for me. Just as sweet as could be. I sometimes would sit in his sports car. While I was high, I went swimming in the nude in their Jacuzzi and swimming pool. I wanted to get into their sauna but couldn't make it work. I went home.

"Later that day, I snuck into their house. I went upstairs in the bedrooms and closets. I saw beautiful red pumps. I wanted to take them home, so I threw them out their bedroom window with several bottles of perfume. They saw me come out of the house but didn't know that I took anything. Their gardener saw me. John came over, went into my house, found the shoes, and had me arrested. John yelled at me, and I told him that I was going to bite off his finger. I went to jail. John was there with his wife, Laurel. I told the judge that I just wanted to try on these pretty red shoes but that they were too narrow. The case was dismissed because John also went into my house illegally. A neighborhood argument. However, I had spent the night in jail before the hearing.

"There are so many incidents. I don't remember them all. I think I was in prison twice and jail ... too many times."

I listened in rapt attention, amazed less by the foolhardiness of Mother's actions and more by her lack of remorse for any of it. To her, it was all just a game. She was having fun: one thrill after another. She laughed and cried at the memories, delighted to be reliving her adventures all over again, delighted that I was sharing them with her.

As I listened to Mother ramble, I was struck by the number of times David drove or flew to wherever she was, sat through court hearings, and made sure she got the care she needed. And sitting there listening to Mother spin her stories, I was profoundly grateful for David's sacrifices.

～०∾

Three years later, her police report listed thirty-three arrests in Hawaii for careless and reckless driving (two), disorderly conduct (four), open lewdness (ten), contempt of court (two), theft (five), indecent exposure (one), criminal trespass (six), harassment (one), and property damage (one), and other offenses under the names Carolyn N. Hicks, Sharolyn, Carol Dona Hicks-Noel, Carolyn Colburn, Carolyn Noel, and Minnie Nowell.

WHEN MY DAD DIED, he left complete control of his company to his board of directors. Fourteen years later, sub-contractors and employees of Hicks Construction Inc. (aka Hicks Homes) told me they thought the company was being mismanaged. They suggested I investigate.

Over the years, I'd received financial statements for my trust that owned one-third of the assets of the construction company but never for the company itself. I asked the board of directors for the company's financial statements. They answered, "It's none of your business."

That was the wrong answer. I pulled the pin and lobbed Mother's third-favorite word at the board of directors like a hand grenade: lawsuit.

Well, not exactly.

But I did start an investigation. A covert operation. On the sly. On the down low. Every week, I asked questions of the company's employees, suppliers, and bankers: "How is Hicks Homes doing?"

I didn't like what I heard.

"HEY, THERE, LITTLE DARLING!" I recognized BJ on the phone, his Southern drawl slipping around me like a warm bath. "Can I please come over?" He missed me. He wanted to try again. He loved me. He wanted to move to Hawaii, to move in with me. The smile in his voice traversed the miles, gathered me in, and embraced me. I melted. Relief opened like a fan. I asked the kids if they wanted BJ to move in with us. They were ecstatic.

"He's so much fun, Mom," gushed eleven-year-old Guy.

So, I told BJ yes. I invited the man who had insisted I abort my baby, who fractured my ribs and collapsed my lung, who drove me to a four-day stint in a mental hospital, back into my bed, back into my home, and back into my life.

Mother was in love with BJ. She wanted to fuck him. That didn't actually bother me, strangely enough. Mother's insatiable desire to fuck indiscriminately became standard operating procedure. And BJ thought it hilarious. He loved her flirting, her free spirit, her devil-may-care attitude, her sense of adventure, if only because it matched his own. BJ asked if I was anything like Mother. I couldn't tell if he was teasing, hoping, or dreading. Still, his question landed like a fist to the gut: "No! I am nothing like her, and I never will be!"

Mother introduced BJ and me to her treasure trove of interests: freshly brewed coffee enemas, iridology (the practice of evaluating one's iris to determine systemic health), Breathariansim (the belief that the human body could live solely on breath, the vital life force; food and water aren't necessary), A Course In Miracles (Mother discovered this at the Unity Church; it stressed the concept of forgiveness—not one of Mother's strengths), Shiatsu, crystals, pyramids, chakras, and body-energy field studies, among others. Mother radiated as she shared her passions with us. She chattered like a chipmunk as she slipped BJ's arm around her shoulders and pressed into his side. I rolled my eyes. BJ laughed. I laughed.

Her mania started to unfurl. I recognized the cluster of signs: rapid, pressured speech, wide eyes, flight of ideas, excitability. But somehow, BJ became a buffer between us, and she didn't scare me as much. I took her as she came, rolled with the punches, as it were. And with BJ around, I felt closer to her, like I had when I was four years old and we would sit side by side on the piano bench on sunny afternoons and sing in perfect harmony.

THE SIRENS SCREAMED LIKE BANSHEES. Or maybe it was the neighborhood kids screaming like banshees. They swarmed our front courtyard, toppling over Julie, Joe, and Guy. "Your tutu just hit a coconut tree at the corner of Hawaii Kai Drive! We think she's dead!"

In that moment, I knew her mania had boiled over—had taken flight.

My children and I sprinted to the corner of our street and Kalanianaole Highway, where a sizable crowd had already gathered. An ambulance sped from the scene, sirens blaring. I hunched over, supported myself on my knees, and tried to catch my breath.

I grabbed the nearest policeman by the elbow.

"What happened? I think the driver may have been my mother."

The officer removed his police cap and scratched his head.

"It was the weirdest thing. I see her driving down the wrong side of the highway, clock her at fifty in a thirty-five. Then she tries to make a turn here—doesn't even slow down—and doesn't make it." He waved his hand at the heap of metal wrapped around the coconut tree. "Looks totaled to me. We tell her help is coming, to stay put. But then she gets out of the car and walks away."

He paused for a moment and had that look on his face that said, "I have something I need to tell you but don't want to."

"And," I pressed. He didn't know there was very little he could say about Mother that would shock me.

"She was naked."

Well, there was a shocker.

"Where did they take her?" I asked.

"Queen's Hospital. Emergency."

I glanced at Mother's beloved yellow convertible Buick GS, now a yellow, twisted hunk of metal, and I wondered how she survived the accident. She loved that car! Her GS. She named Goose Shit.

I waited in the emergency room while the doctor examined Mother. Shortly the doctor told me she had a few cuts and bruises, no broken bones, but he feared she might have a concussion or a sprained neck.

"I can only release her after I've thoroughly examined her," the doctor said. He turned and started to walk away.

I grabbed his coat sleeve. "Excuse me. Wait. Please. You can't release her. Not under any circumstances."

The doctor stepped back and looked at me quizzically.

"She's not well," I said. "She has a history of mental illness—manic-depression. I think she's manic. If you release her without a mental evaluation, she may hurt herself or someone else." My voice hit a special note I liked to call panic. The emergency room doctor seemed hesitant. I was prepared to get down on my knees and beg when he took a pen from his jacket pocket and clicked it.

"Who's her psychiatrist? I'll give him a call."

He wrote the information.

"Do you want to see your mother now?"

Mother sat on the examination table, her hospital gown hiked up to her waist, her bright yellow, blue, and green Gucci scarf spread on a table.

"Sharon, get me out of here! I want to go home!" She was angry, confused, and a little stiff.

"You can't, Mother. You had a car accident. The doctors have to make sure you're okay."

"What the fuck are you talking about?" Doctors, nurses, and other patients in the emergency room immediately turned their heads in Mother's and my direction. I pulled the white privacy curtain around us.

"I feel great!" she crowed. "You must have your car. Let's go!"

Mother shimmied on the examination table, positioning herself to leap.

"Mother, you can't leave. We have to make sure nothing's broken. Your car is totaled, wrecked, wrapped around a coconut tree."

She stopped fidgeting.

"What? Oh, shit! I love that car. It's totaled? Really? My Goose Shit?"

I nodded. She tapped her foot. She couldn't sit still.

"Shit, I love driving my convertible naked with my Gucci scarf around my neck, blowing in the wind. Especially I love stopping at a stop sign next to a bus or a truck so they can look down at me, naked." Mother sighed. Then she burned her eyes into me. Suddenly I became a rabbit. Paralyzed. I hated it when she did this. I hated it more that it still affected me this way.

Then she giggled. "The expressions on people's faces! Ha! Love it!" She shook her head. "People are so fucking fun." She looked at me again. "Can we go home now?"

The doctor pulled aside the white curtain and motioned for me to come.

"Don't go anywhere, Mother. I'm going to talk to the doctor."

"We can keep her here for seventy-two hours," the doctor said. "For observations. After I make sure she's okay physically, I'll transfer her to the Kekela Wing. Her psychiatrist will see her there."

I released the breath I didn't know I was holding.

"Thank you," I said, and I flattened my hand against my chest, overcome with relief. "Is it safe for me to go? Will she walk out? Someone needs to keep an eye on her. She has a history of escaping."

The questions and information tumbled out easily, as though they had been rehearsed a million times. Sometimes it amazed me how effortlessly I slipped back into the role of Mother's caretaker, into the role of Perfect Sharon, devoted daughter, the way it all felt like a well-worn blanket or flannel shirt. It didn't itch; it settled in all the right places, just plain comfortable.

"No, she's not going anywhere," the doctor said with a smile, as though I'd said something funny. "She's too banged up for that. She thinks she can, but she's pretty sore and bruised. I'll give her a relaxant. You can go home now."

I left the emergency room without telling Mother good-bye.

THE NEXT YEAR (SPRING OF 1983), I interviewed Mother again. It was another gorgeous Hawaiian afternoon. We sat on Mother's lanai. The waters of Maunalua Bay glinted like diamonds in the afternoon sun. Today, Mother wanted to talk about nudity. Mother loved being naked. One psychiatrist explained that it was her way of releasing the clutter in her mind. By taking off her clothes, she symbolically disrobed her mind. I pressed the recorder's on button.

"Well, Sharon, you know I belong to that nudist camp on the North Shore."

I nodded.

"One day I was chosen as Queen for the Day. They gave me a crown and everything. Ha! Such fun. Sharon, it is so comical seeing the nudes playing volleyball, dancing, and romping around. The best part is swimming in the nude. No, not really—the best part was when this guy sucked my toes. Have you ever had your toes sucked while you're naked on the beach?"

I opened my mouth to respond, but nothing came out.

"It's the best feeling," she said before my brain could think to form words. "You gotta try it sometime."

Then she told the story about the two men, her next-door neighbors, who were tired of seeing her swim naked in Maunalua Bay, which was their backyard too. They invited her over to their house. Then they tied her to a tree in their backyard.

"Of course I don't have any clothes on. They tied my hands behind the tree so I was facing them. And I'm thinking, *This is going to be fun!*"

Mother laughed. "Do you know what they did next?"

I shook my head. I couldn't possibly imagine. I didn't think I wanted to guess.

"They spread honey all over my naked body! And let me tell you, I loved it!"

A thin smile danced across my face.

Mother leaned forward conspiratorially. "I knew they were mad at me, that they wanted to teach me a lesson, so I didn't say anything. I stood there, very still, a cool customer, waiting to see what they'd do next. But boy was I excited!"

She clapped her hands and hiked up her muumuu.

Nothing but bush.

I sighed and shifted in my seat.

"I tried to act scared and angry," she continued, "because I knew that's what they wanted. I couldn't let them know I was having any fun. They decorated me with sand and twigs and leaves. I must have been such a sight!"

"Yes, Mother. You must have been." My voice was monotone, nearly robotic, even though inside I was enthralled, entranced. I was mesmerized by her fearlessness. I always had been.

"Then they yelled at me: 'You have no respect for people living next to you! We are so tired of seeing you naked! After we get through with you, you won't do it again!'

"I didn't say anything. And they decorated me for a long time. The twigs kept sliding down the honey and falling off. We were there for what felt like, I don't know, hours. I can't really remember. Anyway, all of a sudden I heard a voice yelling from down the beach, 'What are you doing to that poor woman? Untie her at once!'

"I yelled back, '*Leave us alone*. We're having fun!'"

She snorted and hiccupped with glee.

"The two men were so shocked, Sharon! All along they thought they were teaching me a lesson. Ha! So they untied me and said, 'We give up!'"

She grinned from ear to ear. She looked at me expectantly. My head buzzed with indecision. I wasn't sure what she wanted me to say, and I didn't want to disturb this moment of tenuous connection between us.

"That's nice, Mother," I said carefully, going for neutral, not disinterested.

❧

We stumbled through the next several months. The kids were doing well in school; Julie was graduating from high school in a month. I had recently taken a job as administrative assistant for Big Brothers/Big Sisters. BJ couldn't find work—well, work that he enjoyed anyway. He claimed the locals were prejudiced and corrupt. He spent his days sleeping on the couch while I did everything: worked, cooked, cleaned, did laundry, and shopped. This wasn't what I had in mind when I re-opened my home and my life to BJ. He was supposed to provide stability and support, be the man of the house, and not lounge around my living room like a lump while I broke my back. I asked him to leave. I made sure I said *please*. I didn't want him to think I was being rude. He moved back to California.

I started to date. Losing BJ again had left me with a nameless, gaping hole in my chest that I didn't know how to fill. It just sat there, yawning and complaining about its emptiness. So I filled the hole with an attorney, a man with a toe fetish, and a man from Canada who was ridiculously scrumptious. I told myself these sexcapades were nourishing and rejuvenating. They made me feel alive. I told myself it was no big deal—that I was just having fun, that maybe I didn't need a relationship after all, that maybe all I needed was sex. It had seemed to work for Mother, after all. Like a black widow spider, she captured them, fucked them, and terminated the relationship.

∞

One evening, Ginger, a friend and colleague of mine, introduced me to Art while she and I were having drinks at a local bar. Art was mildly attractive, fairly intelligent, and possibly a good fuck buddy. He slid into the booth next to me and started to prattle on about this crazy lady who lived across the street from him and how she'd always walk around the highway naked and even dump her trash into the trash can on the street while she was naked. He went on and on and on, drooling story after story after story about this crazy naked lady on Kalanianaole Highway. I listened in mock indignation, oohing and ahing in all the right places. It was a strange thing to look at my crazy mother's antics through someone else's eyes. He finally took a breath.

I turned to him and said, "You're talking about my mother." The words stretched between us like a tightrope.

Art coughed nervously. "You're kidding,"

"Nope," I said and then took a seductive sip of my drink. A smile slithered across Art's face. His eyes flashed with interest.

"Wow," said Art.

Within an hour, I was at Art's home, stripped down naked, fucking him blind.

IN WINTER OF 1983, MOTHER was arrested for theft in the first degree. She stole three bathing suits from the department store because she was angry at the Honolulu Police Department—at the whole city of Honolulu. I'm not sure why. She didn't make a whole lot of sense then, which was typical when she was that unhinged. The only facts documented were these: She didn't steal all three at once. She took one, shopped around, took another, and so on. It was calculated. She knew she was being watched. She wanted to see if she'd get caught. Her arrest report read, "The defendant stated in good humor, 'I'm guilty; take me to jail and lock me up.'"

This was how it began; the monster awakened. These times were the most difficult, when the mania reclaimed her as its bride like Hades whisking Persephone away to the Underworld and I, like Demeter, had to wait patiently for her release. These times were difficult partially because of their intensity and their unpredictability; I never knew how long it was going to last or what she was going to do. I lived in constant fear that she would harm herself or worse yet, someone else. But they were also difficult because these were the times when her illness ripped our relationship apart, tore it open at the seams, mutilated whatever fragile connection we might have stitched together during her "normal" periods. And each time she spring-boarded into the stratosphere, I wondered if she would come back down or if this time she would be lost to me forever.

∽o∾

A guard called me from the Women's Community Corrections Center, the only women's prison on the island of Oʻahu. It was in Kailua, on the other side of the island from where Mother and I lived. This time Mother was in prison for running a red light and hitting a man on a motorcycle.

192

"Your mother is causing trouble in the cell block, and we want her out. Bail is twenty-five dollars. How soon can you arrange bail and pick her up?" The guard sounded desperate.

"No. No, I will not bail her out. Absolutely not. She is too dangerous when she's out of prison and manic." The guard was nonplussed.

"She can't stay here," he demanded. "You have to come get her. Get her help, do whatever you have to do. We don't want her here."

David had advised me not to rush to free Mother from jail or prison every time she was arrested. "Let the authorities handle it, Sharon. Stop worrying about it so much. You don't have to be her policeman. You have to divorce her, the way I did."

"You don't understand," I told the guard. "I can't get help for her. She has civil rights. She has the right to refuse treatment. There isn't anything I can do. She's safer there."

Silence. Clearly they hadn't trained him for this in prison guard school.

"Well, you have to come get her," the guard said, stumbling over his words. "She's constantly running water in the cell. It's flowing everywhere. She won't turn it off. She called two black inmates lesbians, and we had to stop them from beating her up."

The guard was starting to whine.

"Sorry, sir," I said. "I can't help you."

A few hours later, the phone rang again. "Sharon, what is your problem?" Mother's voice was harsh, accusing. "It's only twenty-five dollars. I know you have the money. Get your ass down here, and bail me out now!"

I took a deep breath and reminded myself: *Let the authorities handle it.*

"Sorry, Mother," I said, my voice tight and even. "I won't do it. You're safer in prison."

"Fuck you."

The phone went dead.

At 4:00 in the morning, I heard something ringing. The phone. I flopped my hand on the receiver and picked it up. Who was calling me in the middle of the night?

"You owe me cab fare," said a deep, male voice in broken English.

"Excuse me?" I slurred, sleep filling my head like cotton batting.

"I just drive your mom home. She say call you. She say you pay all her bill."

At first the words didn't register—not because of his broken English but because the information didn't make any sense. Mother couldn't be home. She was in prison.

"Where did you pick her up?" I asked.

"Downtown, Peanut Butter Ministry."

The Peanut Butter Ministry was a homeless shelter at least forty minutes from the prison by car. How the hell had she gotten there? Better yet, how the hell had she gotten out of prison? Sleep tugged at me like an impatient child, begged me to sink back into its depths, telling me this wasn't my problem. *Let the authorities handle it.*

"I'm not paying," I said through a yawn. Mother was already pissed at me for not bailing her out of prison. I would have had to be insane to go to her house alone at four in the morning to pay her cab fare. There's no telling what she would do. I had seen her leap across the kitchen table and gouge Dad's face with her long fingernails. I had seen her chase him down the highway with a broom in her hand. She had never been physically violent with me, but there was a first time for everything, especially since I reminded her of Dad.

I hung up the phone. I curled into a tight little ball and prayed she wouldn't show up at my door.

⌀

A month later, I got another call from the jail: "Your mother has been arrested for walking around Kahala Mall naked. Do you want to bail her out?"

"No, absolutely not. Leave her there."

This time there was a good chance she would be committed for some length of time. Prancing around naked in a public place means one is definitely crazy and leads to hospitalization. I drove to her house to make sure it was locked and all her valuables were safe. I didn't want a repeat of the Rudy et al. incident.

I walked through the front door and then stopped dead when I saw them. There were clothes everywhere: in piles, hanging from bedroom doorframes, in bags. They were in every size, shape, and color, with the store tags attached from some of the nicest stores in town. There were boxes and bags of fine jewelry. I scooped up all the sales receipts. Seventeen thousand dollars had been spent within the past three days.

I slumped in the kitchen chair. I knew I needed to return all of them to pay for her medical bills. Besides, how had she gotten the money to pay for all this? And the clothes were not even her size. And I knew the jade bracelet was too small for her wrist. She was always crying poor, bitching at David and me: "You parasites! You're probably stealing from me." And now she had spent seventeen thousand dollars in cash when she couldn't even cough up cab fare a month earlier.

I visited Mother at Queen's Hospital in the mental ward. The nurse escorted me through the secured doors, and I went down the fluorescent-lit hallway to Mother's room. When I found her, she was pinging, bouncing off the walls, still manic. This didn't surprise me. Unless they shocked her immediately, it took several days for her to come down from the rafters.

"How are you, Mother? Looks like you've been having some fun."

"Hi, Sharon," she said in that tight, clipped way she had of talking when she was manic. "They're trying to knock me down again. They always try to knock me down when I'm feeling good. Shitheads! I keep spitting the pills out after the nurses leave. They're so stupid. I don't want their fucking medication."

She flopped down on her bed and pouted. A twinge of disappointment shot through me, like it always did when she refused to take her medications and refused to believe that she was sick.

"I have a question," I said, changing the subject. "Why did you buy seven bathing suits in the same style from size sixteen to size four?"

Mother immediately brightened. She liked it when I didn't judge her antics, when I was interested in her side of the story, and when I understood that she was only having fun. I learned this through our interviews. She just wanted to be heard. I had this tiny, fairy-dust-sized grain of hope that maybe I could re-create the togetherness of our interviews here in the hospital. I thought that maybe if I could re-create that intimacy, then I could bring her back from the edge, clip her wings, slay the mania dragon.

"Because I'm going to lose weight! I had to buy it while the stores had it. Cute, isn't it?" She beamed and tapped her fingers on her jiggling knee.

"But you don't wear swimming suits, Mother." I didn't say this as a criticism but because I really didn't understand why she bought them.

"Smarty pants," she huffed, clearly irritated with the fact that I didn't get it. "I wanted them, so I bought them. It's my money. I can do whatever I want with it."

Suddenly she leaned forward.

"I got arrested for walking around the mall in the nude. Isn't that silly? I think I was at Carol and Mary's. I was trying on new clothes in one of their dressing rooms and going back and forth and back and forth to the racks of clothes. What a drag. So I finally just went out in the nude to find more clothes to try on. And then this stupid, mousy little sales lady—she reminds me of you, Sharon— asks me to put my clothes on when I came out of the dressing room. So, I told her to fuck off. I went back to the dressing room, got my purse, hat, and muumuu, and walked out of the store without a stitch of clothing on! And I walked through the mall until they arrested me. It was so much fun! You should have seen everyone's faces! Ha!"

"Well," I said, "I guess when you break the law, there are consequences. You're in the hospital again."

I didn't know why I said this. I knew it was only going to infuriate her, pointing out the obvious like that. She'd think I was taking "their" side, and this would open up a mile-wide chasm between us.

"Oh, don't be so fucking smart, Sharon," she snapped. "Who asked you to come here anyway? It's time for you to leave."

"GIVE UP YOUR RIGHTS, SHARON! Give up your inheritance of Hicks Homes!" Mother was on the warpath. She had sued David and me for control of her trust. Again. She said we had mismanaged her trust. Again. As if I needed this.

"You did nothing to create the company! It's not yours! It's mine! I want my money!" she shrieked.

I knew she wasn't actually interested in the company; she just wanted her due, her fair share. She wanted the world to know how she was wronged in the divorce settlement, how she was victimized because of her illness. For as long as I could remember, Mother had said, "There are no victims, only volunteers." I sometimes thought she chose to be sick, using her diagnosis when it was convenient for her. She hadn't been victimized; she'd volunteered for the life she was living.

"Fine, Mother. I won't write another check to pay your bills. You write the checks, and you decide which bills to pay. I'll sign the checks once you've written them. But I will not turn over my duties as trustee. You'll end up homeless! And I won't allow that. Someone has to manage your money because you sure as hell don't!"

"Oh, forget that, Sharon! You aren't getting off that easy. You know I am sick. You know I can't handle it. You agreed to take care of me!"

Now she was making me crazy.

"Then what do you want, Mother? You don't want me to manage your money, you want total control, but then you tell me you're sick and I have to take care of you like I promised. What is it you want?"

Mother sniffled. "I don't want to have to depend on you. I don't want you around sucking the life out of me all the time."

Her words bit into me, drew blood. Round and round we went, talking in circles. What upset me the most was that I knew it didn't have to be this way. If she would only take her medication. If she would only try a little harder to control her moods. If she would only fight to be normal. If only ...

197

Sometimes I wondered what it would feel like to just turn my back and walk away from her. And then I wondered why I didn't.

My attorney told the judge Mother was mentally ill, and the judge dismissed the case. This only infuriated Mother even more. She didn't speak to me for months.

∾∘∾

I worked for the American Heart Association (AHA) as a special events coordinator. It was a step up from administrative assistant and with more pay. I worked hard. I revived the Heart Ball, an annual fundraiser, which netted ten thousand dollars when it should have been making six figures. I met with the Heart Ball committee from the previous year. The committee members were apathetic.

"It can't be done, Sharon. Don't even try it."

I fought harder. I researched. I discovered which chapter of the AHA had the most successful Heart Ball in the country—Los Angeles. Great. I called LA, got their advice, and asked Mary Lou, the only person on the committee who was interested in change, to be chairwoman of the event, and together our Heart Ball made a grand total of $153,000 the first year.

After the success of the Heart Ball, I began recruiting schools statewide for Jump Rope for Heart, which raised over $300,000. I coordinated statewide walk-a-thons, golf tournaments, and jail-a-thons. I received an award for rookie of the year from the American Heart Association Headquarters in Texas for increasing the revenue in Hawaii by 25 percent my first year. The AHA flew me to Texas to receive the award at their annual banquet. The sudden forward thrust of accomplishment rippled through me and left me tingling. I felt solid and strong. As though I had weight and substance. As though I could do anything. As though I mattered.

∾∘∾

"You bitch!" Joe screamed. "You stupid bitch!"

Joe was fourteen, an athlete, taller than me and stronger. He wanted an Atari. I couldn't afford it. I told him if his dad paid half the money, I would pay the other half. Big Daddy refused. Joe screamed at me, hit the walls with a baseball bat, and called me a bitch again. He told me he wanted to move to California to live with his father.

I didn't know what to do. Joe was out of control. He was angry with me for divorcing his dad, for taking him away from a life of luxury and privilege. He routinely called me names and told me I had ruined his life. Logically, I knew he was wrong, but still my heart twisted in agony that I couldn't provide for him in the way he wanted, the way he deserved, the way my dad provided for me. Guilt, dark and accusing, rose up from the depths, looked down its nose over bifocal lenses, and waved its finger at me. It told me if I had found a man—the right man—this wouldn't be happening. Every boy needed a man in his life, someone who was strong and stable and able to provide. If I had worked harder to find such a man instead of trolling around for one-night stands and having fun, ignoring my most basic responsibility as a woman and a mom, then my hallway walls wouldn't be riddled with holes the size of a Louisville Slugger.

I sent Joe to a child psychiatrist for several months. Then the psychiatrist asked me, "Is Joe anything like his father?"

"Yes. I feel like his dad is still in our house."

"Joe wants to live with his dad in California. Why don't you let him?"

"Because I want the best for him, and I know his dad is not the best father."

"It may be too late. I would let him go because he idolizes his dad. Let him discover who his dad is on his own, and then be free of him. Let him go."

I packed my son, drove him to the airport, and walked him to his gate. My chest clenched and cramped as I watched the nose of the plane lift into the sky, and then, when the distance swallowed the silver jet and I could no longer see my son, a web of cracks slivered across my chest.

SHOCK TREATMENTS (now called electro-convulsive therapy or ect) began in the 1930s. An Italian doctor, Ugo Cerletti, watched electric shock being given to hogs before they were slaughtered. The hogs were unconscious but not dead after being shot through with bolts of electricity. He decided to try it on humans. Since then, ECT has been used to treat a variety of mental disorders, from epilepsy and bipolar disorder to homosexuality and truancy. Although ECT was replaced by psychotropic medications in the late 1960s and reserved as an extreme measure of last resort for the mentally ill, between 1938 and 1968, ECT was administered to hundreds of thousands of people who were either diagnosed with mental illness or who displayed unwanted, nonconformist behaviors. Mother was one of them.

In 1984, seventeen former ECT recipients banded together and formed the Committee for Truth in Psychiatry. Their goal was to participate in the FDA's regulatory proceedings concerning ECT. Essentially, the committee wanted people to know the truth about ECT—the dangers, the effects, how much was known and not known.

"Shock treatments! Sharon, I have had too many to count. The Committee for Truth in Psychiatry wants me to testify. They want to make it a law that all patients must sign an informed consent statement. No one can give an electric shock treatment to a patient without his or her permission."

Mother was tingling with delight. She had decided to talk to me again, primarily because no one else would listen to her rant. She also wanted me to help her testify. It was early spring in 1985. Mother and I sat at the round oak table in her kitchen.

I felt tiny, depleted, as though I was wasting away. Joe's absence carved across me like a scar, a wrinkled, purpled mountain of regret. Not long after he arrived in California, he called and asked for twenty-four dollars. When I asked him why, he told me it was for medication and that he had been hospitalized for an infection.

Panic threaded through me, and I gripped the phone, pressed it into my ear as though this might draw my son closer to me, back to me. Joe said they were homeless, that they had been evicted from their apartment and were living in a friend's living room and then a car. I begged him to come home. Joe refused. "Just send the money," he said and then hung up.

As I was sitting there sharing cookies and milk with Mother, listening to her ramble on, that nameless ache returned—the one where I wanted to crawl into Mother's lap for a short respite and have her protect me from the world. Not likely.

"This is great stuff, Sharon. I have never given my consent and would never give my consent. I have rights! The shock treatments are inhumane, degrading, and dangerous. Always felt like I was treated like some animal waiting to be slaughtered."

Mother rubbed her hands together as though she were washing them. I nodded weakly at her, trying to listen, grateful on some level to be in her good graces again. As odd as it sounded, I drew strength from my mother. If nothing else, she was a survivor. As much as she crashed around inside her own life, she was still standing, which was more than I could say for myself at the moment.

Suddenly Mother's shoulders pitched forward, and she crumpled into her own lap. She sobbed. She shredded a tissue into a little pile of paper snow. I moved to touch her, to feel the warmth of her skin, but then retracted my hand and settled it in my lap. I knew my role: patient observer and listener. This wasn't about me. It was about her.

"It was so awful to be strapped down to a gurney against your will, wheeled into a stark white room with nurses and doctors dressed in white. Everything white! White walls, white coats, white sheets. So much white! So cold and unforgiving." Mother rocked back and forth. She picked at the shredded tissue.

"I would scream in protest. 'Please stop! I'll be good. I promise. Please!' And the harder I cried, the faster I got the stick in my mouth and *wham*! Felt like I'd been hit head on by a train. Strapped down to train tracks and slammed by a train. No muscle relaxants or anything."

Mother was shaking, heaving with the memories, the pain.

Mother sucked huge gulps of air. She cried so hard she couldn't catch her breath.

"It is awful. Barbaric." She shook her head, as though trying to shake the memories out of her. Then she leaned forward. "They tell me it's unlawful to have shock treatments without the patient's consent in California today. They want to pass the same law here in Hawaii. I'm going to help, but most of the time I don't feel like doing anything. If I feel better, I will help." She nodded as she convinced herself this was possible.

"Mother, we don't have to talk about this. It sounds too painful." I inched forward to slip my arm around her shoulder, to try to comfort her. She jerked away.

"Oh yes I do, missy," she snapped.

I recoiled.

She jabbed her finger at me. "And you must take responsibility for letting it happen too. You knew I was sick and helpless. You knew! And you didn't do anything."

Mother let the accusation hang. It morphed with the guilt I felt about Joe, about all my failures, which sat now like a panel of black-robed judges sneering at me, pointing their fingers in disgust. I felt like shit.

"Why didn't you do anything, Sharon?" Mother's voice was softer now, wounded.

"I ... I ... I'm sorry, Mother. The doctors said it was the best thing for you."

"Oh, fuck that shit! I go to the hospital feeling so fucking good and come back a zombie."

Her voice suddenly became smooth, downy. "Don't you remember how confused I was when I came home from the hospital? I didn't even remember how to get to the store. You had to help me. Show me the way."

I started to feel a little nauseous from the pitch and roll of her mood. I fought back tears, fought to keep my face smooth like a pond before the ripple of a thrown stone. "I remember, Mother. I especially remember the times when I was very young and couldn't drive the car. I was so scared! You couldn't remember which side of the street to drive on or where to turn. You would drive so slowly I thought for sure we would get into an accident."

"I didn't know where anything was, even in my own house. Had to learn it all over again. Good thing you were there to help me—my little girl."

She smiled and reached for my hand. I gave it to her. She squeezed it. I dissolved into a pool of unshed tears.

"My little girl shouldn't have had to help me," she said, her voice cracking a little. "I am your mother. It wasn't right."

I clenched my jaw, determined to remain stoic, to allow this moment to draw around me, envelop me. Allow her tears to wash away my guilt like a rainstorm. I didn't move. I didn't breathe. I just watched and observed. I wondered how long it would last. I wondered when she would shift the conversation back to her. The air was thick, pregnant with anticipation.

"My shock treatments were not only electric but insulin induced too. And there was some kind of shock with water. Think they put me in hot and cold water … can't remember … but I know it was some kind of water shock."

Mother flattened her palms on her thighs and rubbed them vigorously.

"I was tortured, Sharon. And all my civil rights were stripped from me."

Now her knees quickly bounced up and down, and she twisted her fingers together and then her hands, as though she was wringing a chicken's neck.

"If I misbehaved or caused a disturbance, which you know I always did, they would punish me by strapping me down and wheeling me into the shock room. I would scream in protest. But that would only make things worse. Now I'm really out of control. If I didn't protest and became very still, they shocked me, too. Now I'm depressed. Damned if I feel good and damned if I'm depressed. Nowhere to turn, nowhere to go. Why couldn't they just leave me alone?"

Her agitation became stronger.

"I'm okay, I'm not sick. I never have been. I was always just having fun. You know that, don't you, Sharon? I was just having fun."

Just having fun. I didn't know how to respond to this. I had always watched Mother bend the world around her, live with fuck-you abandon, operate from a place of unabashed narcissism all in the name of "having fun." I resisted the urge to ask her to define fun. It really hadn't been any fun running after her with a broom and a bucket of soap and cleaning up her messes. Right now I needed her to help me clean up my mess. I needed her to get off the spinning, looping rollercoaster of her illness and be there for me.

"I've always felt close to Ernest Hemingway," she started again. "Did you know that Hemingway had lots of shock treatments too?"

I swallowed a knot of sadness. I shook my head.

She reached over to a stack of deposit slips from a local bank, words scrawled in her hurried hand across the backs.

"Whenever I hear something or think of something, I write it down on the backs of these deposit slips." She shuffled through the pile.

"Here," she said, thrusting one of the slips at me. "Read this one." I glanced at it. It was a quote from Hemingway. Mother leaned back in her chair and folded her arms across her stomach. Her right foot tapped against the tile floor.

Hemingway on his shock treatments:
Well, what's the sense of ruining my head and erasing my memory,
which is my capital, and putting me out of business? It was a
brilliant cure, but we lost the patient.

Her eyes welled up with tears. "We lost the patient," she whispered. "We lost the patient."

"SHARON, I WANT YOU TO come with me to walk on hot coals tonight. Tony Robbins is in town to motivate the University of Hawaii football players and anyone else who wants to fire walk."

The phone call was from Jerry, an ex-boyfriend. Okay, maybe not a boyfriend but someone I dated a few times. And slept with. Once. Only once. Did that make him a boyfriend? It didn't matter. I didn't want to go. I was tired. I'd been working all day. I just wanted to vegetate this evening.

"I'd love to go, Jerry, but I'm a bit cash poor right now. Maybe another time. But thanks for asking."

I hung up and gave myself a pat on the back. Slick. Walk on hot coals? Was he insane? A good book and a dose of dark chocolate was more my style.

I kicked off my shoes and settled into the couch.

The phone rang again. "It's been handled, Sharon," Jerry said.

"What's been handled?"

"You're coming fire walking with me tonight. I took care of the cost. Now you have no excuses. Meet me at Keahi Lagoon at six thirty. Just give them your name when you get there."

Shit. Now I had to go. Why didn't I just tell him no? Why couldn't I ever manage to tell people no? Still, how hard could it be? Walking on hot coals. It was okay. I was cool. I took est. I majored in philosophy. I could handle this.

I arrived at Keehi Lagoon at 6:30 in a cute little red outfit that showed my slim waist and attractive bust. If I was going to walk over twelve feet of flaming coals, I was going to look good doing it. It had occurred to me after I got off the phone with Jerry that maybe this was a sign. Fire equals passion equals love of my life. Maybe I would meet the man of my dreams at the fire walk tonight. A couple years earlier I had read Shirley MacLaine's book *Out on a Limb*. She said you must go out on a limb to get the ripest fruit. Limb. Lit coals. Fire. Burning limbs where my feet used to be. Same thing, right? I tried the astrological route after reading *Love Signs* by Linda Goodman. Anyone for Friday the Thirteenth? No? Didn't think so.

I checked in. All the participants were ushered outside. In the middle of a field was a mountainous pile of coals. With dramatic flair, someone lit the coals with a torch, and the whole thing exploded into flames. The heat was intense, like sticking your head over a barbecue when it was first lit. Who did things like this? Me, apparently. I stood with over three hundred other soon-to-be-enlightened ones staring at the bonfire of hot coals.

I craned my neck to find Jerry. I wasn't sure where he was hiding. I scanned the crowd again, looking to lock eyes with Mr. Right. After a couple of minutes of scouring the crowd and finding neither Jerry nor Mr. Right, I gave up and found a seat in the auditorium.

Tony Robbins bounded onto the stage. He shouted, "What is this seminar *not* about?"

"Fire walk!" the audience shouted back.

"Fire walk!" I echoed, mostly to myself.

"What *is* it about?" he asked, shoving a hand in his pocket and pacing across the stage.

Silence. Bated breath.

"It's about unleashing the power within," Tony said.

The woman sitting next to me nodded her head emphatically. "*Y-e-e-s-s*," she breathed, her eyes fixed on Tony Robbins.

"It's about taking the first step. And since you're taking the first step, you may as well walk on fire too," Tony said.

The crowd erupted into a deafening roar.

Tony leaped forward and high fived the University of Hawaii football players, who sat in the front row.

For the next hour, Tony Robbins talked about our greatest fear. What was my greatest fear? Right then it was walking barefoot across twelve feet of two thousand–degree flaming coals. I was afraid of leaving Keehi Lagoon with a couple of bloody stumps where my feet used to be. I liked my feet. They were cute.

While Tony leaped about the stage, working the audience into a hypnotic frenzy, I looked around the crowd. My event planner brain went into overdrive. I counted the attendance by counting one row across and one row deep and multiplying. I wondered how the organizers of this event got all those people there. How did they advertise? Where did they advertise? How much did each person pay? What would the gross be? Net? Bottom line—how much, exactly, was this guy making tonight?

About an hour into it, we were instructed to partner with someone sitting next to us and discuss our greatest fear.

"What is it you fear most?" Tony asked. "You have ten minutes."

What was it I feared most? I was afraid I would never find a man to take care of me, that I would let Dad down, that Mother's illness was lurking somewhere inside me, that despite all her insistence that being naked was being free, I would never know who she was stripped of her illness, that she would never be able to disrobe that part of herself so I could see her and know her without it. I feared for my children and their future. I didn't want them to suffer. I hoped they had coping skills to deal with whatever hit them in life.

The woman I partnered with smiled at me kindly, waiting for me to go first. After a minute or so, she got fidgety. I was wasting our ten minutes, and she looked anxious to share.

I chewed over a few fears. I decided they were a little too grisly. I wanted to go for the meat. What was I afraid of? Images of Hicks Homes flashed through my mind, of the board of directors dismissing me because I was a woman. Of the investigation I had been undertaking for the past several years. Of Dad walking me down the aisle toward Ronald, indicating that my role was to be submissive and obedient or no man would ever want me—that to be a success as a woman, I must willingly put myself, my needs, and my desires second, behind my man. Of Mother living life on her own terms, strapped down to gurneys and zapped with electricity.

And then suddenly, clarity burned like a violent white light: my biggest fear. My biggest fear was that I was smart and capable, a truly passionate human being. My biggest fear was that I was more than a meek, mousy, obedient woman. My biggest fear was that I was powerful beyond measure and that if I showed this, if I released this flame that had been smoldering inside me, then I would be labeled as mentally ill. Then I would not get the white picket fence. Then Prince Charming would take one look at me, decide I was too much trouble because I was strong and intelligent, because I spoke my mind, and would gallop past me, leaving me standing on the trail, wrapped in a straightjacket, electrodes fixed to my temples, with only a steaming pile of horseshit for company.

The coals were laid out in twelve-foot rows. I stood last in line behind a small boy. I guessed he was ten. Visions of bloody stumps where my feet used to be danced through my head once again. What was I doing here? For a moment, I seriously considered running away. The boy bounced across the coals like a mountain goat. Shit. I was woman. I was strong. Yeah, okay. Also I just had a pedicure. I rubbed the soles of my feet on the grass, taking in the sensation just in case it was the last time I could feel anything with my feet—just in case it was the last moment I actually had feet.

Six-foot-seven Tony Robbins looked down at me. I tilted my head back. I felt like a child.

"Walk softly, walk lightly," he coached. "And whatever you do, don't look down. Look ahead, beyond the coals. This is about breaking barriers."

Don't look down. Break the barriers. My heart hitched and bucked in my chest. My breath wheezed short, spasmodic bursts. This wasn't just about walking on coals. I shook my hands, trying to release the tension. If I did this, it could change everything. If I did this, in addition to stripping the skin off the soles of my feet, the heat from the coals might strip away a lifetime of beliefs about who I was, who I was supposed to be. Then what? What happened after that? That's the part they didn't tell you. What happened when you didn't recognize your life or even yourself anymore? When there was only a smoldering void where familiarity used to live? *Don't look down. Break the barrier.* Excitement and fear twined around each other and wrung their hands. I gasped, took a deep breath, and sighed. I took a step forward. Tony put his hand in front of me, a barrier.

"Not yet," he said. "You're not ready yet. Look me in the eyes."

I sucked in more deep breaths and steeled my eyes into Tony for an eternity.

"Don't look down," he warned.

I nodded my head. Tony glared into me and yelled: *"Go!"*

And I went. *Don't look down, Sharon. Don't look down. Keep going. Doesn't hurt. Feels like popcorn. Like Rice Krispies. Snap, crackle, pop. Doesn't hurt. No pain. Break the barrier. Break the fucking barrier! Almost there. No pain. Eyes straight ahead. Yes! Almost there. Don't look down. Only a few more steps. Snap. Crackle. Pop. Yes, yes! Five, four, three ...*

And then I looked down. A searing pain shot through my feet and up my legs. I howled and jumped off the end of the coal runway, the soles of my feet throbbing with disappointment. The hose people sprayed me down.

They handed me a t-shirt that said: "I Am a Firewalker!"

I thanked them. I looked down at my feet. Thankfully, I wasn't burned, but my soles were black. And my cute little red outfit was ruined, blackened with soot, the fabric warped by the heat. I turned and stared at the last few feet of coals. My heart sunk in a tar pit of chagrin. *Why did I look down? What does this mean—I will always fall short of my goals?*

I MET PATRICK. He was the one. I knew it the first time I kissed him, the way he climbed inside me and his heartbeat immediately synchronized with mine. He was perfect. He was kind and stable, intelligent and laid back, and still had drive. He was affectionate and sensual, spontaneous and strong. He was curious. He was a man who consumed every day and sucked the marrow out of the bones of life. He loved me deeply and honestly. He was everything I had ever wanted in a man. Okay, so I had dated Patrick when I was in ninth grade. But that wasn't the same thing. There was, however, one teeny-tiny problem. When you considered how compatible and in love we were, the problem was really so small. Hardly worth mentioning.

He was married.

✧

Ever since I had walked on hot coals, I knew I was just as capable as any man to run Dad's business—Hicks Homes. I prowled the streets of Honolulu. I saw seven different attorneys. None would take my case. Dad's trust stipulated that a family member couldn't take control of the company. They told me his will was airtight. There was no way to win. The eighth time was a hit. Jim reviewed the will and was appalled that the beneficiaries had never received a yearly accounting of the company's finances, that I was not welcome at the office, and that any questions I had about the company and its health and welfare were consistently left unanswered.

"We're going to hit those trustees over the head with a two-by-four," Jim said. "We'll hit 'em with a lawsuit so big and bad they'll think they were run over by a truck!" I liked his enthusiasm. Besides, what were my choices? He was the only one in town who would take the case.

I filed a lawsuit.

✧

The next few years passed in a series of shuffled jerks and lurches. Julie (nineteen) met a man in a bar named Kevin. He had been dishonorably discharged from the army for drug use. I was thrilled because he was the first man she dated who didn't wear makeup or have piercings. But then I read his tarot cards, which I learned to do a few years earlier for a Halloween benefit at Unity Church. I didn't like what I saw. The cards told me he was waiting for someone to die so he could collect on the inheritance, that he didn't like to work, and that he had an addictive personality. He was not good for her. She fell in love with him immediately. He told her she could move to Texas with him if she had $3,000 and a job there. She asked me for the money. I told her no. She duped her dad, saying that she was going to college in Texas and needed some extra cash: $3000. Julie got a job at a Macy's in Texas. She packed. I begged her not to go. She moved. My heart splintered—another child gone. Julie arrived in Texas to find Kevin hopelessly addicted to cocaine. She stayed there to be by his side. To save him.

As the events coordinator for the American Heart Association, I visited our Maui office to help with an event. Before our business meeting, the manager of the office was anxious to share his weekend.

"I was running in the Honolulu Marathon. I was very excited about being in the marathon because I trained for months and was all psyched up. Leaving the starting line as dawn breaks, rounding Diamond Head as the sun appears, and heading down Kalanianaole Highway toward Hawaii Kai. All the time, my head is down in deep concentration. Then on Kalanianaole Highway as I am concentrating with my head down I see bush, a big triangle of bush! Oh crap, a fat old lady running backwards in front of me totally naked. It ruined me. I lost it. Broke my concentration; ruined my timing and the marathon for me. I wouldn't mind if she was younger and wasn't fat. But she was probably over sixty years old and over two hundred pounds. *Ugh!*"

I calmly said with a smirk, "Peter, you are talking about my mother."

"*No way!* Your mom?"

A board member of the Hawaii chapter of Red Cross told me he was impressed with all the work I had done for the Heart Association. He asked me to apply for the fund development position at Red Cross. I applied. I got the job. It came with a promotion and more pay. I was moving up in the world.

I dated Patrick's close friend who was single.

"Sharon, how can you cheat on me?" asked Patrick. "You are my girlfriend."

Patrick and I made love. He went home to his wife. I went home alone.

✂

Mother was arrested, jailed, and hospitalized.

✂

Patrick and I flew to Maui. We were in bed, lips, tongues, hands, biting, ripping, tearing, clasping, clutching, penetrating, penetrating, penetrating. Released. Ecstasy. Exhaustion. We lay there, slicked with sweat and bliss, the taste of each other sweet and delicious on our tongues.

The phone rang, and I answered. "Party's over, Sharon. I'm in the lobby."

I handed the phone to Patrick. "It's your wife."

✂

Julie flew from Texas, and I flew from Hawaii to California for Joe's high school graduation. I was worried about Julie and wanted to see her. She was pregnant. My knees buckled and groaned with the weight of worry and disappointment. I wanted more for her than living in a trailer in Texas with a drug-addicted criminal. I wanted her to be with a man who had ambition and drive, who would take care of her and provide for her. I begged her to move home. She told me not to worry and that she was happy. She was in denial. Big Daddy came to the graduation. He smiled at me. He was sickeningly sweet. I wanted to vomit.

✂

I slipped into a depression and succumbed to the darkness and heartache of losing Patrick. I couldn't sleep. I couldn't breathe. I moved through the days in a haze of despair, tucked and folded myself into the sheets on my empty bed, an origami of grief. I went to a psychiatrist. He prescribed antidepressants. I took them for a few months and stumbled around bleary eyed and hollowed out. The drugs only served to take the edge off the pain; they didn't help me find happiness, and they didn't help me feel whole. I flew to Molokai for a business trip. I made love, on a whim, to a delicious local boy. And suddenly the sun was shining again. I threw away the pills. Who needed 'em? Sex trumped meds every time.

Later that year, my first grandchild was born. I begged Julie to move home. I offered to pay for the flights, to find them a place to live, to take care of her and my granddaughter. She declined. She was tangled inside Kevin, blinded by love or need—I'm not sure which. I waited. I knew that my daughter would be back; she would come home again.

Guy graduated from high school, moved to California to go to college, hated it, moved back home to Hawaii, and taught water skiing.

I was asked to apply for the executive director position of the Hawaii chapter of March of Dimes. "Sharon, you are executive material," said the chairman of the board. Another promotion. Another pay raise.

"MOTHER, WHY DO YOU HAVE that hook in your ceiling?"

It was spring of 1988. Cyndy was twenty-four years old. We went to Mother's house. I knew I shouldn't have asked, but I did. We saw a giant hook hanging from the beam in her living room.

Mother giggled. "You won't believe this guy. He likes me to tie his hands up above his head so he hangs from the ceiling. Of course he is naked. He loves it when I stick carrots up his ass and put clothespins on his nipples. And then he begs me to whip him with a leather belt. It's the only way he can come."

I gasped and covered Cyndy's ears, even though it was too late.

"Mother, you have no drapes in your living room. People can see."

"What the fuck do I care? You know, Sharon, he is renting one of my apartments on Punchbowl. We have so much fun together. What a character!"

Cyndy cleared her throat, embarrassed, and tried changing the subject. "Tutu, I'm taking a class in religion at the university. I really love it."

Mother loved auditing classes, loved anything to do with religious studies or philosophy. Every once in a while, when she was able to focus, she and I discussed secular humanism, Socrates, Alan Watts, Krishnamurti, and the nature of the mind. I relished those times with her.

Mother crinkled her forehead. "Wait a minute ... who's your professor?" she asked Cyndy.

Cyndy gave her a name.

Mother cackled and then slapped her hand over her mouth. She pointed at the hook. Cyndy looked at me then back at Mother, shrugged her shoulders. We didn't get the joke.

"The hook! Cyndy, this hook is for him. Oh, shit. I'm fucking your professor!"

"Mother!" I snapped.

"What?" Mother said. "It's funny."

∽o∽

Another day Mother was anxious to talk about Dad. Mother was always game to talk about Dad, complain about him, and smear his good name like a bug splattered on a windshield. I thought it was one of the joys in her life, playing the victim and blaming Dad, although I was still not entirely clear what the problem was. She wanted a divorce, she got one, and from where I stood, she had a generous settlement: three homes in Kahulu`u, an apartment building in Punchbowl, a house in upscale Waialae Kahala, and the house on Kalanianaole. The income from her trust would take care of her financially for the rest of her life. I failed to see where she lost.

I missed my dad terribly every day, and I wasn't sure if this interview would resurrect him somehow, breathe life back into him so I could touch him, feel him, and hear his voice again so I could fold myself into the memory of him, wrap it around me like a warm blanket. But how well did I actually know my Dad? Mother's version of Dad was so contradictory to the memories I had of him. To me, he was a saint, the only man I could ever trust. He was my lighthouse, a bright yellow beacon cutting through dense fog, guiding me—guiding us—over the choppy, churning waters of Mother's illness, keeping me from crashing against the slick black rocks of being like her, of failing as a wife and a mom, of failing as a woman. I followed his guidance faithfully, never questioned the path he laid out for me, and believed in it fervently, but still, I crashed.

For as long as I could remember, Mother had railed against Dad's need for her, how he suffocated her with that need. For as long as I could remember, I had rejected her version of him: spineless and needy. I had rejected it because she was insane and because of this, anything she said couldn't be trusted. I also rejected it because I needed to have one parent I could believe in and depend on.

I placed the tape recorder in front of Mother and pressed the red record button.

"It was good in the beginning," Mother said. "I worked as a floater for May Company; they placed me wherever they needed me day by day. Your dad was a buyer for May Company. We took the train from Long Beach, where we were living, to LA and back. After work, I'd wait for him at the train station, and we'd go home together. And then, a few years later, because I knew your dad was sharp in buying, I encouraged him to open the clothing stores. It felt good, doing something on our own, taking the risk. But even back then, he couldn't go to the bathroom without asking me."

Mother shook her head and chuckled. "Your Dad would be a chicken shit farmer without me."

A twinge of guilt pinched me. I didn't like when Mother denigrated Dad. I fought back the urge to defend him, to tell her I always saw it the other way around; without Dad, Mother wouldn't have survived. He carried her, and she rode on his coattails.

"Still, we were doing well as far as our peers were concerned," she continued. "I was twenty-two, Harold was twenty-four. We had a son and a new daughter. We had a car. We bought the house on Marburn. We had all the outward trappings of success." Mother fidgeted in her seat and sighed. "But I knew back then it wasn't going to work."

"What do you mean, Mother?"

"His name was Andy Schulz. He was a neighbor on Marburn. I really liked him, really respected him. I could have loved him easy. I know he liked me, but we never did anything, never had secret talks or anything like that. That's not why I wanted a divorce, though—not for him but for someone like him, the kind of guy I could really live with. I didn't really love being with your dad, but a guy like Andy—that kind of guy I could love being with."

This was the first time I had ever heard Mother talk about a man as though she really loved him, not in the way she did when she was manic and she wanted to fuck someone but in a way that was soft and feathery. There was wistfulness in her voice that unnerved me a little.

"And then I got sick," she continued. "We had to close the stores. I told your dad I wanted to take a trip to Hawaii when I felt better. I thought maybe a trip would help. But it didn't. Because I was living a lie."

"What would have been a totally honest thing for you to do, then?" I asked. The parallels to my marriages were not lost on me—a young woman married to a man she doesn't love, trying to make it work.

"A totally honest thing for me would have been to leave your dad when I first told him I wanted a ... I definitely knew I wanted a divorce at that time. I shoulda just done it." A soft sigh slipped through Mother's lips.

"Was that the first time you thought about divorcing Dad?"

"It was the first time I told him, but I'd thought about it before. And I remember that time very well because before I told him, I took a couple days to wonder—should I really do this? Is it right? And then—yeah, I must tell him. So I did."

"And then what happened? How did he respond?"

"Oh, he had an absolute fit. I never saw anyone act the way he did. He cried and begged and told me he couldn't live without me. So I said to myself, 'You're just going to have to stick with it, kid.' So I did. I lived a lie."

"So you never felt you could divorce him?"

"Fact is, I didn't."

"When he divorced you, how did you feel? Or were you just numb from feeling low?"

The questions tumbled out like puppies, one over the other. Questions I wanted answers for. Questions I was afraid to ask because I might have to really listen to those answers, consider them, and weave them into my worldview. It was easier when the world was black and white—Dad the selfless hero, Mother the narcissistic villain. Colors and shades of gray confused things and made life too complicated.

"Hell," Mother said with a chuckle. "I was glad to get rid of him in that regard. I felt so glad when he said I could have a divorce."

"Why did you need his permission?"

"That was the thing. My hang-up. He had to agree, or I couldn't leave him. If I left him, he'd fall to pieces."

"So you felt responsible? Why couldn't you just let him fall to pieces?"

"Oh, I couldn't do that!"

"Why not?"

"Well, I could today, but I couldn't then. I'm a moral person! I don't hurt people. And the thing is, I never had anyone to talk to. There wasn't anyone to talk to in those days. And I could never talk to my mother. I had to have her think we had a perfect marriage. And she did. I just didn't tell anybody. Fact is, the way I felt when I was with your father, well, I felt like he needed me real bad and I thought, *Well, just keep turning the other cheek, like they say in church.* I figured I'd just keep on letting him need me and then everything would be okay. Except it wasn't. It wasn't okay."

"When you were younger and married, did you feel like you were in a daze? Did you feel like you were in control, or did you just go along with the flow, do what was expected of you?"

"No, I wasn't in a daze. When I look back, it was stupid, getting married so young at sixteen. The whole thing was stupid. But every marriage is, starts out like that, with need masquerading as love. One person needs this from this guy; the other person needs something else. Compared to the way I look at things now, of course I was in a daze."

"You just felt like you didn't have any control?"

"When I was depressed. Certainly when I was depressed. You're sick when you're depressed."

Mother turned her head, looking out at the ocean. She drew in a deep breath through her nose. Her chest heaved and then relaxed. "I think when we live a lie—when we're not honest and we just let things pile up and we think, *Well, that's okay, I'll take it'*—we can only take so much of it and then we're sick. It's all a result of not being honest and open in your life."

I nodded thoughtfully. "Yeah, I was sick a lot when I was married to Big Daddy. Being sick was a way out, a way to get away, to escape."

Mother turned her head back around and fixed me with her gaze.

"Oh, no. No. That's not it. Being sick isn't about escaping. Being sick comes from not being true to you. Remember that, Sharon."

Mother hiked up her muumuu. Her words hovered over the kitchen table. Her words made me wonder, as I always had, about the nature of Mother's illness, about mental illness in general. In the 1960s, Thomas Szasz, a noted psychiatrist and academic, declared that mental illness was a myth, a metaphorical disease used to classify misbehavior as illness. At least that's how I understood it. And from this, I concluded that Mother wasn't sick; she was simply misbehaving, making a rational choice to ignore social and moral mores. The diagnosis of mental illness gave her an excuse to behave irresponsibly. But the doctors were equally convincing, telling us that Mother's behaviors were beyond her control. She couldn't help it. She was sick.

And now, as Mother sat there and told me that being sick came from denying one's true self, I didn't know what to think. *Was this partially Dad's fault? Did he jump on the mental illness bandwagon to make sure Mother never left him? If she were sick, then she would need him as much as he needed her.* I shoved that thought out as quickly as it barged in. *Not possible. So what if he needed her? What was wrong with that? Isn't that what every woman wants—to be needed?*

I SETTLED THE LAWSUIT WITH the board of directors of Hicks Homes in the spring of 1989. I settled out of court, on the advice of my attorney. The understanding was that attorneys for both sides would get paid from the company's directors' and officers' liability policy, only if a settlement was reached. The lawyers representing the directors had been pressuring Jim to settle. Everyone wanted to get paid. It had been nine years.

"Sharon, we need to settle. I have a settlement agreement here for you to sign."

Jim handed me a sheath of papers. I flipped through them and shook my head.

"I don't want to sign this, Jim. It says I waive all my rights to further sue the current directors in perpetuity. That doesn't sound right to me. Besides, we haven't seen the efficiency report yet. What if it indicates that there has been major wrongdoing? We haven't even seen it yet, and you want me to settle."

He grabbed the document from me. "Oh, that. Well, don't worry about that. It's nothing. You're only signing a waiver for information we know now. We can always take them back to court for anything we discover in the future."

It still didn't sound right to me. The "in perpetuity" clause sounded so ... final. But I didn't want to seem like a bitch, and I felt guilty that Jim hadn't been paid, so I agreed. Against my better judgment, I signed the settlement agreement.

The settlement agreement stipulated that the board of directors of Hicks Homes would be increased from three to seven directors to eliminate a voting bloc. Not only was I named as a board member, but I could also choose another board member. The original three board members were to choose another member, and the court would appoint a guardian ad litem to represent all unborn beneficiaries. And perhaps most importantly, there would be no court hearing, no publicity. If the newly formed board of directors discovered any mismanagement, we could simply fire the president. I received no compensation in the settlement.

∽०∾

"Gentlemen," I said, glancing around the table, "this is unacceptable." I was at the Tahitian Lanai, a poolside restaurant located in the Waikikian Hotel, on Waikiki beach. We were having our first board of directors meeting since the settlement. The meeting appeared to be more of a social gathering. I was livid.

The waitress scribbled something on her little pad, shuffled around the table, and leaned forward. "And for you, sir?" she asked one of them.

"Come on, Sharon," an old board member said. "Relax. Do you play golf?" The words slid out of his mouth, oily and greasy, patronizing, as though he was talking to a lower life form.

"No, I don't play golf. And in the future, I request that we meet in someone's office board room, that we have an agenda and financials to review."

Eyebrows were raised and glances exchanged. The waitress tipped her head and tried again. "And for you, sir?"

I continued, "We need agendas, minutes, financial statements, and any other documentation necessary to make informed decisions: the gross profit, the net, the overhead, how many homes we build in a year, five-year business plan, marketing plan. Which model sells best? Who are our customers?" I folded my arms. "And I intend to report to all the beneficiaries how the company is doing. This is a company my father started, and I intend to carry on his legacy."

I pushed my chair back. I stood. I picked up my purse.

"There is an old Japanese saying, gentlemen," I said, looking directly at the old board members. "When a fish stinks, it begins at the head. Good day, gentlemen."

I walked out of the restaurant, butterflies fluttering in my stomach, my head buzzing with the concussion of the bomb I had just dropped. I squared my shoulders and held my head high, heels clicking on the pavement. As I left, I heard the befuddled waitress. "So, what can I get you gentlemen today?"

⌒∞⌒

A few months later, the efficiency report Jim ordered for the lawsuit indicated Hicks Homes had not made a profit in eight years. Even though hundreds of homes were being built, there was no profit. And every year, bonuses had been given to the board of directors.

Land assets had been sold—at least a million dollars in company assets.

"We've got proof!" I shouted as I burst into Jim's office. "Let's sue!" I slammed the efficiency report on his desk.

"Can't," he said simply. He twirled a pen in his left hand. He didn't even look up from what he was reading.

"Excuse me? What do you mean can't? We've got proof."

"You signed a waiver."

Oh shit. My knees began to buckle.

"Wait a minute, Jim. Wait just a goddamned minute. You said that waiver only applied to the information we knew at that time. You said not to worry about it, that we could sue based on new information." I grabbed the efficiency report and shook it in front of him. "This is new information." I let the report drop to the desk with a slap.

"Read the waiver," he said. "It states that you waive your right to sue in perpetuity. Sorry, Sharon. You signed it. Now, if you'll excuse me ..." He waved me toward the door. He never looked up from his desk.

I seethed and grew claws. I breathed fire. I put on a red suit. I sprang into action. First step: all the board members except my board choice had to resign. I needed to get control. I targeted each board member, invited him to lunch, and told him I was holding him personally accountable to all the beneficiaries and I would no longer allow any stonewalling.

The first to resign was the board member chosen by the original three. "I was told this wasn't going to be messy," he said. "This is messy. I didn't sign up for any mess."

The board was now six.

I met with the guardian ad litem. He argued with me. "What are you doing, Sharon? The president is a fine Japanese gentleman. He must save face."

"I don't particularly care. I'm only interested in what is best for Hicks Homes."

He shook his head. He resigned.

The board was now five.

At the next board meeting I circulated the efficiency report and made a motion to "retire" the president and CEO of Hicks Homes. The motion was passed.

And then there were four.

Privately, I asked my board choice to nominate two of my high school classmates as board members. They were both highly respected in the community and in the construction business. I pretended I didn't know them and remained very quiet while the original two board members voted for them.

Now the board of directors was stacked in my favor: Four to two.

At the next meeting with our two new board members, I was nominated as chairman of the board and president. My first order of business was to select an executive committee. I stacked the committee with my friends and omitted the two original directors, making them impotent. When the original two board members realized that I had taken control of the board, they resigned.

I settled into the president's chair, pressed myself into the lumbar cushion, and gripped the arms. I twirled around a couple of times like I had when I was a little girl visiting Dad at the office, watching him, marveling at the way he moved effortlessly through the halls, conducting business on nothing more than a handshake and his word. I leaned my head back, closed my eyes, and drew in a deep, satisfying breath. Dad was immortalized in my mind and heart as all that was good and right with the world. Mother's recent rant had done little to damage that image of him in my mind. I understood that he was flawed, that he made mistakes, and that maybe he wasn't perfect. But he was perfect to me. And now, as I sat in his chair, rescuing his company, it felt as though something had come full circle. It felt as though I was back at the beginning, where I was supposed to be; we were a team again, Dad and I, the two of us taking care of each other.

"MOTHER, WHAT ARE YOU DOING?"

"Sharon, come on in. I'm trying to figure out what to do today."

I had stopped by on the chance that Mother might see me. It had been a while, and I missed her. There was so much I wanted to share with her: how much I missed Joe and Julie, how much I worried about them, and the titanic effort it would take to turn Hicks Homes around. The battle for Hicks Homes had taken its toll on me. Even though I was happy with the end result, I felt like a wounded soldier returning home from war, slashed and battered and bruised, head bandaged, a black patch over one eye, one arm in a sling. I had been told countless times over the past nine years to give up, throw in the towel, that I was in way over my head, and that I was only a woman and no one would blame me for quitting.

I knew Mother would understand. I thought if she might take the time to listen, she might even be a little pleased. When she first started taking est, she constantly encouraged me to stand up and speak my mind. "Stop being so mousy, Sharon!" she would snap. "Say what you have to say! Without fear!" And then she would tell me she wanted me to become a powerful motivational speaker and that she'd always wanted more for me than being a subservient housewife, dissolving myself around the whims of men. I was not a motivational speaker, but I was the president of a company. I thought she might like that.

"Sit down," she said, patting the empty kitchen chair next to her. "I am making a list of eleven things I'd like to do, starting with number two: going to the movies, taking a walk, making cookies, and making cheesecake."

"I love your cookies, Mother." I slid into the oak kitchen chair. "We call your cookies fart cookies. Do you have any?"

"Fart cookies! Ha! It's true. They will make you fart." She pushed a plate of cookies toward me. "Here. Have all you want. What else should I put on my list?"

"How about reading, driving around the island, going to the mall, and going to the art museum—Bishop museum." *A conversation with me. Ask me how I'm doing. Ask what you can do to help. Tell me that you are proud of me.* Tears blurred my vision. I pinched my eyes shut. *What's the point?*

Mother scribbled on a piece of paper.

"Okay, that's all good," she said. "What else?"

I swallowed my tears.

"Why are you starting your list with number two?"

"Oh, because when I am finished, I will roll the dice. Whatever number appears on the dice is what I'm going to do today."

"A roll of the dice?"

"Yes, exactly. A roll of the dice."

A roll of the dice. Everything left to chance. No planning. No preparation. No struggle to bend life into the shape you wanted it to take, the shape you thought it was supposed to take. Throwing your desires into the wind and letting fate decide. It seemed irresponsible somehow—so typically Mother.

I took a bite of a cookie.

"Mother, these cookies are good. What do you put in them?"

She snorted. "If anyone can guess, I'll give 'em one hundred dollars." She flung her hand toward me. "Go on," she demanded. "Guess."

"Well, I think you take a basic chocolate chip recipe but use whole wheat flour and then add carob chips, oatmeal, sunflower seeds, walnuts, pumpkin seeds, raisins, pine nuts, and macadamia nuts."

"Mmhmm. What else?"

I took another bite.

"Some spices: cinnamon, cloves, ginger ... some nutmeg, maybe. Knowing you, you probably add wheat germ. Am I close?"

"Yep. Pretty close. Still missing some ingredients. Keep trying."

"Come on, Mother. I'd really like to know the recipe. Can't you just tell me?"

Mother rolled a pair of dice across the table. "Six!" She looked at her list. "No, no. Don't really want to do that." She rolled again. "Three!" She looked at the list. "A walk on the beach. Now that sounds nice."

Mother looked at me. "I'll tell you the recipe before I die."

I couldn't resist. "And when will that be?" A smile flitted across my face.

Mother winked at me. "Oh, I'll let you know. I belong to the Hemlock Society. It was the poison Socrates drank to end his life. He chose to die in dignity, as will I."

She scraped back her chair. "Let me find my membership card." Mother shuffled through a stack of cards and pulled one out. She handed me the card.

> The Hemlock Society, USA,
> Encourages, through a program of education and research,
> public acceptance of voluntary physician aid-
> in-dying for the terminally ill.

Mother plunked herself back into the kitchen table chair. "I love Socrates. Wish I could have met him." She giggled. "Of course, he lived in four hundred something BC." Mother looked at me. "I'm so glad you majored in philosophy, Sharon. Now we have something to talk about."

Like a child on Christmas morning, I filled up from the inside, tingling with delight and anticipation. I loved these talks with her.

Mother leaned back in her chair and grabbed a stained, scribbled piece of paper: "Here. Look at this."

It was a quote by John Stuart Mill:

> *It is better to be a human being*
> *dissatisfied than a pig satisfied;*
> *better to be Socrates dissatisfied than a fool satisfied.*
> *And if the fool, or the pig, is of a different opinion,*
> *it is because they only know their side of the question.*
> *The other party to the comparison knows both sides.*

I put the slip of paper on the table in front of me. "Mother, if you are a pig satisfied, you probably have no worries. But as a Socrates, who always question the establishment ... constantly questioning, was he ever happy?"

"Sharon, why can't you be happy questioning? The quest, the journey—that is the excitement. Know thyself. Now that is a quest."

The journey. The quest. The excitement. Sometimes I'd rather be a pig satisfied. No worries. No struggle. Happiness. Wasn't there something to be said for that—for getting off the hamster wheel and resting in a pile of fluffy wood curls? What was gained in the struggle?

Mother paused, tapping her fingers on her lips. She shifted in her seat and leaned forward. "You do know your dad was going to turn me into a pig, right?"

Oh shit!

"That's what the lobotomy would have done. I'd be a pig satisfied." Her voice was sharp, bitter.

I slid my chair back a little, putting some distance between us. Existing with Mother was a bit like an elastic band: it stretched you to the point of almost breaking. Then it snapped. The recoil was a bitch.

"Your father died of a brain tumor. Good for him. He got his." She cackled.

"Mother, Dad died of a melanoma. And he didn't agree to a lobotomy for you."

"Still," she hissed, "the cancer went to his brain. Serves him right, messing with my brain." Her eyes iced. "I want you to go now. You remind me of your father. I'm pissed off."

"Fine, Mother." I got up to leave. And then: "Mother, I have just taken over the construction company after a nine-year legal battle. It is taking all of my strength to turn it around. I'm a single working mom and a grandma. I don't have time for this shit anymore. For your shit. If you can't choose to speak to me positively, to leave the past in the past, to stop blaming me for what happened, I will choose not to see you." The words spilled from me, a torrent of irritation. They took me by surprise, but I was powerless to stop them. I'd had enough.

Mother shrugged her shoulders. "Okay," she said. "You can go now."

Yes, Mother, I thought. *Yes, I can.*

I WORKED HARD TO UPDATE Hicks Homes. The home designs and construction materials hadn't changed since Dad's death in 1967, twenty-three years earlier. A large contractor in town shook his head. "Sharon, you are taking a speeding train going downhill and trying to push it uphill. I don't know how you are going to do it."

Family pitched in. Guy worked cleaning job sites; he began an apprentice program with the Carpenter's Union. Joe returned from California and worked in the Hilo office. He wasn't quite home but almost. Cyndy worked as my assistant in organizing the company: forming a five-year business plan, actions plans, and organizational charts and updating old house plans. I met with employees. Like a sponge, soaking up information, I analyzed the structure and culture of the company. I requested reports, information, and advice. I held staff meetings, the first in over twenty years. I met with bankers and suppliers. I structured for efficiency. Forty employees were fired. I was ruthless. The man I was dating called me Dragon Lady.

Within four months, Hicks Homes turned a profit for the first time in eight years.

My father's company, although wobbling like a newborn foal, was getting stronger every day. Ever so slowly, my life stopped feeling out of alignment, stopped pulling toward the ditch on the side of the road. The wheels were straight and true, the asphalt humming beneath the tires.

Then Jim, my attorney, hit me with a five thousand–dollar bill for legal fees. I tore it to pieces and tossed the scraps in the trashcan. He sent me another bill; I shredded it. And another; I shredded it. Then I received a summons to appear in small claims court.

After hearing Jim and me tell our stories, the judge peered at me from behind his polished wood desk. He told me to get an attorney and not to pay the bill. I realized Jim had just opened the door to a lawsuit. I could now sue Jim for all the monies the beneficiaries should have had in the original lawsuit, somewhere in the neighborhood over a million dollars.

227

Jim and I rode the elevator down from the courthouse. Beads of perspiration gathered on his forehead, glistening in the fluorescent lights. He stared straight ahead, a muscle jumping in his jaw.

"You shouldn't have billed me, Jim," I said, also staring straight ahead. "Now, I'm coming after you." My voice was smooth, like a millpond. The elevator glided to a stop on the ground floor. I looked at Jim as the bell dinged to announce our arrival. "You're fucked," I said simply. The doors opened. I walked into the foyer of the courthouse, heels clicking on the white marbled floor. "Have a nice day," I called over my shoulder and then stepped into the warm afternoon sun.

∽o∾

"Please tell David Schutter this is Sharon Hicks. Please tell him I am not my mother, I am nothing like my mother, and I would like to make an appointment with him."

"Just a moment, please," said the receptionist.

I had been calling the law offices of David Schutter for weeks. He didn't return my calls. Given what Mother had done to him, I couldn't blame him. Mental illness was genetic, right? Still, Schutter was the only attorney in town who would sue another attorney, and I needed him to sue Jim. After that day in small claims court, I had done some digging and discovered that Jim had made a tidy little arrangement with the opposition. If Jim could get me to sign the waiver, then he would get an extra $160,000 for processing the directors' and officers' liability insurance policy, known as a conflict of interest.

"Okay, Ms. Hicks. Mr. Schutter will see you."

Fabulous.

The day of the appointment arrived. I was giddy. David Schutter was something of a celebrity in Hawaii. He was ruthless, a real bulldog. He was exactly what I needed. I dressed carefully, with purpose. I wore a black trench coat over my naked body and a large hat. Okay, that's not entirely true. I also wore a black lace garter belt, black seamed nylons, and spiked heels. I sauntered into Schutter's office, flipped my hat on his desk, and flashed open my coat. "Surprise!" I said in my sexiest bedroom voice: "I am exactly like my mother!"

Just kidding. I wasn't crazy, and I didn't think Schutter had a sense of humor regarding Mother. I couldn't afford to piss him off, no matter how entertaining showing up naked at his office might have been. If he didn't take my case, I was screwed. I dressed in a navy suit with sensible pumps. I was nothing like my mother.

Schutter greeted me in the reception area and escorted me to his office. I was feeling a little overdressed—not in the amount of clothes sense but in the style of clothes sense. Schutter actually looked like a pimp. He was dressed in a black velour jogging suit with no T-shirt, tennis shoes, and gold jewelry—a large gold medallion that hung down his bared chest, rings on most of his fingers, and diamond earrings. His office was a shrine to sports—posters, pennants, and pictures. Behind him on the wall hung a huge sign that shouted, "SUE THE BASTARDS." No wonder Mother liked him so much.

Schutter waved me to a seat on the opposite side of his desk. He sank into his swivel black leather chair. I sat carefully, perched on the edge of my seat, feet crossed at the ankles, knees shut. I was proper and demure, soft and without edges. The Dragon Lady slinked into the background, and Perfect Sharon emerged. There was over a million dollars at stake here. I wasn't taking any chances.

"Before we begin," Schutter said, "I want to tell you a story about your mother. However, I want to bring in another attorney to hear it as well."

I groaned inwardly. I knew what he wanted to say and was interested in hearing Schutter's version of it. (Mother had told me her side years earlier.) Schutter talked on his phone, and a few minutes later another attorney came into his office. There were introductions; diet drinks were offered and declined. Then Schutter told his story.

The short version: In 1967, Hyman Greenstein, the attorney Mother hired to defend her right to the widow's share of Dad's estate, failed to appear in court after David called him and told him Mother was mentally ill. When Greenstein was a no-show, the judge dismissed the case. Mother, of course, was livid. She hired Schutter to sue Greenstein for $1,000,000, the amount to which Mother felt she was entitled. Schutter was new in town and the case sounded promising, so he took it on a 40 percent contingency fee. It was supposed to be an easy case. Greenstein had malpractice insurance for $1,000,000. They were going to settle out of court, and then Mother refused the settlement. She wanted her day in court. She wanted to tell her story. Schutter tried to convince Mother this was a bad idea. Mother ignored him and insisted on her day in court. The jury awarded her $40,000 dollars. Schutter was livid. He got 40 percent of $40,000, not 40 percent of a $1,000,000. But this wasn't the most interesting part of the story.

Schutter took a sip of his diet drink. "And then, after all that," he said, more to the other attorney than to me, "Carolyn becomes obsessed with me. She calls my office constantly, sits in my waiting room eating hard-boiled eggs, spreading shells all over the carpet. She tells my other clients she is in love with me. She finds out where I live, harasses me at home, and drives me fucking crazy.

"One night," Schutter continued, "I wake up to find Carolyn standing over me, totally naked, wearing a huge floppy hat and carrying a big bag. I sleep in the nude and am afraid to move from my bed. I am unarmed except for the phone. I'm convinced Carolyn has come to kill me—that she has a gun in her bag."

I chuckled softly to myself, making sure to keep my face still. This part of the story never failed to tickle me. Schutter lived in a $22,000,000 mansion that was gated, armed, and patrolled by guard dogs. Mother managed to get past all that, into his house, and into his bedroom. It was funny to see Schutter, big, bad defense lawyer that he was, rattled like this by a manic woman. And then suddenly it wasn't so funny. Schutter became more agitated; his face purpled. He looked a little like the picture of the Los Angeles Laker hanging on his wall: all purple and gold. I started to get a little concerned. *What if he doesn't take my case?*

Schutter continued: "I grab the phone and dial the police. I yell 'Help! There's a naked woman in my bedroom!'" Schutter shook his head. "The dispatcher laughs to his buddies, 'This guy has a naked woman in his bedroom!'"

Schutter flicked his eyes at me, as though he was gauging my reaction. Nothing. If I even hinted that I found this story funny, he'd probably not take my case. I needed him.

He continued, "Frustrated, I tell the dispatcher, 'No, you don't understand. I didn't invite her.' Now the dispatcher is hysterical. 'Heh, this guy didn't invite her!' I hear another cop yell back, 'So, what's the problem?' The dispatcher is laughing so hard he can't catch his breath.

"Meanwhile, Carolyn is pushing her way onto my bed, her tits in my face and that big fucking hat flopping around. I scream into the phone, 'This is David Schutter, and I want this woman arrested now!' The cop on the phone yells very slowly: 'It. Is. David. Schutter!' Forty-five minutes later, the police come to arrest Carolyn."

Schutter whistled a sigh. "Longest forty-five minutes of my life. You see, I am not popular with the police because I get the bad guys off after they arrest them. Besides, I have threats on my life. And I was sure your mother was sent to kill me."

He turned to me. "Sharon, this is why I didn't take your calls. I hope you understand."

I cleared my throat and smiled sweetly. "Oh, of course," I said, my voice dripping honey. "Of course I understand." *Please notice that I am nothing like her. Please take my case.*

"Anyway," Schutter interrupted, "I can see you're nothing like your mother, so I'll take your case."

Relief flooded me. I stood and shook Schutter's hand. If he could survive Mother, then Jim didn't stand a chance. Besides, the sign mounted above his head shouted, "SUE THE BASTARDS."

∾◦∾

I couldn't resist. I called Mother. "Mother, I saw David Schutter today."

"Oh, sure. I remember him," Mother said brightly. "He has some beautiful carved tiki gods on either side of his fireplace. And he sleeps in the nude between beautiful satin sheets."

I rolled my eyes. "Yes, well, he agreed to take my case against Jim."

Mother giggled. "I don't understand what Schutter's problem was," she said, as though I had called to talk about her. "I just wanted to fuck him. That's all. Why did he make such a fuss?" She paused. "You know, Sharon, he's your age. You should go out with him."

A few months later, Schutter called.

"Sharon, I've got bad news. We can't pursue Jim for damages because he has no malpractice insurance."

My knees went weak. This couldn't be happening. Jim was going to get away with this.

"Furthermore, on paper, he owns nothing," he said. "All his assets are recorded in someone else's name. There's nothing we can do. I'm sorry." He hung up.

I sank into the cushions on my couch. I buried my head in my knees. Nothing. I got nothing. At least Mother got $40,000 and a good story from working with Schutter. I got nothing.

∾◦∾

March 1992. There was an article about me in *Hawaii Business* magazine about how I saved Hicks Homes. It detailed how, under my leadership, Hicks Homes had the potential to thrive again. It outlined the changes I had made and how I cut overhead by 50 percent. I relinquished country club memberships and luxury company cars. I instituted better pricing controls, computerized the accounting and estimating systems, devised a business plan, wrote a personnel manual, and hired an architect to redesign the homes and a real estate company to sell the homes.

Harold Kawasaki, the treasurer, was quoted, "If the company had not been restructured, there wouldn't have been a company in two years."

The interviewer asked me about my most difficult obstacle with regard to breathing life back into Hicks Homes. "Being a woman," I said. "I was questioned at every turn because I am a woman. That never would have happened if I was a man."

A full-page picture of me was featured prominently opposite the full-page article. In the picture, I sat on a paint-splattered ladder at one of our job sites. It was flecked with all manner of white paint: off-white, crème white, ecru, eggshell, matte, and satin, semi-gloss and high-gloss. It was crusty and used, dented and wobbly. It was an old ladder. It had character. I wore blue jeans and a tailored shirt. I was fifty-one years old—the same age Dad was when he died. I was smiling. I was happy.

The title of the article: "You Can Go Home Again."

SUMMER OF 1995. The company was in trouble—big trouble.

First there was an increase in the lease where the Hicks Homes offices were located from $5,000 to $25,000 a month. I had tried to sell the lease interest on the property when I became president five years earlier. No one wanted to buy improvements on lease land with only ten years left. I was upset with the prior board members for not planning for this increase that was clear in the lease agreement. And why didn't Hicks Homes own the land for their offices—Hicks Homes that had built over twenty thousand homes in Hawaii?

Second, Hicks owed $80,000 for two months' dues to The Hawaii Carpenter's Union. I called them to make arrangements for payment, but instead the Union took a lien on the lease interest on the property, which did them no good because termination of the lease was imminent. However, they thought the lien would include the two model homes on the property.

Third, Hicks owed a $100,000 in Workers' Compensation insurance paid in advance. That was a surprise, since the prior years we had been billed monthly and we had an excellent record. I went to the banks and material houses for help. They were sorry, but construction was slow. Because Hicks didn't have Workers' Compensation insurance, I laid off the union carpenters. The Carpenter's Union was furious with me. They filed lawsuits. I threw them away.

Finally, Hicks Homes owed taxes. I sold the model homes located on the lease land, rushed to the tax office, and used that money to pay the taxes. I told the IRS that the Carpenter's Union thought these model homes were real estate that belonged to them.

The IRS agent said, "No, they are considered personal property, and we will take the money. Let them fight us if they want."

The Carpenter's Union arranged house movers to have the model homes, which they thought they owned, moved on a Friday. But on Friday at 2:00 a.m., house movers I contracted moved the

234 • Sharon L. Hicks

model homes from Hicks Homes' lot and delivered them to the new owners in Waimanalo. The Carpenter's Union came Friday morning—no model homes. Threats. More lawsuits. I threw them in the trashcan.

Every morning, I woke up, put on boxing gloves, and fought with the unions, the banks, and the creditors. I never knew what each day would bring. Hicks Homes lost its contractor's license. We ceased to do business as a contractor. We became a sales office.

〜⚬〜

Mother was manic, again. She walked to the office with her knees bloodied. She couldn't remember what had happened. She thought she might have fallen down. Her hair was a mess, her muumuu was short and torn and dirty. She was sweaty, sloppy, confused. She mumbled, "Where is my car? How did I get here?"

Joe responded, "Why can't you be a regular grandma and bake regular chocolate chip cookies?"

〜⚬〜

"My son, Kevin, is going to kill your daughter."

It was the middle of the afternoon in August of 1995. I sat at my desk at work. A husband and wife sat across from me. We were discussing the plans for their new home. They were young, newly married, and filled with endless newlywed hopes and dreams and optimism. I knew we could build them the home they wanted, the home they expected, the home they could afford. Hicks Homes hired reputable contractors to build homes under contract, and I continued to operate Hicks Homes as a sales office until I could determine the best course of action for the company.

"Excuse me?" I said into the phone as I swiveled my chair away from the young couple.

"He's sharpening his knife right now! He says the knife is for your daughter!" The voice on the other end was shrill with panic.

My mind spun into an electric frenzy. Julie was four thousand miles away in Texas. I hadn't spoken to her in two years. Whenever I called, Kevin answered the phone and told me Julie was "unavailable." For two solid years she had been unavailable. She was either at work, the store, or in the bathtub.

"They are homeless. Kevin's grandmother has paid for a one-week stay at a motel, but when that ends, they will be on the streets. Do something!" she shrieked.

I swiveled back around to face the couple. I cupped my hand over the phone and forced a smile. "Do you think we could do this another day?" I asked.

They looked startled. "Is everything okay?"

"Oh, yes, fine. I just need to take this call."

"Yeah, sure, we can come back another day."

"Thanks so much."

I didn't show them to the door.

"Where are they now?" I asked the woman on the phone, Kevin's mother.

"They're staying at a motel in Conroe."

"I'm not really sure what I can do from Hawaii, but thanks for the phone call."

I hung up. I jackknifed at the waist and grabbed my stomach. Images of the O. J. Simpson trial flashed through my head. I, like the entire nation, had been transfixed on the trial for the past eight months. Bloody gloves. Stab wounds. Children who had lost a mother. Parents who had lost a son, a daughter. I couldn't breathe.

The phone rang again.

"Hi, Mom. How are you?"

It was Julie calling from Texas. Words stuck in my throat. I wanted to reach through the phone and pull her through, pull her out of danger. Then I wanted to shake her. What was she thinking staying with a drug addict for ten years?

"Can you please help us? We need money for the kids to go to school."

Lies. All lies. I hadn't heard from her in two years, and now she called me asking for money, pretending it was for the children.

"Of course, honey. I'll send it today," I lied too. "Julie, where are you?"

"At a motel. You should see our room. It is great, Mom! We have free ice!"

"That's wonderful, honey. Glad to know you and the kids are doing well." I didn't tell her about Kevin or the knife. I didn't want to alarm her. Besides, she might confront Kevin, and that could only end in disaster.

"Talk to you soon, Mom," she said, a little too cheerfully. The phone went dead before I had a chance to say good-bye.

I rallied the troops. I called Guy to leave his jobsite and quickly come to the office. I then told Joe, who was already at the office, and Guy, "Julie's in danger! Kevin is threatening to kill her. We need to leave now!" They did not hesitate.

I called Cyndy. She agreed we needed to leave at that moment and bring Julie and the two children home to Hawaii, to safety. She would check local agencies in case Julie needed drug rehabilitation.

Two hours later, Joe, Guy, and I were in the air, on a red-eye headed for Houston. For the entire flight I worried. *Will Kevin kill her? What condition will Julie be? Is she on drugs? If so, what kind of drugs? Will she leave with us? If not, what are we going to do?* Around and around and around, questions chased after one another in my mind. I closed my eyes and tilted my head back against the headrest as the plane sliced through the air. I knew one thing with absolute certainty: Adri (seven) and Mykel (five) were coming home with us. I didn't know how, but I knew in my gut my grandchildren were coming home.

The plane landed. We rented a car and drove to Conroe, forty miles north of Houston. We stopped for breakfast. I flipped through the phonebook, found an attorney, and made an appointment to see her. We raced to her office, called Kevin's mother, and told her to get her ass down there.

Kevin's mother was ten years younger than me and looked about twenty years older. She was unkempt, with stringy gray hair. She was obese. She had no teeth. Julie told me once that this woman had Kevin smoking marijuana at age five. Then she gave birth to another son in the toilet. She was the poster child for trailer trash. Her name was Sharon.

Sharon told us in the attorney's office, "My son told me he is going to kill Julie. They are homeless. I am not sure if Julie is on drugs, but Kevin is a junkie. He takes whatever he gets. He likes crack because he can get it easy and cheap." Her voice was dull, flat.

Then Sharon turned to me. "I am so glad you are here. I need some money from you to support the grandchildren. I will take Adri and Mykel home with me."

She couldn't be serious. I stared at her, slack-jawed. She cleared her throat and excused herself to go to the bathroom. When she was gone, I took a wad of cash from my purse and counted it by twenties on the attorney's desk. Two thousand dollars. The attorney simply stared.

"I understand Texas law indicates a grandparent can take custody of her grandchildren without the parents' consent if the children are homeless," I said, my voice even and direct. "Those kids are mine. She is not to get possession. What will it take to get those kids on a plane with me to Hawaii?" I shoved the stack of twenties closer to the attorney.

A smile flitted across her face. "You got 'em," she said as she opened her desk drawer and slid the money in.

Without saying anything to Kevin's mom about the grandchildren moving home to Hawaii with me, the attorney took her deposition and then dismissed her. Before she left, I asked her not to call Kevin or Julie. She agreed.

"Whatever it takes to get my grandchildren," she said with watery eyes.

The attorney told me we would go to court Monday morning, and that I would get custody of Adri and Mykel. It was Friday. Monday was three days away. It felt like forever.

The boys and I rented two adjoining rooms at a lakeside resort. I couldn't really afford it given the state of affairs at Hicks Construction, which was teetering precariously on bankruptcy. Actually I was teetering precariously on bankruptcy. As President of the company, I was personally liable for all the company's debts. Like Marc Antony, I would take the golden sword and plunge it into my midsection. At that moment, though, I didn't care. All that mattered was getting my daughter and grandchildren home to safety.

I called Julie at the motel where she was. I told her that we had come for a construction convention and would like to see her. She was excited and gave me the address of the motel.

The motel looked exactly how I felt: dismal, dilapidated, and on its last legs. Where there should have been windows were plywood boards spraypainted with graffiti. The walls of the motel were in varying stages of disrepair, chunks of rust-orange stucco missing or falling off like scabs. I knocked on the door. Julie opened it and nearly toppled me. She was skeletal. I stifled a cry, forcing back tears. She hugged Guy and

Joe in turn. No one looked anyone in the eye. I poked my head inside the room and saw one double bed with no bedding for the four of them, a small cooler in the corner of the room, and stained and torn carpet patched in places with silver duct tape. There were no suitcases and no clothes in the closet. Adri and Mykel stared at me from behind Julie's legs, eyes wide as saucers. The only thing in the world they owned were the clothes on their backs. My heart shattered.

"We're staying at Lake Conroe," I managed, and the words stuck together with unshed tears. "We'd love for you to join us there, to spend the night."

Julie darted back into the room to talk to Kevin. Words were exchanged, tensed and clipped. Julie darted back out.

"Kevin has to work, but I can come with the kids." She smiled, but it didn't reach her eyes.

The weekend passed at a glacial pace at our motel. The kids swam in the pool. Guy and Joe took them for boat rides. The second night Kevin joined us for dinner. Guy and Joe cracked their knuckles at the table. Their faces colored with rage. Still, they said nothing. One misstep and Julie would be gone again, this time, I feared, forever. I asked Kevin to come with us to the hotel to spend the night. I knew he would decline, but I wanted to throw him off guard. He did decline.

On Sunday morning, I watched Julie on the phone whispering in code, her eyes darting back and forth between the phone and me. She hung up.

"Mom, I want to borrow the car you rented. Just for this morning."

I sat her down in a chair.

"Julie, here is what's happening. We are not here for a construction convention. We came to get Adri and Mykel to take them home to Hawaii. We go to court tomorrow morning to get custody. They deserve a good home, good schools, and a loving, supportive family around them. You have a choice to make. You can either stay here with Kevin or come home with us."

Instantly, her eyes narrowed and filled with hate. "You bitch!" she yelled. "You cannot take my kids away from me!" She leaped from the chair and put her face in mine. "How dare you!"

I didn't flinch. "Julie, you are a bad mother," I said, smarting inside and wanting nothing more than to gather my youngest daughter in my arms the way I used to when she was a little girl, to rock her in my lap, tell her everything was going to be okay. "You are not providing for your children. You have a choice: come home with your children and us or stay here with your man. You must choose: your children or your husband."

Immediately, memories of Big Daddy crowded me: the abuses, the way he constantly picked on Julie, how I stayed for nine years, desperate to make the marriage work. I spent more energy trying to figure out how not to make Big Daddy angry and upset than defending my daughter against his cruelty. And I stood there calling Julie a bad mother. I suddenly felt like a hypocrite.

I stood my ground. This wasn't about me; it was about her.

The color drained from Julie's face. She pushed past me and went into the bathroom. I heard the shower, and I waited. She came out and dialed Kevin's grandma. Her face started to fall by degrees. She hung up; fat tears streaked down her cheeks.

"Okay," she said between hiccupped breaths. "No one is leaving with my kids without me."

Immediately, I woke Joe, Guy, Adri, and Mykel and told them we were leaving in fifteen minutes. No showers, no food, no dilly-dallying: "We need to leave *now*."

A few hours later, we were on our way home via San Francisco. Julie and I constantly looked over our shoulders, searching the crowds at the Houston airport for Kevin, wondering if and when he would come and follow through on his threat to kill us both. (He told me once he had a special baseball bat with my name on it at their front door if I ever tried to see my grandkids.)

At the hotel in San Francisco, Julie and I shared a room. She told me Kevin wanted the car that morning to go to the pawnshop. He had stolen something from work and wanted to pawn it. She told me Kevin always told her she couldn't leave Texas with her kids. When I told her I was going to court to get the kids, she said the thought was surreal. While she was taking a shower, something inside her clicked, but first she wanted to call his grandma. Granny told her to leave with me because her grandson was no good.

She talked for hours about how he used the children to hitch rides by putting them on the street and then hiding in the bushes. And he took them to see the candy man. And he was planning to pimp Julie for drug money. When she undressed for bed, I saw the bruises, purpled stains for which I couldn't help but feel I was, somehow, in part, responsible.

∽∽∾

The Carpenter's Union continued to file lawsuits, and the IRS and the state of Hawaii demanded back taxes. The sheriff served me with papers more than once. At one point, I backed into a sheriff. I didn't back into his car but into him. It was an accident. I never saw him standing there. I hid and filed for bankruptcy. I lost nearly everything: my car, my credit, and any inheritance that was due me from Mother's estate. In an act of mercy, the court allowed me to keep my leased townhouse.

Joe decided to keep Dad's legacy alive. Joe never knew my dad because Dad died a year before Joe was born. To know Dad's business would continue into a third generation, that his legacy would live through my son—well, that nearly undid me. Joe started a new entity and called it Hicks Enterprises, Inc. He bought the name Hicks Homes from me. He hired me as sales manager. I had no financial interest in the company. I was simply an employee. I drove the car I bought for Joe when he was in college. It ran; that's all I could really say about it. I sat on broken springs; there was a hole in the floorboard where I could see the moving pavement as I drove. It was a far cry from the BMW I had surrendered in the bankruptcy. I was single and broke. I was fifty-five years old.

LANI, MY CHILDHOOD FRIEND, lived a few houses from Mother. Because Lani was a saint and because Mother had categorically declared that she didn't want me around, didn't want to see me, Lani checked on Mother periodically and called me with updates.

"Oh, Sharon. Your mother's at it again! She walked down to my house, plopped herself in a chair, hiked up her muumuu, and spread her legs wide in front of my husband—a clear beaver shot!" Lani laughed. She thought Mother was endearing and cute.

I tried to laugh, only I didn't really see the humor in it. Mother had kicked me out of her life. She preferred her friend Sarah's company or Lani's company—anybody's, it seemed, but mine. The upside was not hearing Mother ramble about how unfair her divorce was. The upside was not hearing her call me a parasite and a shithead. Still, I missed her. Mother was seventy-eight years old. She wouldn't be around much longer. I had hoped age would mellow her—that the madness might grow tired, wear out, give up, and let me have her during her last years.

◈

I was co-chairing our fortieth high school reunion, planned for August 1988. It was my brainchild: the first statewide reunion for all those graduating in 1958. We expected over two thousand graduates, including our very own Hawaii Governor Cayetano. That night we met to finalize our plans for an affair to remember. It was a scene from *Grease*—a blast from the past. Poodle skirts and saddle shoes and crinolines. The bunny hop. The jitterbug.

Someone handed me the phone. I heard Lani's voice. "Sharon, you have to get over here now."

My fingers immediately tingled with panic.

"Why? What's wrong?" I excused myself from the reunion committee meeting, the phone pressed tight against my ear.

"Your mother needs your help. She won't get off the floor. She's been there for days, and she won't let me help."

241

I told her I'd be right over.

Francois offered to go with me to Mother's house. I nodded and squeezed his hand. "Yes, thank you. I'm afraid of what I might find."

Francois and I arrived at Mother's. I wasn't prepared for what I saw. Mother was lying on the living room floor nude, her legs spread eagle.

She glanced up at Francois and me. "Hey there, kids. How ya doin'?"

I grabbed Francois by the elbow and dragged him into the kitchen. "Wait here. Let me get a sheet to cover her." And then, blushing, I said, "Sorry you had to see that."

Francois smiled, shook his head. He knew.

After I covered Mother, Francois came back into the living room. Mother looked up. She was unable to move.

She looked at Francois: "How come you never married my little girl?"

She hiked the sheet up to her waist. I pulled it back down. She pulled it up. I crossed my hands to my chest and retreated a few steps. I gave up.

Francois knelt next to Mother's head. "Mom, we've been good friends since sixth grade. I've always loved Sharon."

"I know." Mother pressed. "But how come you never married her?"

Francois chuckled softly and looked at me. "Because she never wanted me."

It was true. I had never been attracted to Francois. I didn't know why. He was fundamentally decent, caring, and good. Still, there had never been a sexual attraction. He was my good friend.

Mother's face turned serious. "Now, Francois," she commanded, "this is what I want you to do: go to Long's Pharmacy and buy two Fleet enemas. I'm stopped up like a busted septic tank. I need an enema. Badly. And I want you to give it to me. Only you." Mother looked at me askance and pursed her lips. "Do you understand?" she asked, flicking her eyes back to Francois. "Oh, and while you're there, buy me some Haagen Dazs. Eight cartons. Rum raisin and chocolate. Four of each. It's on sale. Now, go!" She jabbed her finger toward the front door.

"Mother, why don't you let Francois and I help you to bed? The floor must be very uncomfortable."

I fought to stay emotionally detached. I promised myself I wouldn't get tangled in her chaos again, that if she didn't want me in her life, I would honor her request. Still, I couldn't just leave her on the floor.

Mother said, "No, no, no. I'm fine here." A beat. And then, "Well, okay. But Francois is going to give me the enema, right? I don't want you touching me, you parasite!"

I stomped the urge to walk away. "Yes, Mother, he will. But first, let's put you to bed."

Thankfully, Francois was over six feet tall and a retired fireman. He handled Mother's ever-growing bulk with ease. Surprisingly, she didn't fight him. After a few minutes, she fell asleep. Francois and I left.

In the driveway, I said, "Thank you so much. I could never have gotten her into bed without your help. Don't worry about giving her an enema. She'll forget we were even here."

"Sharon, I have done some crazy things in my life and I will do almost anything for you, but giving your mom an enema ..." Francois settled his mammoth hands on my shoulders and kissed me gently on the cheek. Then he got in his truck and drove away, leaving me standing there.

～∽～

"I'm not going, Sharon," Mother said, crossing her arms over her chest like a defiant six-year-old. "I don't need to go to the hospital."

It was the next day. Cyndy, Julie, and I were at Mother's house. I brought my daughters as back-up, reinforcement, in the hopes that she would at least listen to them. Mother was propped up against several pillows on her bed. The room reeked of urine. She hadn't moved since the previous night.

"But Mother, I'm worried about you."

"Too fucking bad. I'm not going."

"Come on, Tutu," Cyndy said. "You need a physical exam to make sure everything's okay."

"Nope. Absolutely not."

"Please, Tutu?" Julie implored.

Mother clamped her mouth shut and shook her head vigorously from side to side.

There was nothing I could do. When I was a child, it was easy to get her to the hospital, to get her help. Now the laws had shifted. No more men in white coats, no more being strapped to gurneys. Now she had the right to be sick, to refuse treatment.

Cyndy, Julie, and I made dinner and forced water into Mother to try to relieve the constipation. Mother drifted in and out, disappearing for long spells into her own little world. I gave Mother her enemas. She didn't fight me too much. This was our new intimacy—doing what needed to be done, tolerating one another. I bought her a little porta-potty and set it next to her bed. Hopefully she would use it. I didn't want to give her an enema again.

I called Adult Protective Services, hoping they would do something, anything, to get Mother the help she needed. She fought them and me at every turn, ever determined to live life on her own terms, bullheaded to the last. The report from APS didn't surprise me. Mother was dehydrated, impacted, lying on the kitchen floor for days on end, feces and urine on her, on towels, in bed. Collected urine in glasses were lined up on the kitchen counter. She couldn't remember what she had said immediately after she said it. She thought people were stealing from her, thought people were after her for overdue bills, was afraid to open her mail. She refused to seek medical attention and became very violent and abusive when anyone tried to interfere.

She refused to cooperate. Without her cooperation, even with the report from APS, there was nothing I could do. She had civil rights.

THE NEXT YEAR MOTHER was lying on the floor again; she had been there for four days. Sarah, Mother's friend, discovered her and called me. She was lying in her own excrement, unable to move. Urine and shit and maggots were everywhere. Dirty dishes crusted with rotted food were piled in every corner of the house. Clothes, rags, towels, expensive Gucci scarves, and fine jewelry were spread on the floors, over chairs and tables.

"Mother, looks like you need some help. Cousin Julianne is here with me." I said this offhandedly, hoping she would respond favorably if she thought I didn't really care. Sometimes I thought she refused help just to spite me, just to prove she didn't need to depend on me. Over the years, Julianne, a registered nurse, had helped Mother. With her there, perhaps Mother would cooperate. Mother didn't seem to think Julianne was a parasite or a shithead.

Mother turned her head and smiled a toothless smile. Where was the olive-skinned beauty I used to so admire? The reality of Mother's decline crushed me.

"Oh, hi there, girls. No, I don't need any help. I'm just fine. My boyfriend from the north shore is making me some beef stew. He'll be here soon. You can go now." Mother turned her head and resumed staring at the ceiling.

There was no boyfriend. Mother didn't eat meat.

"Okay, Aunt Carolyn," Julianne said, giving me a knowing look. "We'll leave."

I tilted my head and crinkled my brow in confusion. Julianne motioned me outside to the backyard. I stepped onto the lanai, and just like that, I was ten years old again, watching Mother sunbathe, enraptured by her beauty, her lithe figure, and her vitality. The way the house was always flawless. I looked back to see Mother lying in her own shit, smiling her toothless smile at the ceiling, waiting for a boyfriend and beef stew that didn't exist. My heart hurt. And then I was suddenly exhausted, withered, and atrophied from years of circling around Mother, trying to find a way into her life, trying to cobble together some semblance of intimacy between a mother and daughter. I was tired of trying to get her to stand still for once, to stand still in the same spot with me, to stop twisting away.

Black waves of anger rushed me. *Why won't she let me help her? Why does she insist she doesn't need me, doesn't want to lean on me? Why doesn't she fight for our relationship?* It was in that moment that I realized I had been standing in the ring alone. I had been the only one fighting—fighting for a mother who didn't exist, a relationship I could never have. Time was running out. Mother was slipping away. I could see her end, and there was a part of me that thought, guiltily, that it would be better for both of us when she was gone.

I swiped away an errant tear that had escaped. "Well, what should we do?"

"Call the crisis center," Julianne said without hesitation. "This is definitely a crisis."

I made the call. We waited outside in the backyard. Mother was still lying on the floor in her kitchen, unable to move.

Two hours later, a social worker arrived. "So sorry I am late. I was on the north shore and it is Saturday and we are light handed, and ..."

She went inside to talk to Mother. Then outside with us, she called a judge. She asked for a court order to have Mother committed. She nodded into the phone. She nodded some more. Her face fell. She hung up.

"I'm sorry," she said. "As long as family is here, the judge cannot issue an order for commitment."

"What?" I asked. "I don't understand. She needs help."

"I'm going to call an ambulance," the social worker said. "That way, once they see her condition, we can get her to the hospital."

Fifteen minutes later, the medics arrived. They rushed into the kitchen to help Mother. "Hello, Mrs. Hicks. How are you today?"

Mother's face crinkled into a smile. "I'm fine. How are you?" Mother winked at the medic and tried to hike up her muumuu. She couldn't close her fingers around the fabric.

"Will you let us take your blood pressure? It's just routine. We won't stay long." His voice was cool and soothing, a salve, a balm.

Mother nodded her head. "Okay. My boyfriend is coming soon with beef stew."

"That sounds wonderful," said the medic as he wrapped the blood pressure cuff around Mother's arm.

"Her blood pressure is so high that she could stroke at any moment," the medic told us in the backyard. "She needs help now. Unfortunately, we can't do anything without her consent. She refuses to go to the hospital."

I threw my hands in the air. "What can we do? She needs help now!"

The medic replied, "Call the police. They have the authority to help her."

I called the police. I told them Mother needed help immediately. Julianne and I walked back into the kitchen.

Mother turned her head. "Oh, hello girls. Are you still here?"

"Yes, Mother. How are you feeling?" I resisted the urge to stroke her hair, her face.

"Oh, I'm fine," she said cheerily, still flat on her back. "I think someone else was here, too. But I can't really remember ..." Her voice trailed off. She hummed a tune to herself.

Within minutes, the police arrived. And I recognized Derek. He had dated Cyndy once upon a time.

"Hi, Mom," he said, hands perched on his duty belt. "You need some help?"

At this, I cracked. Relief broke through the dam of stoicism and flooded down my face. "Oh, Derek," I sobbed. "It's so good to see you. My mother is lying on the kitchen floor. The medics say she will have a stroke if she's not rushed to the hospital." I was momentarily embarrassed at my display. It wasn't like me at all in a crisis situation. I cleared my throat, squared my shoulders, and pulled back the tears.

Derek flashed a soft smile. "No worries, Mom. We'll get her to the hospital. Where do you want her to go?"

"Queen's," I said, matter-of-factly.

Without delay, the medics loaded Mother into the ambulance. I darted out the front door to watch the ambulance leave. Derek was on his motorcycle, heading in the opposite direction of the ambulance.

I yelled after him, "Derek! Follow the ambulance! Once she gets to Queen's, she may resist treatment. Please! Catch up with the ambulance!"

Derek flashed me a thumbs-up and turned his motorcycle in the other direction.

I collapsed on her couch. It was silent except for the pull of the waves on the shore, the rustle of the trade winds in the palm trees. I looked around at the mess Mother left, the avalanche of clothes and food and decay, and I was struck, in the middle of all this, by how empty it felt, the way a room always felt as though all the energy had dissipated whenever Mother would leave—as though without her, there wasn't a reason to stay. And then I wondered if that was how my life would feel when she was gone.

MOTHER WAS DIAGNOSED WITH DEMENTIA, along with an old infarct, hypothyroidism, hypertension, and possible diabetes. All of these were complicated by the bipolar disorder. That was the bad news. The good news was that with this new diagnosis, the judge granted me full guardianship over Mother's person and property. I could now make decisions for her without her permission. I could now authorize medical treatment and manage her personal finances in addition to handling her trust's financial matters.

The social worker at Queen's recommended the Ponds at Punalu'u. It was a beautiful facility nestled against the mountains on the north shore of O'ahu. It was clean and cozy and well-staffed. The entrance foyer resembled any fine hotel lobby, with vases of island flowers under a vaulted rotunda. The atmosphere was serene and calm. And there was a locked ward for those with dementia.

I was escorted through the locked doors and taken to Mother's room. Afternoon light filtered in through the blinds. Mother sat on the edge of her bed. I hardly recognized her. She was clean, her nails done, her hair washed and styled. If I looked carefully, I could still see the breathtakingly beautiful woman with the coffee-colored pageboy, red lips, and flashing green eyes around whom men melted into little pools of lust and desire, desperate for a small piece of her attention. If I looked carefully, I could see the mischievous nymph who grabbed life by the balls and swung it toward the moon. If I looked carefully, I could begin to see her stripped of her mental illness. If I looked carefully, I could begin to see parts of her within me—not the crazy, mentally ill parts but the bold, daring, and adventurous parts.

I crossed through the doorway and set a new robe, a nightgown, some dark chocolate, and a potted plant on her bed. Mother smiled when she saw me.

"How's my girl? How's my Sharon?"

Her question was sincere. She was clear, lucid. I thought of all the years I had spent wishing for moments like this, wishing I could

249

count on them, having to learn to live without them. And in that moment, she genuinely wanted to see me. Mother patted the empty space on the bed next to her. I sat down and folded her hand into mine. It was warm and comforting.

"I like your room, Mother. You have a lovely view overlooking the mountains and the garden. It's really very beautiful."

Mother nodded.

"I brought you some things." I scooted so she could see the pile of goodies on the end of her bed. She giggled and reached over me to grab the chocolate, which she hid among her things in her end table. She put the potted plant on the ledge under her window. I hung her new nightgown and robe in her small closet.

She turned to me. "Let's have lunch."

The dining room sat in the main part of the hospital, outside the locked facilities. Mother moved slowly, shuffling her feet. I offered her my arm for support. She pushed it away. "I can do it," she muttered.

We sat at a table on the open lanai. Mother looked out at the verdant landscape and sighed. I wondered if she knew where she was, if she knew what year it was, how much of our life together she remembered. She was eighty-one years old, gray, overweight, and without teeth. It amazed me how much she had changed over the years, the way her illness robbed her of her beauty and left behind an old woman—the way time flew out the window and didn't bother to tell us it was leaving.

"Mother, I've been keeping notes for the past forty years about you. Remember when I sat on your lanai and taped you for hours? I want to write about you. Is that okay?"

Mother's face lit up, as it did whenever attention was on her. "Sure! Include all the stories I have told you." She waved her finger at me. "I always wanted to write a book. Remember? The title was *Fuck, For You See Clearly*. But never could get it together." Mother tapped her finger on the side of her head and laughed. "Just too much going on in here, I guess."

I smiled and nodded.

"Mother, don't you think taking medication would have helped you to have a normal life?"

The question wasn't planned; it just sort of slipped. I figured there wouldn't be too many lucid days with her, days when I could poke and probe and try to understand why she chose her madness over her family.

"Ha! Who wants to be normal, Sharon? I loved being high. I always thought if I could ride out the lows, I would be okay."

But Mother, I wanted to ask, *did you ever wonder if the rest of us would be okay?*

Mother sipped her water.

"Sharon, did I ever tell you about the time a man, a stranger, knocked on my door in the middle of the night?"

I shook my head.

"Of course, I'm naked. I invite him in. And there we are, sitting opposite one another in the living room, just staring at each other. I ask, 'What do you want?' He laughs. 'Well, I came to rape you, but now that I see you naked, I think I will leave.' Ha! Sharon, remember when I ran the Honolulu Marathon in the nude, backward? That was on the front page of the paper."

Mother laughed, tickled to death by her stories.

"One guy called me after I got home from jail. He said, 'I saw you in jail, and I can tell you want it. I am a male prostitute by night, and I work for the electric company during the day. I can come over and show you the best time in a bubble bath.'"

Mother had a twinkle in her eye. Then she said, "Sharon, he was fabulous. Some of the best sex I ever had. But you know, I wouldn't pay him. Why should I pay for something I can get for free?"

"Mother." I wanted to change the subject from sex and ask about her younger years before I was born. Maybe her illness hadn't started with my birth. "David said you tied him to a clothesline when he was little, before I was born. Do you know why you did that?"

"Because I loved him. I didn't want to him to get hurt. Besides, he liked it."

"What do you mean, liked it?"

"Well, every morning I cooked oatmeal for him. And if he didn't finish it, he had the same oatmeal for dinner. I didn't even take it off the table. He needed to learn to eat what I fixed."

"Mother, David told me he hated to eat that same oatmeal for dinner. He said it was all gooey and mushy."

"Well, he shoulda eaten it at breakfast."

"What happened after breakfast?"

"David ran outside and stood under the clothesline pole. He waited for me to tie him up. There was a hook on the line and he could run the length of the clothesline, and besides, he could see the boy next door through the fence and talk to him. Then I didn't have to worry about him."

"Mother, you tie animals, not children."

"David didn't care."

"How old was he?"

"I don't remember. Two, three?"

"Did you ever think you were sick?"

"No, just misunderstood."

⌒⌒

Another day, another visit, another chance to connect. At lunch, I asked her, "Mother, do you remember one of your psychiatrists, Dr. Amjadi?"

"Oh, yes. I liked him. Why do you ask?"

"He told me that you are obsessed with knowing the truth. What do you think he meant by that?"

"Hell if I know. But maybe I told him that because he was always interested in philosophy. You are too, aren't you? You majored in it. Are you obsessed with knowing the truth?"

"I find philosophy stimulating. I wouldn't call it an obsession. But there were times, Mother, that it was difficult to discuss anything with you because you always thought you had the answer, the truth. You thought everyone else was a dummy." I cringed a bit, a little afraid of her response.

Mother paused and sipped her iced tea.

"Well, Sharon, most people are dummies. They just don't get it. They sleepwalk through life, afraid of whom they really are. They spend their time hiding, covering themselves up, and covering their inner conflicts. They need to be truthful about their feelings." She creased her forehead. "I hope you're reading Alan Watts, Krishnamurti, and Buckminster Fuller."

"Of course I am, Mother." My mind tripped over her words, and I wondered, momentarily, if I was one of the sleepwalkers, if I'd spent my life hiding, covering myself up. I turned my head away so I didn't have to face the answer.

"Is it okay if I bring Kathy to visit you?" I had remained friends with my stepmom over the years.

"Oh, sure. I'd love to see her." A beat. And then, "You know she got the leftovers."

"Yes, Mother. I know."

"Your dad was so needy. Need is not love."

We finished our meal in silence.

MOTHER FELL OUT OF HER bed. She was rushed to the emergency room at Queens Hospital, and then, because she had a stroke and was medically unstable, she was transferred to Ann Pearl Nursing Facility in Kaneohe.

I could tell she was in pain.

"Mother, don't you want to just let go? It's okay to let go."

When Dad was dying in the hospital, someone told me that sometimes the dying need permission from their loved ones to let go of this life—that they wouldn't leave unless they knew the ones they were leaving behind would be okay.

Mother moaned and shifted around on the bed, trying to get comfortable. "Absolutely not!" she snapped. "I don't know what tomorrow will bring."

"I remember you telling me you belong to the Hemlock Society. Are you getting close? Is there something you want me to do?"

"None of your business!" She rolled over on her side, her back to me. She winced. The pain was excruciating. "This is shit, Sharon," she groaned. "Nothing like I thought it would be." Mother twisted and writhed as the pain surged through her.

"What do you mean, Mother?"

"I mean it's shit. Just plain shit!"

That was it? That's all she had to say? I desperately wanted her to share with me some private wisdom in her last moments, some final thought, some final gift just for me, the way Dad had. I had always been enamored of Mother's mind, the way it ignored the banal and wrestled with the infinite, the things that matter— truth, philosophy, metaphysics, the workings of the universe, how to be content. I had never known anyone besides Mother who was so absolutely content with being alone, with who she was—no hiding and no apologies. And I wanted to understand that; I wanted to know the secret to such naked bliss before she died. Because if she didn't give it to me, then who would? *Fuck*. For. You. See. Clearly. Everything was so fucking clear. Not to me it wasn't.

The next day, a staff member at Ann Pearl called me at work. "It's time. You better get over here. Your mother doesn't have much longer."

Julie and I rushed to Ann Pearl Nursing Facility. My heart pounded against my ribs as I drove there. My mind spun with imaginings of what our last moments together would be. As I drove into the parking lot, I was suddenly afraid. I didn't know what I was supposed to feel. My mother was dying, and I didn't know what I was supposed to feel. For the past ten years, I had willed myself into a place of detached compassion for Mother. And it worked, for the most part. It allowed me to exist near her, to take care of her without being drowned by her. Only now, in her final moments, I wasn't sure I wanted to feel detached. The problem was, I couldn't remember how to feel anything else.

Julie and I jumped from the car and ran through the double doors, down the hall to Mother's room. Cyndy was standing by Mother's bed, looking down at what once had been my mother. We were too late. Cyndy's face was slippery with tears. Cyndy told us she had climbed in bed and held Tutu in her arms, whispering in her ear: "You are perfect the way you are." Then her tutu had smiled and died.

～o～

A few days later, Cyndy and I went to the mortuary to identify the body before it was cremated. Mother was no longer a she. She was an it. That bothered me. My mother was not an it. She was ... beautiful and flamboyant, theatrical and talented. She was narcissistic. She was an imp, a puck, mad as a hatter, absolutely bats. And I loved her more than words could say.

Cyndy and I were escorted down a long hallway into a room that smelled of death and emptiness. Finality. The silence in the room crushed me, weighed me down, flattened me, and reminded me that she was gone—that my life was now filled with her absence. When she died, I went about my daily routines as though everything was normal, as though there hadn't been some monumental shift in the axis on which my life spun. Quite simply, I forgot that she died. And then, for no particular reason, I would remember, and the sting of it drove me to my knees. And so it went. I forgot. I remembered. I forgot. I remembered. I wondered when the moment would arrive when I would cease to forget and always remember.

The mortuary director wheeled in a large, rectangular cardboard box. He lifted the lid. Cyndy laced her fingers through mine and squeezed. We approached the box slowly, timidly.

I peeked over the edge of the box and screamed, "That is not her! That is not my mother!"

The it inside that box was shrunken and gray, emaciated, shriveled. A shell. A husk. Too small to have ever contained the vibrancy of Mother. It was some kind of sick joke. And then I recognized her muumuu. *Anyone could be wearing her muumuu.* I covered my mouth with my hand.

"I don't know who that is," I whispered, shaking my head.

Cyndy leaned into me. "Mom," she said softly, "look at her hands."

I looked. I flicked my eyes back to her face. I looked back at her hands. Yes, they were her hands. I grasped the side of the cardboard box. I looked down at my hands. They were my hands too.

"IN HONOR OF TUTU," David's oldest son said. "Let's take off all our clothes!" A wicked grin was plastered across his face. He started to unbutton his shirt.

Mother's loved ones laughed as Mother lived: out loud. We all had our own special memories of Mother naked in public. Our own stories. Our precious memories flooded us warmly as we came to spread her ashes in Maunalua Bay in front of her home.

David and I piled into my nephew Michael's beautiful forty-foot boat. Other friends and family piled into canoes. We made a circle in the middle of Maunalua Bay, where Mother loved to swim naked. I opened the koa wooden box and removed the bag with Mother's ashes. I untied the twisty thing. A few ashes escaped on the wind. As usual, she couldn't wait to get away, to be free. I handed the bag to David. He leaned over the side of the boat and gently released Mother into the deep, blue water. Cyndy, Guy, Julie, and my grandson Mykel leaped from their canoes. Mother's ashes swirled around them. My children and grandson splashed, laughed, and frolicked with Mother one last time, a final farewell.

I sat on the stern of the boat. I didn't put my feet in the water. I watched the current steal Mother away. I braced myself for sadness, for grief, for that inexorable loss that accompanied the death of a loved one, for that sinking feeling to grab hold and drag me under. It didn't come. I felt nothing except relief. There would be no more midnight phone calls. No more panicked charges to the jail or the hospital. No more living on the edge of constant emergencies. No more name calling. No more insults. No more. It was over.

Every breath I had ever breathed, every step I had ever taken, and every choice I had ever made had been about not being my Mother—about proving that I was nothing like her. It was a singular, relentless pursuit. I had spent the entirety of my life running away from her, turning away from her insanity, pushing her to the farthest corners of my existence while at the same time clinging to her for dear life, hoping for answers to unanswerable questions.

No matter how hard I tried to escape, Mother invaded every part of my life. I grew into her, and she grew into me. She and I blurred at the edges. I didn't know where I ended and she began. Such was the nature of madness. And as I watched Mother's ashes drift away on the salted ocean current, as my life necessarily untangled from hers, as I learned to exist without her, there was only one more question, which, like all the others, I had asked over the years and had no satisfactory answer to: *What do I do now?*

*If you change the way you look at things,
the things you look at change.*

—Wayne Dyer

Epilogue

MOTHER DIED over ten years ago. Of course, she is still around. I feel her energy every day: in her china hutch that sits in my dining room; in her hand-stitched Hawaiian quilt that spreads across my bed, the one I wrap myself in every night as I fall asleep; in her silver pendant I carry with me everywhere. At first glance it looks like an angel with wings, and you think, *Oh, how sweet.* But then you take a closer look and squint your eyes in disbelief. *No, it can't be,* you whisper to yourself. Then you feel the heat creeping into your cheeks when you understand that you are, in fact, looking at an erect penis, complete with tight balls and yes, wings.

Once I'd asked Mother about it. Her lips had curled back into a smile. "It's great, isn't it?" she said, fingering the shaft as it hung on a silver chain around her neck.

"I don't get it."

"Oh, come on, Sharon. Think about it." Her eyes sparkled with mischief. She waited.

I shook my head.

"Who gives a flying fuck!" She cackled, and her whole body shook with delight.

That was Mother. She was, for the entirety of my life, brazen and rash, unreliable and self-centered, irreverent to the core. Still, it's the thorn in your side that leaves the biggest hole.

❧

A lot has happened in the past ten years. I left Hicks Enterprises in 2002. I worked as executive director of the Honolulu County Medical Society for less than a year and then worked with Governor Linda Lingle to help her fulfill a campaign promise to provide medication to the indigent population of Hawaii. I retired in 2005.

Dad's legacy, however, was not forgotten. In September 2006, Harold E. Hicks was inducted into the Hawaii Building Industry Hall of Fame, nearly forty years after he died. He was chosen as the most influential contractor of the past fifty years. I imagine, had he been alive, he would have graciously accepted the honor and then gone on about his business. That was just his way. He wasn't much for the spotlight.

∽

It's April 2011. I'm standing on the edge of Maunalua Bay, tiny waves tickling my toes. The sun is warm on my bare skin. I raise my hand to shield my eyes from the bright Hawaiian rays. I draw in a deep breath. Seventy years. Seventy years spent running. Seventy years spent hiding. Seventy years spent sculpting a life that would prove I am nothing like my mother. And all along, she was there, inside me, rattling around, whispering, sometimes yelling, "Release me." A soft wind blows, prickling my skin. I take a step forward. The warm water caresses my ankles. Seventy years.

I smile. How do you grab a naked lady? You don't. You let go.

∽ ∽ ∽

CPSIA information can be obtained at www.ICGtesting.com
Printed in the USA
BVOW08s0435190314

348121BV00001B/135/P

9 781458 206190